AF449022
AKI92B
DOT BARDARSON

BOARDWALK FOOTSTEPS

Memoir of an Artist at a Remote Alaskan Cannery

By
Dot Bardarson

Ghostwritten by
Tara Neilson

Cirque Press

Copyright ©2024 Dot Bardarson

Published by
Cirque Press

Sandra Kleven — Michael Burwell
3157 Bettles Bay Loop
Anchorage, AK 99515

Print ISBN:
979-8-89619-760-7

cirquejournal@gmail.com
www.cirquejournal.com

Cover art/photo: Dot Bardarson
Author photo: Linné Bardarson
Author back cover photo: Sandra Wassilie
Book design: Signe Nichols

DEDICATION

To my three children Dori, Blaine, and Rolf who, as adults, thanked Linné and me every day for their amazing and adventurous childhood and who allowed us to see Chatham Cannery through their young eyes.

Rolf, Blaine and Dori share stories about Chatham.

INTRODUCTION

My husband and I often talked about milestones. We noted that we could remember a year by a milestone that set it apart from the rest of our lives. Certainly one of those was our five summers at a remote salmon cannery in Southeast Alaska in the 1960s.

The first year there we had three children all under eight years old. The children and I were allowed to go to Chatham Cannery because Linné, my husband, was superintendent.

As outlying canneries disappeared and were replaced by modern canneries on the road system, I gradually realized that we were part of Alaska history, a part that needs to be told. I felt a responsibility to write about this before our generation is gone and memories recede into obscurity and details are reported wrong.

I was also a photographer and had the reputation of being a documentarian. I ceaselessly photographed and recorded the day to day lives of what we now call an "off the grid" settlement that was in the business of putting salmon into cans.

Most of these remote canneries were built in the late 1800s and had used Chinese labor to process salmon. In the 1960s our workforce was made up of Filipinos, white or black laborers, Japanese technicians, and Alaska Natives (mostly from the Tlingit town of Angoon across the strait from Chatham Cannery).

I never realized until later the privilege my family and I enjoyed being exposed to all of these cultures and ethnicities. Of course, since it was the Sixties, we had a lot to learn about "white privilege" and institutional racism.

At Chatham, my family lived in the superintendent's house at the highest point of the entire community, looking down on everyone else. I never thought about the symbolism at the time, mostly I regretted the 79 steps I had to climb to get home. But the hierarchical system was in everything, even in how the cannery was laid out.

My references to Natives and Filipinos in the following pages are made with caring and respect. So many people from Chatham became personal friends who widened my horizons and enriched my life. My husband, Linné, was given a Tlingit name while at Chatham and he remained longtime friends with one of his hotshot fishermen, Herman Kitka, who eventually became the Tlingit chief in Sitka, and his wife Martha, who was the energetic forelady in the cannery.

Through the years I have enjoyed visits by folks from Angoon. That was where most of Chatham's workers lived when they weren't working at the cannery. Our daughter, Dori, was old enough at the time to make life-long friends in the Chatham Native Village. In 2001 Linné and I visited Angoon and looked up old friends. In the writing of this book, I was very fortunate to have several Native friends from Chatham answer my questions and participate enthusiastically in phone interviews. I have always loved their humor, their spiritualism, work ethic, and most of all, their friendship.

As for those of African-American descent who shaped part of my younger life, to be true to the time period I've used the term "Negro" as it was the vernacular of the day, before we even heard the term "black" or "African-American." I used the term with esteem. My father, a Coast Guard Commandant, flouted convention in his attitude toward the racism of his time, as did my mother. They often entertained African Americans at their home or even a Japanese acquaintance—which, considering it was just after World War II when Americans hadn't yet got over seeing someone of Japanese descent as "the enemy"—was pretty remarkable.

My father was keenly interested in and supportive of one of his black officer's writing endeavors, a book that explored the man's African *roots*. It was the saga of his family's experience in America, from slavery to modern times. This petty officer (in the rating of steward, one of the few ratings open to a black person at the time) was named Alex Haley and the book became *Roots* and eventually an award winning movie. One day a Coast Guard cutter would be named after him and stationed in Alaska.

My apologies are warm. We've endeavored to come a long way in our struggles with racial biases, which I would like to believe and hope I never had, and don't today. But I have left these terms in the manuscript as I wrote them in the 60s.

Canneries were so isolated that when I first arrived in Chatham, we didn't even have a telephone. If there was an emergency, one could call on the one way radio for a plane to come from Juneau, 55 miles away. If the "supe" didn't want other people listening in he'd have to take a float plane to Sitka (40 miles away, over a mountain range) to make a sensitive phone call.

As an emerging artist, I found a little time to paint on location, observing picturesque scenes that I was only able to capture because of being privy to a self-operating civilization that perched on the edge of the wilderness. How could I have been so lucky? I sold my very first watercolor at Chatham, launching a career that culminated in 2019 with the Alaska Governor's Lifetime Achievement in the Arts Award.

To us, the whole thing was an adventure, from amphibious planes to brown bears, and we got to see firsthand what Linné did to earn a living that we'd only previously heard about in his letters home. As our children grew there, they learned how to make their own entertainment, learned other cultures, and developed friends from multiple ethnicities, some of whom are friends with them to this day.

Our children thank us every day for this adventure that expanded their cultural horizons in their early formative years. Chatham wasn't the only cannery where we lived, but we spent the most time there. I feel drawn to tell the story.

My main cohort in writing *Boardwalk Footsteps* was Tara Neilson. I found her after reading her book, *Raised in Ruins*, her account of growing up amidst cannery ruins in remote Southeast Alaska with only her family.

We had similar experiences.

After we got our heads together to compare notes, I asked her to be my ghostwriter. I sent her letters I had written to my Mom during the 1960s, many photographs, three cans of 8-mm movies I'd taken of my family's experience at Chatham, a video documentary about my art that had been created by television station KAKM, and a hand-bound book I had already put together about Chatham Cannery in 1998.

Almost every day, for months, Tara would send me e-mails asking me questions. I looked forward to them and poured out a verbose response of memories. Tara said, countless times, "You cannot give me too many details."

Then she would take what I had written and re-word it sometimes to create sensory-filled scenes drawing from her similar experiences. She immersed herself in my vernacular, my humor, my emotions, my family, my history, my aspirations, and my connection to the fishing industry in order to be able to write in my "voice."

In the telling, there are flashbacks that include bits of my childhood, but mostly the first years of our marriage living aboard two cannery tenders where Linné was skipper and I was his deckhand working out of Juneau and Petersburg, delivering salmon to Kayler Dahl Fish Co.

But mostly this book is about an Alaskan cannery operating in one of the most remote areas of the world midway through the 20th century.

This history should not die. Alaska deserves to understand its outlying canneries with entertaining stories told by a family who lived in one.

Chatham Cannery, summer of 1963.

PROLOGUE

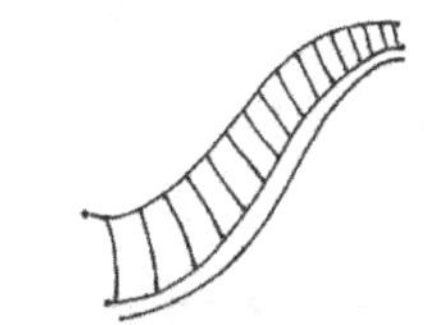

Chatham Cannery

September 10, 1996

Civilization fades in our wake.

We're surrounded by the mountains of Southeast Alaska's Inside Passage. The skirts of the unending forest touch the tide as bald eagles wheel overhead and humpback whales lie on their sides and slap the water with their house high fins.

Linné's brother and sister-in-law, Baird and Peggy, are with us on our maiden trip aboard the *Bardy*. Our plan is to visit the remains of our past: Chatham Cannery.

We anchor in Sitkoh Bay, located midway between Juneau and Sitka. On one side of us are rolling hills covered in shaggy evergreens, unmarred by man's touch. On the other side are a variety of weathered buildings nearly overtaken by time and autumn-colored foliage, scattered along the shoreline. An army of weary, blackened pilings stagger out from the beach.

Up with the misting rain and tucking into a captain's breakfast of pancakes, bacon, fried eggs, coffee, and freshly squeezed orange juice, we contemplate the proper protocol for getting permission to come ashore.

Linné calls the watchman on the radio to explain our pilgrimage. "I was assistant superintendent and then superintendent at Chatham Cannery for eight years in the Sixties," he explains. "My wife and kids lived here with me for five summers."

"That's amazing! We'd love to hear your accounts of the cannery when it was operational."

We're delighted to hear an enthusiastic welcome and don full raingear.

Armed with cameras of every description we board the rigid inflatable raft for the short trip to the airplane float. We walk past Herman and Martha Kitka's house, the home of a hotshot fisherman and canning forelady during Linné's time.

We climbed up to the dock and recognized the Native Village.

There are a couple of families in Joann Jacob's old house across from Mathew and Bessie Fred's in what was once the Native Village. The families in the house, we are told, are here to care-take Chatham. They're all related, and they intend to spend the winter home-schooling the kids out here. They invite us in. The watchman tells us to call him Willy.

In remote areas all over Southeast Alaska, this scene—of strangers being welcomed like rarely seen family—has been repeated endlessly and will be repeated again. It's in the wilderness amidst the raw, stunning grandeur and sometimes life-threatening wild animals and weather, that we are reminded that the human race is a family.

We barely get started sharing the history of Chatham when a light dawns in the mind of one of the mothers.

"Your daughter's name wouldn't be Dori, would it?" She disappears into a back room and emerges holding a notebook. On it in childlike scrawl is "Dori Bardarson" written with large letters. On the back cover are Japanese phrases—*watashi wa, anata wa, onamaya wa,* obviously learned from our Japanese house guest, Toshiko, in 1967. Toshiko had come to see her brother, thinking that Chatham was a town where she could stay in a hotel. Instead she found a roadless outpost with nowhere to bunk so we took her in.

"That's amazing," says the woman when I explain. "When I saw that name, I couldn't believe it. You see, my name is Dori too, and I spell it the same way." It's somehow fitting to know that a Dori once again calls Chatham home.

With this we begin our journey back in time, exploring through the light mist the next building on the boardwalk that extends from one end of the cannery to the other. It's the Filipino Mess Hall where they used to clear away the tables for a dance to celebrate a rare day off from canning.

Linné and his brother pick their way past leaning structures. Linné is on the right in red ski suit.

**Scene from the staircase that led to the house.
The Superintendent's office still stands.**

The building itself leans precariously with the ravages of the passing years, but it seems secure enough, for the moment, to support our investigation of every nook and cranny.

We enter the galley, where they made the delicious, gooey donuts for the cannery coffee breaks called "Mug-Up"… and where someone was murdered.

Food is still on a plate, as though it's in the process of being devoured by a worker before they return to work their shift. I could almost see the ghostly outline of someone I'd once known and chatted with in passing, someone who might have swung me out onto the dance floor to the accompaniment of the mish-mash local band. The music floats in the distant hallways of my mind, just out of reach.

As we proceed down the boardwalk we watch for bears. Our footsteps echo, recalling all the boots and shoes that have walked these boards before us. I wonder where those people are now, if they still walk the earth.

We halt abruptly and catch our breath. The full impact hits us of the devastating fire that destroyed and eliminated the huge New England Fish Company (NEFCO) warehouse and statuesque cannery building, as well as all the connected boardwalks.

There is this huge void in front of us—sky, where the building had stood. It's so weird. A hole in our hearts. Linné and I stand there, unable to process it. It feels like such a personal loss.

The main dock stands silhouetted in the rain-dimpled water, isolated, stark and useless, with no connection whatsoever to the remaining structures. Once the 422-foot Liberty Ship *Southport* had docked there and I'd sat on the wharf with my stretched paper and watercolors and painted it. Where was the *Southport* now?

Our three children on boardwalk in front of Linné's office, 1963.

Linné's office still rests on its pilings. Precarious as it is, we make our way inside, long enough to catch a quick photo of Linné re-enacting radio communications with his fishing boats.

His call letters ring familiarly: "KWF57. This is Chatham cannery. Do you read? Over."

I capture it with my camera, exactly as I had thirty years before.

Linne re-enacts office radio communication.

"This is the Hetta, come back, over." Almost I can hear the captain of the cannery's tender responding. Our oldest son, Blaine, had been allowed to travel on the boat during a fish buying trip. I remember him coming back with a string of halibut on his line, beaming with pride that he'd caught them himself.

Next, we climb the steep steps, all 79 of them, to the superintendent's house up on the hill that overlooks the bay and the entire cannery.

I regale Peggy with an account of Blaine walking up the handrail and plummeting off into the bushes on the sheer slope. I remember how we carefully carried him up to the house. A visiting doctor friend was so sure he had hurt his kidneys, but there was no keeping Blaine down, or

Moss covered steps to the house.

quiet. He was at it again, practicing, the next day. All three kids used the handrail to slide down.

We put our weight on the outer edges of the steps, which seem more secure, and deftly dodge the ones that are missing.

After the long climb up those moss-covered steps, sweating in our full rain gear, we finally make it to the large covered front porch where I spent so many hours at my Smith-Corona typewriter banging out daily letters to my parents in Seattle, regaling them with remote Alaska cannery life.

Dot and Linné on the porch of the house, 1996.

The house is as we had left it, rich with dark paneled walls and paneled ceilings, friendly with big bay windows in the living room. Time has taken its toll, but we can easily see past the deterioration and remember when it was ours. The dining room still has the feel of warmth and love where we spent so many hours with guitars, brojects…and there was the nearby day bed.

I say to Linné, "I don't know what you would have done without that daybed. You'd come up in the afternoon, huffing from the steps, and exhausted from 'putting fires out' at the office, and head to the dining room where the family 'hum' put you to sleep instantly."

He nods with a smile. "I just loved sort of hearing it in the background, where I could still be part of it even though I was unconscious."

Dot and Linné in the dining room, 1996.

"I suppose it was kind of like when we were living on the *Alma*." I suggest. "You used to say you liked the sound of the Atlas engine in the background."

"Yes, that was exactly the same feeling. Life is good. And we're so lucky."

"I never worried about interrupting your sleep, you slept so soundly. But I do remember that if I did, I had to do it gently, because you would spring into action, startled and almost attack the person who woke you. Seems like the stress of running the cannery had you on high alert even in your sleep."

"No doubt."

The kitchen is, as usual, a mess of wires that doesn't quite reach destinations. I remember them well. "Oh, the first time I tried to do a load of laundry in that washing machine with its hand-operated wringer. Do you remember, Linné?"

"I remember you telling me. You were practically in tears…and from what you told me it's a wonder you didn't electrocute yourself, you and Blaine." Linné guffaws as he remembers the details of my battles with the washing machine.

He's always laughed at my mishaps, until pretty soon I'm laughing with him at my own frustrations. That's the way it's always been. He never lets me wallow in misery.

I show Baird and Peg the kitchen's back door where I had, after hearing noises on the back porch, sneaked up to peer through the window in it and went eye-to-eye with a grizzly. I remembered the terror I'd felt knowing the kids were outside and Linné was down in his office with the nearest gun.

Then it was on to our bedroom. It's at the front of the house, with its entrance into the living room. The only trouble had been if I went to bed while we had visiting dignitaries in the living room, there was no way to get to the bathroom unseen at the back of the house to enjoy privacy while performing my evening ablutions. "But," I show Baird, "It had a sink in a corner, which sometimes came in handy when parading through the living room was too awkward."

We take one last look around.

"This is really a beautiful house," says Baird, eyeing the built-ins.

Linné follows his gaze. "We know. We always loved the woodwork. Look at the parquet ceiling. And the old glass windows in the dining room above the window boxes. You know how you can tell they are old?" he asks his rhetorical question assuming Baird won't have a clue. "You see the distortion, the way the glass looks wavy, and it's thin? That's old. River boats on the Mississippi back in the 1800s never used windows in the pilot house because that distortion disguised telltale currents that indicated a barely submerged sandbar or snag."

"Well, with age we'll look that way too before long," quips Baird, ignoring his brother's superior knowledge. (He's not one to be one-upped, even if Linné had been the almighty superintendent.)

We have to be extra careful coming down the 79 steps to cannery level. It hasn't stopped raining and the steps are slippery. Some are missing. We don't see any No Trespassing signs to "protect" us, but we purposely don't look either.

Next are the carpenter's shop, and the Ways, which had been the subject, along with the cannery building behind them, of my very first commissioned painting. Gone are the two giant fuel tanks the beach gang had worked so hard "Egyptian-style" to move and mount.

The Mess Hall looks the same, a little older but still wearing one of the signs I'd painted in 1963. It's well-preserved, "Like us," I say in an aside to Peg.

**Dot and Linné reminisce about all the meals
they ate at the Chatham Mess Hall.**

Gone is the aroma of freshly baked pies or the anticipation of seeing Smokey and Elizabeth in the kitchen. We traipse through the mug-up room where yummie leftovers had been available as between-meal snacks. Then comes the dining hall where we not only ate three squares a day but watched

16-mm movies at night on rental from Juneau.

On down the boardwalk is the still-standing bunkhouse with 30 private rooms. Linné shows us where he lived during the three summers before he was superintendent, before the kids and I came to stay with him.

By this time, we're saturated, even in our rain gear. There is nothing quite like 'sploring in a Southeast Alaskan rain mist.

Avram Gross owns Chatham now and has built a nice house in the style of the old cannery houses, trimmed with contemporary teal. The artifacts he has gathered are on display as in a museum in one of the old Native houses.

We say "Goodbye" and thank Willy and return to the *Bardy* via Zodiac.

It's pouring rain when we pull anchor. The rain almost, but not quite, obscures the leaning buildings and long boardwalk that once supported busy and productive Chatham cannery.

I look back as our wake splashes against the shores of our past. And I remember…

PART I: 1963

Boardwalk Footsteps

CHAPTER 1

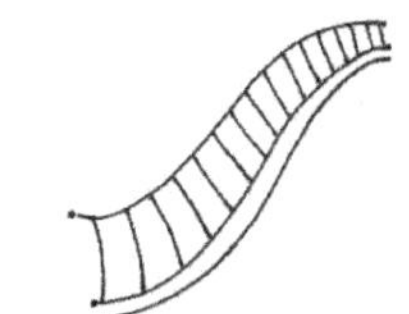

Choosing Chatham

How I wish I were at Bardvilla so that we could all play together... We sure are getting a lot of fish up here this year. Some day you can come up and help Daddy can all these fish.

— Letter to Blaine from Linné, July 9, 1961

Seattle, Washington
April 29, 1963

"The superintendent of Chatham Cannery in Alaska has had a heart attack," Linné announced through the phone's receiver.

I was disconcerted by the undertone of triumph in my husband's voice. When I'd answered the phone I'd wedged the receiver against my ear with my shoulder, leaving my hands free as I ironed laundry by the overcast light glooming through the window that overlooked our backyard at the north end of Seattle's urban sprawl.

I needed to prepare myself for something momentous. I could hear it in every word he spoke. "Is he okay?" I took a breath, tested the Hotpoint iron with a wetted finger, and then picked up a boy's shirt to give my hands something to do.

Linné became more subdued, "He's dead."

I dropped the shirt. "Oh, no! I'm so sorry to hear that."

"It's rough. But there's always an upside to even the hardest parts of life, isn't there? Change is good."

I set the ironing aside and held the phone to my ear. "And the upside to a fatal heart attack is…?"

"I've been promoted to superintendent!"

"Oh Linné, I know how much that means to you." I hoped I sounded as pleased for him as I should. He'd put in three seasons of hard work at Chatham, cut off from his family, as assistant superintendent for the New England Fish Co. at Chatham Cannery.

Inside I felt suspended above a drop off, waiting for the fall that I sensed was coming.

"Don't you understand, Dot? Now, you and the children can come to Chatham!"

There it was. I saw where it was all headed now.

He didn't notice my silence.

"I'll have the superintendent's house with space for you and the kids. How wonderful that we can at last be together in the summer, during the salmon season!" Linné rattled on, full of plans and purpose, compelled by an irrepressible drive for larger-than-life adventure. I'd been hauled willy-nilly, into his adventures before. But that was then.

I was older now and I had three children, all under the age of seven. And there was nothing we loved more than leaving the rainy suburbs of Seattle behind for our little summer getaway that we had so lovingly and laboriously built on Washington state's idyllic San Juan Island. How could I turn my back on it to live in a rough cannery in a remote, roadless region of Alaska?

The summer home we'd created on San Juan Island was my paradise and I didn't want to give up a fourth straight summer there. And what about the kids, who spent every waking—and sometimes sleeping!—hour outside happy as larks? The kids swam, hot-dogged on the beach, explored the island, sang songs with me on my guitar as accompaniment, hosted the girl scouts, and made friends with children on the island. Their favorite pastime was to sit on the hood of the car while they held nets to scoop up the island's innumerable bunnies.

I was right there with them, rejoicing in the banana-belt weather. We didn't have much, not that anyone cared. We gathered treasures of driftwood, rock, shells, and flotsam from the beach, and I arranged them artistically on the back deck and back wall of the house.

We drove an old junker car and scavenged for home décor at the "Community Exchange" (San Juan Island's dump) and bought rough-hewn deck furniture from a roadside vendor. The kids had their own small outside table made from a sawed-off tree round with driftwood legs. We'd found a bathtub at the dump and positioned it at the back door. We all used it, though we had to be careful of the severe water shortages on San Juan Island. In addition, friends gave us furniture every time they visited us, and visit us they did…big time.

We hosted one family after another. Everyone shared with food, and helped make repairs on the cottage, once helping to re-shingle the entire roof. We dubbed it—after experimenting with "Bardvista"—"Bardvilla" (since our last name was Bardarson) and every person who stayed became an honored "Bardvillain." I'd be saying goodbye to folks leaving at the same time folks were arriving. It was so much fun.

Bardvilla Cottage.

How could I and the kids give up the enchantment of Bardvilla this summer?

Not that I didn't want to be with Linné. People use the term "the love of my life" so lightly that it's become a cliché, but Linné was that for me. He never failed to make my heart skip a beat when I was near him. He was the only man for me, and I'd known it during the first minutes of a blind date with him.

It was my second blind date of the night. The first had been a bust.

I opened the front door after the bell and there he stood on the bottom of two steps. We were at eye level. Then he stepped up, all 6 foot 7 inches of him. I mentally checked "tall" off the list of characteristics I wanted in a husband.

No wonder I fell in love, December 1953.

The fact that he was as handsome as could be with Nordic good looks, a gift from his Swedish mother and Icelandic father, also didn't hurt. It was from the Swedish side, I later learned, that he got his unusual name. It was taken from the famous Swedish botanist known as the "father of modern taxonomy," that is, the system of naming organisms: Carl Linnæus, later (after his ennoblement) Linné.

To my dismay, on the night of that life-altering blind date, my dad came into the living room just as I was diving into my jacket, in a rush to get Mr. Linné Bardarson all to myself.

Dad, a captain in the Coast Guard and a good judge of men, sized Linné up and immediately said, "Won't you stay and have some ice cream? We were just dishing up."

An hour later, Linné and I took off in his new Ford car. Mom, Dad, and Aunt Edna went into the kitchen and assured each other that "if she doesn't like him, there's no hope for her."

There was plenty of hope for me, as it turned out.

After 58 years of marriage, one day I asked Linné, "When did we first kiss?"

He answered, "Oh, about a block from the house."

It had been that way for both of us from the start.

No, being with Linné wasn't a problem for me or the kids, who adored him. It was being banished to the hinterlands of the 49th state that was the issue. As much as I'd once enjoyed being Linné's deckhand on a fish tender, times were different now. I had children.

Early on Linné had a way of getting me all excited about a new adventure. When we were courting during our attendance at the University of Washington, he would regale me with stories about buying fish in Southeast Alaska on the fish tender he skippered in the summer, the *Estella*.

I was not raised to be a deckhand on a slimy fish boat, but that's what I became.

In fact, if my life was the subject of a documentary, here is where the narrator would say: *Little did fashion-conscious, New York City girl Dot Bardarson know that she'd never wear triple needle shoes again.*

Right after our brief honeymoon Linné had been called back to Alaska while I stayed behind to write thank you notes for wedding presents. I followed him a couple weeks later. As I descended the portable steps from the prop plane at the Juneau airport, I searched the waiting groups of people and waved when I saw Linné there to meet me.

Being a young woman trained to be a model in New York City, knowledgeable about the travel etiquette of the 1950s—and the necessity of dressing for the occasion—I'd donned a picture hat with a broad brim. My dress was chartreuse with black trim, fitted to the waist with a flared skirt with large black buttons down the front. Perfectly matched to the outfit were delicate, open-toed, ankle strap black heels. To top it off I wore black elbow-length gloves, attention-grabbing large clip-on earrings, and clasped my black clutch bag. I was as "well put together" as any East Coast debutant.

How I flew to Juneau.

As I swayed on my heels toward him, Linné thought to himself, *I think I've made a horrible mistake.*

Or so he liked to claim whenever he teased me about my background that was completely unsuitable, and had not prepared me at all, for being the wife of an adventurer like Linné Bardarson.

The *Estella* was docked at the Juneau Cold Storage. It was low tide and I had to climb down, in my fashionable high heels, a vertical, slick dock ladder that dripped with seaweed. When I reached the deck of the *Estella*, Linné swept me off my feet with a flourish and carried me in his arms on to my new diesel- and fish-smelling home.

We "cast the lines loose," as Linné would say, and somewhere between Gastineau Channel and Haines we made love on the flying bridge. I never wore the dress and its accoutrements again.

Around 5 o'clock of our first trip he suggested I go down to the galley and cook my first meal. I knew nothing about cooking. But he said he had thawed out some pork chops and that I could fry them on the oil stove. I somehow muddled through, and our honeymooner enchantment made the meal edible.

We bought salmon from a gillnetter and hauled them to a cannery in Petersburg. I had never known such fatigue. But Alaska was beautiful, and we were in love.

After stowing my dress, I realized I was "home," that I'd left behind forever the remnants of a New York City girl. Life on the *Estella*, with her cabin newly painted white and brick red, was fabulous. I realized why Linné loved it so much.

We lived aboard the 57-foot *Estella* and later the 95-foot *Alma* for two and half years. I never imagined during my blind date with Linné that one day I'd be climbing 26-foot ladders off the deck of a fish tender in Alaska while I was eight months pregnant. Or that I'd be nursing and ministering to the needs of my baby, Dori, for the first six months of her life while also tending to my deckhand chores.

Leaving the *Alma* to give birth.

It soon became apparent that I couldn't continue to share Linné's Alaska life. We needed a shore home—Dori needed a place where she could crawl.

We sold the *Alma*, sold our 1953 Corvette, and bought a cute little two-bedroom house in the North end of Seattle. We paid $14,000 for it at payments of $85 a month.

When spring of 1957 rolled around, Linné took off for Alaska. My dad had been transferred to Curtis Bay, Maryland by the Coast Guard to be the commandant of the shipyard. My folks suggested I come for the summer since I would be alone.

I also went there in 1958 and 1959 after Linné headed for Alaska. But it was a long trip with two children (Dori and Blaine) and by then I was pregnant with Rolf. The twelve hours on a prop plane to cross the country with small children while "expecting" were not conducive to my continued sanity.

In 1960, Linné and I discussed this, and came up with the idea of a vacation home on San Juan Island, where the kids could have a summer in the country. We found a cabin on False Bay with 300 feet of waterfront; five acres altogether. Perfect. It cost us $5,500, which we couldn't afford so Linné's mom made the $50 a month payments at first. It was more than worth it for everyone involved even if it meant struggling to make ends meet.

Every summer, I rented our house in Seattle to visiting professors at the University of Washington and happily headed for Bardvilla.

Our three summers in False Bay were the perfect place to raise children. I also taught art classes, painted watercolors, and signs. Water was always in short supply, and to pay back the neighbors for being given access to theirs, I painted signs for them. We bought raw milk from a farmer who had livestock on the island, including horses. It was a healthy, bucolic life for the children and a custom-fitted one for me.

Sundstrom Farm on San Juan Island.

Although San Juan Island was beautiful, it was Bardvilla itself that had the magic, a magic I'd lovingly molded with my open hearth hospitality, hootenannies, and the freedom the children had to safely explore on their own.

The thought of sacrificing our time at Bardvilla never occurred to me until Linné called me that gloomy April morning.

I stood at the ironing board, endlessly re-arranging a pillowcase on it, as I listened to Linné talk about how much we'd enjoy it, the kids and I, abandoning Bardvilla for a raw cannery in Alaska.

I pretended to embrace the idea, hoping that Linné didn't sense my inner resistance and disappointment.

We hung up and I unplugged the iron and thought, *this is an emergency that requires a Fran consultation.*

Before heading out, I checked myself in the mirror. I wore a blouse and long pants—I'd learned to give up dresses and heels to be comfortable going about chores as a deckhand on the *Estella*. Despite that, my appearance was blameless, as though I always expected somebody to stop by. There was never a moment of my waking life when my makeup wasn't done perfectly, a result of those early modeling lessons. Since I had naturally curly, dark hair, I didn't need to worry about that. I wore it short since it was the most becoming style for me.

I flicked a comb through my curls and headed outside after double checking to make sure I'd turned off the iron. Fran was my dearest friend and lived just around the corner.

I had first met her when I'd heard there was a four-year-old in the house named Ralph. My Rolf was four. So I went over and knocked on her door, introduced myself and Rolf, and immediately Fran and I became fast friends.

She had four children and was expecting a fifth and she and her family were regulars at Bardvilla. No one knew better than Fran what a perfect place it was for children and how much joy I took in creating its open-door conviviality with friends coming and going. She'd understand what a sacrifice it would be for me to have to give it up.

As I left, I frowned at the development on the street at the side of our house, where five streets came together. Dayton Avenue was a dangerous street, an arterial, where cars drove way too fast. We lost a cat on Dayton. Once, I even had to spank Rolf for heading toward the street, after quietly explaining things to him. I shivered thinking about what might have happened to him. Thankfully the impact of my talk with him, even more than the spank, served to impress on him the need to never go near Dayton again.

That was one more reason to look forward to going to Bardvilla, where the children could roam free and be perfectly safe. Could it possibly be the same in the Alaskan wilderness, where great brown bears had the run of the beaches and woods where the cannery was situated?

I was thankful as I reached Fran's house that her children were all in school. She and her husband had a relationship more reminiscent of the 1860s than the 1960s. She made it work, finding pleasure in focusing on the kids and cooking and letting her domineering husband take charge of everything else. He was under the impression that he completely ran the show, but she had her way of getting what she wanted for the family. She and I spent a lot of time laughing, mostly about human nature.

I wasn't laughing now.

Fran took one look at my face when she opened the door and said, "What's happened?"

"Oh, Fran," I said, "We've got two hours to convince me that I want to go to Chatham Cannery in Alaska instead of Bardvilla."

Her eyes widened as she took in the idea of me losing Bardvilla for the summer. "Wow, that's a tough one."

I nodded. "When Linné comes home tonight, I need to be enthusiastic."

Fran was the right person for the job. She martialed her resources, plying me with tea and home-made chocolate chip cookies though she knew I was a health nut. The circumstances demanded extreme measures and I went with it.

She seated herself across from me and laid a note pad and pencil on the table.

"What's that for?" I asked, mid-sip.

"Positivity. We already know what there is to love about going to Bardvilla. Let's come up with all the pluses we can think of on the Chatham side of the equation."

Were there any? I didn't allow the negative thought to gain traction. Instead I thought about what Linné had said about all of us being in one place this summer. I knew how much Linné missed being with us; it showed in the letters he'd write from Chatham, like the one he wrote to me on Dori's 5th birthday:

"Today we have a five-year-old girl. How I wish I could be there to celebrate with you all. Good times, happy times, times to remember. How lucky I am to have someone like you at the controls while I'm gone.

I'm in love with my wife. She is the finest thing I have ever known… The watchman is about ready to turn out the lights so it's goodnight sweetheart. I wish it were with you. All my love, Linné."

My heart warmed by the memory of his letter, I said to Fran, "Having the whole family together."

"Good one." Fran scratched it down. "How about having an Alaskan adventure? I know you've had some already, but how many have the kids had that they'll remember?"

That was a good point, and it got easier from there. We added: the kids would learn what their daddy did to earn a living, and we wouldn't be able to spend any money while there because all our needs would be met. We would get to eat in the mess hall—I wouldn't have to cook.

"More time for your art," she pointed out.

"That would be a big plus," I agreed, my spirits lifting more.

Best of all, we realized that we could still go to Bardvilla at the end of the salmon season.

There was one other plus that came to me after I returned home to wait for Linné, after making sure the house was picked up and the children were in clean clothes. (Mom had drilled it into me that when your man comes home from work, you make him feel like a king.)

As I cooked dinner, I thought of all the times Linné stopped by at a bar on the way home. Dinner would be ready, and he wouldn't come, and dinner would get cold. I'd end up having to put the children to bed without them seeing their father. I wrote about it:

> *I'd wait and wait, so looking forward to having him home with his family, and for me an adult to share stories with. I'd look longingly from the kitchen window, expecting two headlights beaming toward the house, and finally have to feed the children and sometimes myself as the hours dragged on. I was always on the alert not to take my anxiety out on the children because*

I instinctively knew the damage it could do.

I'd wept many quiet tears over the years about it. At least at the cannery there would be no bars.

Thankfully, this night Linné arrived home right on time. He must have been concerned about how the kids would feel about giving up Bardvilla. He was capable of understanding and responding seriously to childish concerns. He wrote a letter to Dori on her 5th birthday from Chatham, apologizing for seeming to miss her birthday because his present to her was late, explaining that because the moccasins he'd commissioned from a Native Alaskan worker were made by hand they took longer than buying them from the store. "I hope you don't think that I forgot your birthday… I miss you very much Dori, I'm sorry that I have to go away each summer. Take good care of Mommy. All my love, Daddy."

To Blaine, that same summer, he wrote: "Gee! How I wish I were at Bardvilla so that we could all play together. Wouldn't it be fun if you and I could go for a ride on our raft in False Bay? I'll bet when I get home you will be a great big boy. We sure are getting a lot of fish up here this year. Some day you can come up and help daddy can all the fish. This fall when I get home I'm going to take a vacation. Then you and I can play together every day. All my love, Daddy."

Over dinner, after we introduced the idea of going to Chatham for the summer, Linné told the kids alluring stories about flying in a small plane, seeing bears, and making friends in the Native village. He left Bardvilla out of the conversation, and I made no mention of it either.

The children were at the most adaptable and resilient of ages: almost seven (Dori), five and a half (Blaine) and three and a half (Rolf). They were easily enticed.

That summer I made one last trip to San Juan Island with friends after renting our Seattle house to the University of Washington as usual. A couple of families offered to take care of Bardvilla while we were away. *Lucky them.*

And then we flew off to Alaska for a new adventure.

CHAPTER 2

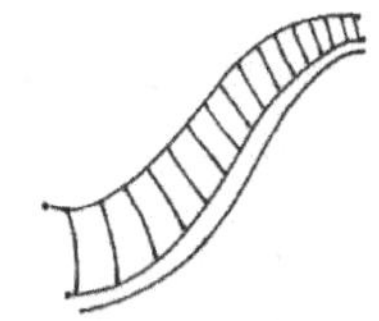

An Understanding Wife

You are undoubtedly the most understanding wife in the world, and the sexiest and the most loveable.

—Letter from Linné to Dot, June 21, 1960

Pan American jetliner
Seattle - Juneau
July 9, 1963

Shortly before the children and I left for Alaska, I got a letter from Linné that opened with the words *We just had an experience here that made our blood run cold.* And as I read it, my blood ran cold. It was all too easy picturing myself and my kids in the situation he described:

A huge brown bear came out of the woods and was milling around in front of the guest house by the lumber pile. Smoky saw it first and got Hugh and I out of the office. Elizabeth Hansen and Mathew Fred were in the warehouse. We all went over to the windows to watch the bear at close range.

Mathew and Elizabeth were three or four windows down, closer to the village. All at once Elizabeth screamed THE CHILDREN — THE CHILDREN. Mathew screamed RUN RUN. Four six and seven year old girls had come skipping up the walk and had just reached the lumber pile before they were noticed. At this point bears are supposed to run off into the woods, but not so. In one jump he was on top of the lumber pile and after these four girls. It was the most horrifying sight I will ever see. Four little girls running for their lives. It was a close race, the girls had a head start and they won by a hair. As they blew into the far end of the warehouse Mathew slammed the door shut behind them. The bear then came back up to the boardwalk to the guest house. I went charging into the cannery looking for someone who owned a rifle. By the time Buckley and Mathew got their rifles, the bear had disappeared.

It didn't exactly endear Chatham to me. My stomach went weightless every time I thought about it.

Keep positive, I reminded myself as I settled into my seat on the Pan Am jet, and mentally went over the upbeat list Fran and I had come up with earlier.

The engines revved, vibrating our seats and the fragile metal membrane enclosing the fuselage. The jet rolled forward faster and faster until we parted ways with the ground. Finally, the kids and I were off, flying out of Sea-Tac airport.

Seattle miniaturized below us as we arrowed upward through blue sky and into a fluffy white cloud bank before the plane leveled off and people were allowed to wander around the cabin and unwind with a calming cigarette. Not me, I hated smoking and never ceased wishing Linné would stop.

The Pan Am stewardesses were very attentive to the kids (who were extremely well-behaved during jet travel), plying them with snacks, beverages, cards, and wings to pin on.

Towards the end of the flight, I felt the ever present need to document the moment. I reached for my camera. I wasn't called "The Paparazzi" by my family for nothing.

"That's a nice camera," my neighbor across the aisle said. "You'll find that Alaska rewards and frustrates the amateur photographer with breathtakingly beautiful, but all too vast, panoramas. Where are you headed?"

I was abundantly familiar with Alaska's panoramas up close and first hand after being a deckhand on a fish tender for 3 years, but at the time, it was normal for men to assume they knew more on every topic than any stray woman they happened across. I didn't hold it against him and explained that the kids and I would be taking a floatplane to a remote cannery about sixty miles south of Juneau.

"Your husband is superintendent?" He looked at me curiously, and I knew what he was thinking—I always looked young for my age. When I was 15, I'd been able to ride the train to Baltimore, when my family lived in Linthicum, MD, for only 11 cents because I looked like I was under 12. Nowadays my short dark hair and slender build tended to take years off my age.

My air travel neighbor apparently assumed Linné was likewise lacking in years because he added, "Isn't your husband a little young for that?"

"Not when you consider that he started working when he was twelve."

Right then the pilot announced that we would be landing in Juneau shortly.

I got the kids in shape, putting away toys and blankets and pillows from the upper bin.

Sheer, snowy peaks dominated the capital of Alaska with its unimaginative, boxy high-rise architecture. The city of Juneau was wedged between the mountains and the glittering ribbon of the channel. As we traveled through the downtown area by cab to Alaska Coastal Airlines (the seaplane company that would fly us out to the cannery), I entertained myself by planning what I'd write to my parents:

> *Naturally I arrived minus a few items, namely our coats*
> *which were left at the Juneau terminal in the hands of the ticket*
> *agent, and the green suitcase with Blaine's clothes. I don't know*
> *where that is, presumably just overlooked on the plane. We had*

to wait 3 hours in Juneau after our bus trip from the airport. So I thought of the library. I read three books to the children which was the perfect activity except that I got so drowsy. We went in search of food, which we didn't really need, but I thought would keep us occupied. I was quickly reminded of the exorbitant prices in Juneau.

I swiped a menu to send to my parents to scandalize them with the food prices in the Last Frontier. At home sirloin steak was $.63 a pound, here a simple hamburger on a toasted bun, with a side of fries or potato salad, cost 95 cents, and if you added a slice of cheese it would bump up the cost to a dollar and a dime. On the drinks menu a milkshake or malted milk cost 60 cents (nearly twice what we'd pay back in Seattle), while phosphates and buffaloes would run you from thirty to 50 cents respectively. Even a Bromo Seltzer cost 35 cents!

We arrived at Alaska Coastal Airlines where we'd take a floatplane out to the cannery. After I settled the kids into the plastic chairs in the lobby, I tried to imagine what life would be like at Chatham. I had always been game for anything, and now, thankfully, the kids were just old enough to be brought along on an Alaskan adventure.

I did wish Linné was with me, but he'd gone to Chatham several weeks earlier to prepare the cannery for the new season. He'd had three years before that when he was assistant superintendent, but now I'd get to see in person what he'd written about in his frequent letters home.

The kids of course were taking it all in stride, as kids do. They were easy travelers, taking it all in and helping with luggage and finding things to keep them busy as we waited.

Their suitcases didn't include toys which turned out to be okay. That stimulated a kid's imagination. They made up their own games. Dori, of course, had Chatty Cathy. She couldn't go anywhere without her doll. Maybe the boys' had a small truck but that was all.

Yes, this would be a grand adventure into the unknown. Oh, I had seen canneries before, but always with a town attached or nearby. This would be different. It was all by itself, a little space off the grid, a self-functioning salmon cannery.

My parents liked to shake their heads in amazement at the exploits that took me to the wilds of Alaska. Linné had assured me, however, that it wouldn't be too "wild." There was, he'd assured me, a comfortable house there for us with electricity and water.

I'd always had to cook three meals a day. What would it be like to eat in a mess hall? I looked forward to that. Would the food be nutritious? Because of my mother-in-law, I had been heavily influenced by her to feed the children good, honest food, avoiding the pitfalls of excessive sugar.

I was ahead of the curve, already taking vitamins, just a few. I had been raised on cod liver oil, so I was putting drops in the kids' juice. When Blaine was born two weeks before Christmas in 1957, I had picked up a staph infection from the hospital that developed into a breast abscess, so I had to stop breast feeding.

Linné's mother had rushed through Seattle traffic to bring me blackstrap molasses, Lugal's Solution, and Brewer's Yeast. As soon as Gertrude arrived, she concocted a brownish awful looking formula with evaporated milk and all the "goodies" to feed the new baby. She had to enlarge the hole in the rubber nipple to accommodate the extra nutrition.

I barely had the kids settled in the chairs in the seaplane base's waiting room before *"Chatham!"* was called by the woman behind the desk.

We gathered what gear we hadn't already sent down to the dock to be loaded into the nose of the plane and stepped outside into the salt-fresh air.

Sea gulls shrieked as we made our way down the wooden ramp with its triangular floor stops to keep clients from sliding down its length. We reached the main float where a variety of seaplanes were lined up, bobbing on the channel chop like horses on a carousel. Their pontoons, wings and fuselages glinted blindingly in the high latitude, afternoon sunshine.

Excited, we were directed to one of the big flying boats, the Consolidated PBY Catalina, which was larger than the Grumman Goose but had a similar hull. I learned that it had been bought from military surplus meant for the war in the Aleutians during WW II. It was white with black stripes the length of the fuselage, had red and gold engine cowlings mounted high above the flying ship, and the seaplane's logo of a mirrored flying goose gleamed on the nose.

Years later I discovered that our pilot was Ray Renshaw, one of Alaska's famous pioneer bush pilots. Among many hair-raising adventures, he'd flown PBYs during the war in the Aleutians, so we were in extremely capable hands.

We scrambled one after the other into the oval open door next to the gigantic, retracted wheel. When it came my turn, I gathered up my skirt and endeavored to enter the fuselage with grace and modesty. Whether or not I succeeded is best left a mystery.

The plane could seat twenty in small but comfortable chairs that looked out picture windows. Rolf and I sat below the peaked ceiling embedded with high windows that flooded the cabin with light but that no one could see out of. It was where the flight engineer would have sat during military operations. Dori and Blaine were thrilled to sit in the observation blisters where the waist gunners would have sat. Dori called them "the bubble" which perfectly described each bulging window on either side of the tail end of the plane.

When the plane took off, the spray sloshed up over the top of the blisters and Dori exclaimed that it was like being in a car wash. Rather than facing forward, the seats faced each other across the aisle, but the blisters gave a near 360-degree view of the sky, glaciers, sea, and forests we flew over, and narrow mountain passages we climbed through within foot-dragging distance of the rocks and snow.

The PBY was infamous for being "a tank to drive" partly because it didn't have flaps, and it took a lot of strength to keep it from sliding around in the air. I couldn't help imagining what would happen if the hull dropped just a few yards and made contact as the tips of the broad wings seemed to scrape snow off the Alaskan mountainsides.

How would we survive up here in this barren, cold world until help came? If we survived the crash. It made me think of when my mother flew for the first time. Most people at that time bought insurance that would pay beneficiaries in the event of a crash. Mom wrote a letter to us four kids, with fear embedded on the pages, telling us how much she loved us.

It was a relief to drop down from the cold, monochrome heights toward the temperate and colorful broad snaking pathways of our section of the Inside Passage.

We flew over miles and miles of spruce forest, some of them with logging roads. We approached from the land side behind the cannery and as the pilot banked the plane and dropped altitude, all of a sudden there was this tiny settlement, largely built on pilings at the head of a slough sided by evergreen-covered, steep rolling hills with mountains in the background.

It was the only sign of human habitation, and looked tiny from the air, but more and more buildings individuated themselves as the pilot lowered the retracted floats from the wings and we circled down toward the water for a landing.

I was surprised at how small it was. I guess I had expected a more sprawling campus. All the buildings were connected with wooden boardwalks. The artist in me liked the orderly design of that.

I had no idea Chatham would be so picturesque. Why hadn't I brought my watercolors? Well, I wouldn't have time to paint anyway with three small children and a husband. Linné and I hadn't seen each other in several weeks, and I was eager to spend lots of time with him.

The main processing building and warehouse stuck way out from shore on pilings. Large vessels were anchored out in the bay waiting to take on loads of canned and labeled fish to be freighted down to the Lower 48. (Chatham was one of the rare canneries that did their own labeling, affixing the logo that said New England Fish Co. which showed a salmon with a harpoon behind it and the trademarked legend below it: *Packed with the wiggle in its tail*.)

I could see a variety of tenders out the plane window as the big seaplane's hull met the water. We were jostled around in our seats as the PBY roared toward the cannery.

I was familiar with multiple canneries since I'd worked on a fish tender, but Chatham struck me as different because of how isolated it was.

In addition, as the cannery grew in scope in front of me, I felt that there was something all new and inspiring about Chatham. Maybe because I knew my husband, as superintendent, was lord, mayor, justice of the peace—and even coroner—of this remote outpost.

That makes one's perspective a bit grander.

When we docked, I busied myself with getting the kids and their things organized and out of the plane. But as soon as I set foot on the airplane float with the huge red and white buildings towering over it on a forest of pilings, I only had eyes for the tall blond man with a wide smile stretching his handsome features.

He greeted the kids happily then turned to me and my heart thumped hard. I couldn't tell if he looked tired or not. As I later wrote to my parents: *As far as I can see he looks WONDERFUL!*

Linné swept me into a hug, and we kissed passionately. I had a feeling it would have to hold me for a while with how busy he was, so I put a lot into it and he returned it in full measure, making my toes curl. Maybe giving up Bardvilla hadn't been such a sacrifice after all. I could hardly wait till this evening when I had Linné all to myself.

As he set me back on my feet, I happened to catch the be-spectacled eyes of a stocky businessman in slacks, open suit jacket over a polo shirt, and on his head a brown, wool felt hat. Linné introduced me to him: Jay Gage, General Superintendent of the New England Fish Co.

Perhaps I should have been embarrassed by our public, ardent embrace, but Linné and I had never made a polite pretense of our relationship. In an era when it was absolutely verboten to kiss on a first date, we'd kissed within an hour of meeting each other.

Jay Gauge, Linné, and Mike Goodman holding Rolf.

"I'll give you the complete tour tomorrow," Linné said. I could see in his eyes and hear in his voice how much he looked forward to that, how proud he was of his cannery, and it melted my heart. "Sorry I can't do it today; we're way behind. I might not see you the rest of the day."

"Okay." I tweaked his rumpled T-shirt and raised my eyebrows and he admitted he'd been so rushed for time that he hadn't bothered with washing his clothes in the washing machine, he'd simply tossed a couple shirts off the dock and reeled them back in to dry in the sun.

It made me impatient to get to our house and turn it into a real home for him, using all of the wifely arts Mom had trained me in so that I'd be able to provide the housewifely benefits that were, as she insisted, all important to a man's health, happiness, and comfort.

We waved as the PBY taxied away from the dock and then roared off between anchored vessels, leaving behind the lingering urban scent of its exhaust. Linné's attention was snagged by the kids who were rambunctious after the long flight. He was a tolerant father for the most part, but his tolerance had its limits. One thing he didn't like was for the kids to disrespect me or cause me too much trouble, and he took the opportunity now to lay down the law with them to be helpful and not cause trouble for me.

He was gone in the next instant, after another quick kiss for me and the words, "I'll see you later… maybe." I didn't get the chance to be disappointed because Jay Gage stepped in front of me, cutting off my view of Linné loping up the steep ramp to the cannery wharf.

"Don't be too disappointed that you won't see that much of him. He's super busy right now," Jay said.

I knew he was. In our phone conversations, Linné had mentioned that he'd been sleeping on a bare mattress in the office the past few days, fitting in naps here and there where he could find 10 minutes.

Jay made small talk with me, asking about my flight, showing interest in whether I had home help or not (NOT), and took pains to assure me the kids would be happy here with so many other kids to play with. All the time we were talking, I sensed he had something on his mind and he was circling around the point, studying me intently through his thick, black-frame glasses.

I studied him curiously. He was the general manager over all of the New England Fish Co.'s canneries in Alaska, so Chatham was a regular stop in his constant tour overseeing every operation. Linné had told me Jay didn't like Chatham and never stayed long. He spent as little time there as possible. Linné wanted to make Jay feel completely comfortable and satisfied that everything was under control with Linné at the helm, so as a supportive wife I nodded along to everything Jay said.

"I was relieved to find out about all the children here from Linné's talks with me on the marine radio," I agreed, trying to put him at ease with me. Maybe he was concerned that I wasn't the kind of woman who could handle living in such a small population. "Though they're very good at entertaining themselves, as am I."

"Good, good. That's good to hear… I guess you heard about the bumper year we are experiencing in Chatham," he added abruptly.

The wake from the PBY reached us and slapped against the float and much to the kids' delight slopped up onto the deck almost catching their feet. I kept an eye on them and said to Jay, "Yes, I know, Linné told me. I gather he's having a hard time keeping up, coming on the heels of the general strike."

My words appeared to light a fire in him. "I've never seen anything like it! Chatham is going all out, both lines running, but still the fish keep pouring in. Excess fish are being sent to Petersburg for processing by Petersburg Cannery. This cannery," he swept a hand toward the large buildings above us that lined the shore on endless black pilings, "hasn't shut down this season before three a.m. and many times as late as five. The workday starts at eight regardless and the cannery runs six days a week."

I looked around, taking in the double-moored lines of fishing boats at every available space and anchored out on the bay. Tenders were offloading fish and freighters were taking on countless wooden pallets stacked with boxed canned salmon. I could see men driving forklifts on the wharf above us and the constant motion of the giant arm of the crane swinging the product out to be caught by deckhands and put away in the hold. Steam vented continuously from one building and the muffled, mechanical roar of the processing equipment was a constant noise obliterating all wilderness sounds.

"It does seem busy." I offered with a deadpan understatement.

"The office has had one catastrophe after another. Bookkeepers have been flown in from other less strenuous areas, but one has already succumbed to a bad case of nerves and has been flown to Juneau."

It brought home to me the stress Linné was under. It was my pleasant job to encourage him any way a wife could. The more lovingly, the better. I could hardly restrain a smile at the thought of getting my husband to myself again, finally.

Jay added, "They are behind not only in the office but in the post office. Linné is the postmaster too, by the way."

"Yes, he—"

"The fish are piling up and some of the boats are disgruntled because they can't get them unloaded fast enough. Linné is juggling the briners trying to hold fish, but at the rate they keep coming in, we see no end in sight or a chance for a break. Perhaps you don't know—" he delivered this with a weighty look, "—but Linné's dragged a mattress down to the office and is sleeping on the floor. I'm afraid he won't be much of a…*husband*. So don't expect… *much* of him."

I got it then, what he was—to his mind—ever so delicately trying to get across. That I shouldn't be a demanding wife outside of the bedroom, and certainly not inside of it.

I managed to say matter-of-factly, "I totally understand. Remember, Linné and I used to run cannery tenders. It was like that for us sometimes too, and we were newlyweds. We slept together in a 30-inch-wide bunk our first year on the *Estella*."

"Good, good, so glad you understand. It's important for a man in Linné's position to have a wife who understands the situation and knows what's expected of her. It is all very complicated." In his relief at getting his "sensitive" point across, he went to great lengths to assure me that Linné was thought much of and got encouragement from other "big wheels," who made such comments on the radio as "Well, Linné, if anyone can handle it, you can."

This was good to hear, of course. Jay went on to add, "Linné is well known in Southeast Alaska, respected and liked. And I think everyone is delighted he has attained this station."

Did he think that my marital demands might in some way undermine it?

"How nice," I said with a polite smile. It was not unpleasant, when I asked him how long he was staying, to hear that he had to be off tomorrow.

"Every New England Fish Company cannery and buying station is plugged. My job is to check up on them. I need to find out how things are going at the other places. It looks like Linné is handling the crisis as well as can be expected—even better. The cannery can't possibly keep up, but Linné is making good decisions about rationing the amount of fish we can handle. I get good vibes from the fishermen, despite the fact that they are madder than hell at being restricted in what they can deliver. I've never seen anything like this."

He was like the survivor of a catastrophe, repeating himself to make it all seem more real.

I escaped him as soon as I could. I'd have to deal with what I felt about his marital advice later. Right now I had to get settled in our new home.

The kids and I made it up the ramp and to the boardwalk that served as the cannery's main street. We could see it stretching in either direction, lined with buildings and power poles with lines sagging between them. I came to the bottom of a steep flight of stairs. Seventy-nine steps in total I was to find, up to the superintendent's house which overlooked the entire operation.

The stairs to the house, carpenter shop, bookkeeper's house, and Blaine.

Our luggage was brought as far as the bottom step, but we were promised that the "beach gang" would take them up for us when they had a break in their other chores.

Rather than take the men away from more pressing duties, I decided to haul them up myself. The kids were thrilled to help bring the luggage up for me. Even little Rolf made it up with one of the boxes. I didn't know how they managed it. The more I yelled, "Don't try to bring THAT up those steps!" the harder they worked.

The brown shingled house with white trim, teal painted steps and deck, was technically one story but had a high, spacious attic that was almost a second story. It also had a wonderfully large, covered veranda with rocking chairs situated to take in the view of Sitkoh Bay. Stepping inside, I was delighted by how roomy, comfortable and beautifully old-fashioned the house was.

Everything was cozy, much as Linné had described it, with the classic dark wood paneling I loved—gorgeous fir wainscoting and woodwork throughout the first floor, which had a living room, kitchen, dining room, two bedrooms and a small bathroom. The ceiling was also paneled in dark wood between criss-crossed beams. There were built-ins with wooden posts and glass panels.

The living room was positively stately with its bay windows that overlooked Sitkoh Bay with all of its comings and goings. In the dining room old-fashioned, double-hung windows that were clear on the bottom and multi-paned on top looked out into the woods.

Upon closer inspection, the linoleum-floored kitchen did not inspire much love or even hope, but then I wasn't supposed to be spending much time in there. On the list of pluses that Fran and I had drawn up for Chatham, not having to cook and being able to eat at the Mess Hall had been high on the list.

Which was just as well. When I turned on the faucet, the water labored and dribbled pitifully. Apparently with the cannery running night and day it used all of the water, leaving precious little to make its way up the hill to the Superintendent's house.

I could live with it. When we'd lived on the fish tender the *Estella*, I'd had to adapt to a sink controlled by a push button pump with a limited reservoir of water. (Linné told me he'd never run out before my advent aboard the boat, but I managed to do it, so in Haines where we had to beg water from a competitive cannery.)

I noticed the ominous looking wringer washing machine was set up in there and I eyed it with a goose-pimpling sense of foreboding. How would it cooperate with the crippled water pressure? But that was a question for another time.

The kids clamored for sustenance, so we tramped down the dizzying set of steps to a landing just off the main boardwalk where a small white building (the bookkeeper's house, we were to learn) sat. When we knocked to ask for directions, we were confronted by a frazzled accountant. He told us we needed to go past the red-painted carpentry shop on our right with an overturned dory and sawhorses in front of it, and straight ahead to the White Mess Hall. The only building beyond it at the end of the boardwalk was the large White Bunk House.

It might have been supposed that they got their names because they were painted white, unlike the majority of the red-painted buildings, but that was not the case. They were the white people's mess hall and bunkhouse. And they were as far as it was physically possible to get, I was to discover, from the Native Village at the other end of the boardwalk.

Since it was a little before dinner was to be served, I made my way into the galley to chat with the cook. As it turned out, the head cook was dominated by his assistant, a woman with an overbearing attitude. She apparently wasn't very keen on attending to the usual duties of a galley assistant, such as applying soap and water to surfaces. I tried not to look too closely at the state the place was in for fear of losing my appetite.

"Hello, I'm Dot Bardarson," I said cheerily and caught the shared glance between them that seemed to say, *Oh, fun, an interfering superintendent's wife.* I wondered if bringing up my stint in catering would cut any ice. It would at least let them know I was understanding of the difficulties they faced in an operation of this size. Before I could modestly mention it, I was cut off.

"That's nice," the assistant said, in a way that wasn't nice at all. "I'm Marla." She had a rasp that was brutal on the ear.

"I'm glad to meet you," I said warmly. "I wondered if it would be possible to feed the kids ahead of the others. They've had a long day traveling and—"

"This is a busy time for everyone, Mrs. Bardarson, and we have to maintain a regular system to feed everyone on time," the head cook said, politely enough.

"Yes, I understand that; I've worked in catering and—"

Marla shoved herself front and center, arms akimbo. "How do you come stomping in here, trying to rearrange things on your first day, and expect us to upset our routine? Do you have any idea what it's been like around here? We've been slammed and we don't need any extra meals being demanded in between the main ones!"

I refrained from contesting the "stomping" accusation, but I did try to reason with her. "We can't expect children—"

"They'll just have to wait!"

The head cook seemed a little more willing to compromise. "We could feed them after."

Having them wait even longer to eat wouldn't work, but I didn't need to say that since Marla nixed that idea with all the subtlety of a meat cleaver.

I beat a retreat and was forced to admit to the children that they'd have to wait for the dinner bell to be rung to eat with everyone else. To keep them occupied, I took them down to the beach below the white-painted mess hall with its blue trim on window and door frames.

There we breathed in the cannery scents of seaweed, fresh caught fish, gas fumes, and sun-heated creosote and the less pleasant whiffs of rotting fish viscera dumped under the cannery buildings. Over by the main wharf we could see an enormous rusty cylinder, one of the cannery's retorts that had apparently been shoved out of the cannery when it came to the end of its natural life to corrode away on the beach and provide high rise living for barnacles, hermit crabs, and mussels.

The children pounced on mounds of brightly colored starfish which I promised to preserve by boiling them. Even such an unappetizing image as that made our stomachs growl.

Fortunately, the bell rang soon after and the boardwalk was trampled by a seemingly never-ending horde of hungry workers. We got caught up in the rush.

I caught glimpses of Linné at the head of a very long table in the dining hall as he participated in fascinating "cannery talk" with his immediate neighbors. I was marooned on the Siberian end of the table, tasked with the job, Marla informed me with a smirk, of supervising the children's eating. Not that they required supervision; they were always well-behaved during mealtimes.

I foresaw that I wasn't going to eat with Linné at all, the entire time I was there. How far was I to go with this "understanding wife" routine? I might give up my marital rights to his attention at night, but I was determined that I would receive some of his time during the day, especially when he wasn't actively on the job. Or why, after all, had the children and I sacrificed our beloved Bardvilla to come here?

After dinner, I took my dissatisfaction out on the house, rearranging the furniture, disposing of lace doilies and other eyesores, cutting off vines that had grown through the windows into the living-room, and washing by hand one of the two shirts that Linné had brought to Chatham.

In between this whirlwind of activity, the children provided their own entertainment. Rolf, not yet four years old, beckoned me to check out the backyard and once I was there, he yelled, "Here bear, here bear, come on and eat Mommy up!" Blaine joined in the fun by drawing a picture that showed a bear devouring me and Linné hitting the bear on the tail with a stick.

We were all pretty tired, possibly delirious. It had been a long stretch getting here with a lot of excitement, including the kids' first jet and floatplane rides. After getting the kids unpacked, they settled down to bed in their unfamiliar room.

In the living room I removed the wooden barricade in the unused fireplace, cleaned it out, and built a shingle and log arrangement to light upon Linné's arrival home.

A little fireside romance with one's very busy superintendent husband wasn't too much for an understanding wife to ask, was it?

CHAPTER 3

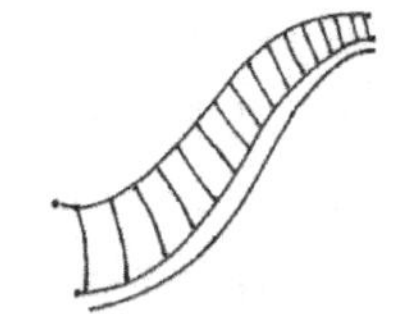

Fireside Romance

*There are many love stories in the fishing industry,
some as fleeting as a school of herring, some as
long lasting as summer salmon.*

—*The Fishes & Dishes Cookbook*
by Kiyo and Tomi Marsh and Laura Cooper

**Chatham Cannery
Sitkoh Bay, Alaska
July 9 and 10, 1963**

After the kids were settled in bed, despite it still being broad Alaskan daylight and would be for hours into the twilight evening, I took a moment to rest in one of the rocking chairs on the veranda. It was hard to take in that every building in sight was subject to my husband's rule. Even the boats moored at the dock, and the larger ships anchored out in the bay, were attuned to Linné's schedule and impacted by his every decision.

The trenchant, high latitude light bathed the white buildings in water-reflected ripples and bestowed a ruby glow on the red-painted cannery buildings. From up here on the hill, the constant racket of the machinery was a mellow rumble.

Chatham was a remote settlement, a mechanized outpost of civilization, built on the west shore of remote Sitkoh Bay at the southeast tip of Chichagof Island. The bay was only a mile wide and about seven miles long.

Sitkoh Bay had historically been an important area for the local Natives, the Tlingits who lived in Angoon and were now ferried by barge every summer across Chatham Strait to work in the cannery.

Not quite a mile above the cannery was the site of an old abandoned Tlingit village called "Sit'qo" or possibly "Sit'xo." In their language the word meant "among the glaciers." The village had been built just south of the mouth of Sitkoh River, on a terraced knoll.

For generations Tlingit families with their animal-named kwáans (clans), subdivided by matrilineal descent, had lived on the sockeye river that drained Sitkoh Lake about four miles inland, and caught and smoked fish for winter. They fished for halibut and cod in canoes up to 60-feet long, burned and carved out of enormous cedar trees, or they stretched traps across the river to catch salmon. They submerged hemlock branches to attract herring in order to harvest their eggs, a treasured delicacy.

This area would have been exclusive to the tribe living on the Sitkoh River and any infringement on it by other tribes would have been grounds for war or bloody retribution. They'd have had their own trade territories and routes along the coast and would have conducted skillful bargaining trips with northern tribes like the Athabaskans, exchanging otter furs, dried fish, and woven robes for caribou skins, fox furs, jade, and copper—things they couldn't find in their part of Alaska. Before each big fishing or trading expedition, they'd have had a big ceremonial dance.

Within a century, from the Russians' colonization of the area in 1799, much of this life would be forever gone.

Anthropologist and ethnologist, Frederica de Laguna, dug test pits on the site a few years after WW II and discovered what she believed to be an ancient house pit, and in it she discovered a human skull and other bones belonging to an elderly individual. "The human bones were not charred; it was not a cremation," she recounted. "We do not know whether this was an intentional burial, an abandoned corpse, or a slave sacrifice (under a house post?)."

The first cannery to be built on the site was in 1900 by August

Buschman. It was known as the Sitkoh Bay cannery, but the community that developed around it came to be called Chatham for the strait it was on, named by the English explorer George Vancouver in 1794 for William Pitt, the Earl of Chatham (a famous British statesman).

Chatham post office, of which Linné was currently postmaster, had been established in 1906. The letters I'd send to my parents would have the Chatham postmark on them and would one day become a collector's item when the post office closed forever.

In 1901 the Pacific Packing & Navigation Company bought the Sitkoh Bay Cannery, and three years later they sold it to George T. Myers. In 1929 the New England Fish Company (NEFCO) bought it, and 37 years later my husband became the superintendent of Chatham cannery.

We had an 85th anniversary edition of the story of New England Fish Co. called *NEFCO: From Sea to World Markets,* and I opened it up as I rocked on the front deck with the cannery below me. I found reading it pretty interesting.

You never think how the Civil War impacted the fishing industry, but according to this book it prompted important changes in the industry: "Some of the fish dealers in Boston, while serving in the army, became impressed with the value of orderly conduct of affairs, and resolved to apply it to their own business."

Apparently, before that, the selling and buying of fish had been haphazard with no system universally used. But in 1868 eleven wholesale fish dealers organized the New England Fish Company, establishing a system of cooperative buying and distribution.

Once railroad track was laid to Tacoma, Washington in 1887, the West Coast fishing possibilities opened up. NEFCO established their first base on the Pacific in Vancouver, British Columbia in time for the 1894-1895 fishing season.

I read, with raised eyebrows: "In those days," stated Grier Starratt, "the grounds had too many halibut upon them—the fish were eating one another. We caught big halibut having 2 or 3 or 4 small ones inside their stomachs." He described one submarine valley as having its side "simply solid with halibut."

NEFCO came up with the genius idea of shipping fish back to the East Coast on refrigerated train cars like the meat packers did in Chicago: "The venture was successful from the very first. By October 16, 1894, three carloads of fresh halibut already had been received and sold, having arrived in good condition. Three more cars were enroute with more to arrive a week later. For the second season, 1895-96, another steamer was chartered, and the catch came to 1 ½ million pounds for the season."

In addition to the railroad cars, NEFCO built a steamer in 1897-98 designed especially for halibut fishing in the North Pacific, pioneering a new and distinct type of vessel. During the ship's first trip from Boston to Vancouver via Cape Horn it was almost commandeered for the war with Spain as an addition to the auxiliary fleet, but it escaped to arrive in Vancouver in time for the Yukon Gold Rush. Its first cargo south was not fish, but fever-mad miners with their pockets full of gold dust. They carried the first Alaska gold to Seattle.

In 1904 NEFCO began building onshore ice plants in British Columbia. They built their first freezing and cold storage plant in Alaska at Ketchikan. In 1907 nothing like it existed so far from any railhead, right on the fishing grounds.

The writer of the book, Harry R. Beard, sounded a bit triumphant as he wrote: "The Company was… roundly criticized for going so far afield, but this Ketchikan plant… soon justified its existence."

According to the book, the ice plant output eventually became enough to supply many of the vessels in the halibut and salmon fishing fleets. It was also in Ketchikan that NEFCO built their first salmon cannery in the U.S. in 1923.

During World War II, NEFCO helped meet the demand for non-perishable protein food with their canned products. "All canned salmon went to the armed forces or was shipped overseas to Great Britain and the other Allies. Fish meal and oil and vitamin oils were expanded to the utmost as were fresh and frozen fishery products."

During this time, the company expanded throughout Alaska, blanketing the huge pre-Statehood Territory with fish industry plants of every description including, of course, Chatham cannery. The book (in the 1953 edition I was reading), reported: "This cannery is located in Chatham Strait, four miles inside Sitkof [sic] Bay, at the east entrance of Peril Strait. It is midway between Juneau and Sitka, Alaska. Good fishing abounds in all directions, and with easy access to Chatham. The pack consists principally of Pinks and Chums, a fair share of Reds, and comparatively few Cohoes and Kings. Chatham cannery has developed nation-wide acceptance for quality. This is a large cannery, packing up to 7500 full cases a day."

It was so strange to realize that this book detailed a part of Alaskan history and we, the Bardarsons, were now becoming an ineradicable part of it.

I was tired to my bones after such a long day and went inside to lie down for a nap. I found it hard to sleep. A part of me was wide awake to hear Linné coming home. And I couldn't stop my mind from going over the events of the day.

Even in a day so filled with new, exciting, and yes, abrasive experiences (Marla's grating voice echoed in my ears), one scene stuck out more than everything else.

Jay Gage taking me aside and ever-so-kindly making sure I didn't think I was going to enjoy my husband's attention to the full. "I'm afraid he won't be much of a... *husband*. So don't expect... *much* of him."

I turned over restlessly. I supposed I could ignore Jay Gage's words. It really wasn't anyone's business how we conducted our marriage.

As I lay there on the bed in my new home in the middle of the Alaskan wilderness with the cannery's machinery pounding away steadily in the background, my mind wandered back in time to when Linné and I were in college and first dating.

Linné would, in front of my parents or other adults, suggest we go to Grandma's, and I would demurely accept. We often stayed late at Grandma's, but how could anyone mind? Little did they guess that the college-age youth of the area were actually gathering at a place for carousing, an empty house that had nothing to do with Grandma. Or we'd head out to "the library," i.e., the Montrose Bar.

We drank beer and loganberry wine. Linné and I talked for hours in the car, stopping at the drive-in for hamburgers or hot dogs drenched in chili. But when it came to a fraternity dance, he would forget to invite me until the last minute.

Nothing had been said about "going steady," so one time I decided to teach him a lesson.

I accepted another date for that night.

Linné arrived right on time.

"Oh, I'm so sorry," I said, all dressed up in my best dancing outfit, "I wasn't expecting you… after you didn't call. I have a date with someone else tonight."

It was a foolproof scheme to teach Linné not to take me for granted. At least that's what all the agony columns and my girlfriends assured me: *It doesn't hurt to let a man know that you've had plenty of boyfriends and you could get another.* It was true I'd dated quite a bit: some young men I'd even been in love with, others had been in love with me.

But no one made me feel like Linné Bardarson did.

Let him know that you're in demand, counseled the romance experts.

Standing in my finery, confident in my tactics, I looked Linné right in the eye… craning my head back, even in heels, to do it. I could have, as the experts dictated, said ever so sweetly: *Next time why not call so we can avoid this awkwardness?*

I didn't suggest any behavior on his part, instead I just let him see that he hadn't committed and what the consequences of that were.

He got it. I saw it in his eyes. But for some reason he didn't look, as the experts had forecasted, deflated. He looked purposeful.

"Be right back."

He disappeared out the front door. Before I could guess what he was up to, he returned bearing a bottle of Chianti, the kind that had a basket around the bottom.

"What's that for?"

"I brought it for our date, and I don't want to waste it. After all, it was meant for you."

I melted, as what girl wouldn't? While I marveled over how romantic he was, he busied himself pouring the wine down my throat as we huddled together on the couch, giggling.

By the time my date showed up, I was a mess.

Linné had insisted on meeting my date, but when my date arrived, he disappeared into the kitchen to spend the evening with Mom and Aunt Edna. He told them, "I don't want to be here when Dot gets back." When they told me this, I couldn't help but be touched by his sensitivity, which I saw much more of later.

Needless to say, I never again attempted to manipulate Linné into paying the proper amount of attention to me, and I decided I wasn't going to now when he was so stressed and his job demanded all of his attention.

But that didn't mean I couldn't enjoy some romantic encounters with my husband. I visualized his return to the house tonight—which he would notice felt already more like a home after my flurry of housekeeping. I'd light the fire I'd set in the fireplace, and we'd cuddle together in front of it and enjoy a moment or two entirely to ourselves.

My dozing, heartwarming visions were interrupted by Rolf, crying in the other bedroom. When I checked on him, I found him sobbing in a large pool of vomit.

Too much travel and too much excitement, I diagnosed. Though with the state the Mess Hall galley had been in when I visited it earlier, it was perhaps surprising we weren't all throwing up and in the last stages of terminal food poisoning.

I reassured poor little Rolf who was barely out of toddlerhood, not yet four years old. When he was calmer, I cleaned him up, and changed the bedding.

A half hour later, after settling back into my anticipation of Linné's arrival, I heard retching in the other bedroom. I found Rolf once again swimming in vomit.

When Linné came home, he didn't have a chance to be charmed by my homemaking. He walked in on the scene of Rolf standing in the middle of the dining room's floor without any clothes on, vomit splashing on his feet.

I'm sure it wasn't Linné's idea of what it would be like having his family with him at the cannery when he'd been so enthusiastic about us being able to come. I barely had a chance to say anything to him as I made a second attempt to clean up the bed and wash out pajamas. I quickly used up all the towels in the house trying to protect the bed. We finally got Rolf settled for the night.

By then I was famished, but there was nothing but beer and soda in the house.

"That's okay," Linné said, "when the cannery is going full tilt like this, there's a midnight dinner."

"Dinner?" I questioned whether I was in any shape to have another encounter with Marla after a long day ending in vomit cleanup.

"I'll go grab you something," Linné said.

I melted. After his own long day, no doubt filled with every kind of cannery crisis, he was willing to traverse those 79 steps, roundtrip, in order to bring me a little sustenance.

While he was gone, I lit the fire and made a comfortable place for us in front of it. He returned bearing toast and an enormous, thick slice of fried ham. Thank goodness, it was exactly what I needed.

In the kitchen I smiled mistily at him—tall, blond, handsome, competent, and all mine—as I reached in the fridge for a root beer. Finally, we were together.

I opened the can. "It's so good—" The root beer exploded.

Thoroughly doused and speckled brown, I mopped up the sticky floor and counters.

Maybe I should have taken the hint and given up on the idea of romance, but I was the furthest thing from a quitter.

Linné and I settled down in front of the crackling fire, its warm light flickering over the dark wood of our new Alaskan home. At this latitude in summer, it was still light outside with a sunset glow that never faded, but the fire made it cozy and intimate inside the dark paneled house.

Gazing into the flames with Linné beside me reminded me of Timberline Lodge at Mt. Hood where Linné took me skiing.

He'd taken me up the chair lift and taught me how to do a zip-turn, but that was all. After falling in contortionist twists countless times, I was exhausted, and I remained squatting in the snow. I announced, "I just can't do it." No amount of persuasion could elicit another attempt on my part to traverse the steep slope. Exasperated, he said to me, "Well, I'll see you at the Lodge." And he disappeared in graceful zigzags. I made it down by sitting on the skis, reaching Timberline Lodge all sweaty and out of breath, but that didn't discourage his ardor. We made love for the first time that night.

Now, in our new Alaskan home, I met Linné's eyes and said softly, "Doesn't this fire remind you of *that* Mt. Hood skiing trip?"

"Kind of…" He returned my gaze. "Dot, the cannery is going to stink from fish offal—" he misunderstood my stunned expression and went into greater detail about the waste parts of fish, and how they piled up under the cannery and below the docks and stank as they rotted. "You and the kids need to be wary of bears, since they get pretty brave with the pungent odor. They'll come right onto the boardwalk, and they'll definitely roam the beaches."

What was a woman to do? I did what I always did and fitted myself to his world and found romance in the sharing of it, in being an involved and invested supporter.

Despite all the ups and downs of the day, we had a lovely time discussing the fantastic record-breaking run of fish in front of the dancing flames. We were a part of living history and what's not romantic about that?

During the first couple weeks of the season, Chatham had been the only cannery operating due to a massive strike among the fishermen. Linné wound up directing all the tenders in Alaska. He'd ordered at least four brine boats up here from another area to hold the fish. Both lines in the cannery had been operating continuously with the many usual start-up problems.

On Saturday alone, 320,000 fish were brought in which amounted to 15 percent of the total pack during 1960, which up to that time had been the largest run of fish on record.

Many nice things had been said to Linné in response to what had apparently been his expert handling of labor problems as well as mechanical issues, including problems that had affected the entire industry and involved all companies. I focused on that in our conversation to encourage him, but nothing could assuage the terrible churning in his stomach at the weighty responsibility this unexpected season had thrust on him.

I even told him the good things Jay Gage had said about him (not his unsolicited marital advice), but I could tell Linné was still stressed. I was glad I hadn't pushed him to be "romantic." He would have his family here, even if he didn't see that much of us, and he would feel our support and know that he had us no matter what else happened.

As I listened to him talk, I thought: *We are two such different people.*

Linné had taught me how to laugh, tell a story, see things in another way, how to be independent, and how to spend money. He'd altered my military upbringing, teaching me to break the rules and face challenges head-on. He understood hard work and long hours and taught me to embrace it.

When we started our marriage on a fish tender, I was his deck hand, standing long wheel watches and peughing fish. (A peugh was a pole with a curved spike on the end. Linné insisted on peughing the fish in the head so as not to damage the meat, but it took longer so the fishermen didn't like that rule. Nevertheless, we all did it Linné's way.) I was not paid, and somehow it never occurred to me that I should be. I thought he was God.

Me peughing fish on the *Estella*, 1954.

He told me he never wanted me to have to go out and work. He was the bread winner and after the kids came, I was the stay-at-home mom. Fortunately, I loved motherhood and I found other moms without paid jobs to enjoy it with.

In fact, my ideal of womanhood was the pioneer woman who helped found this country. She fought and worked at her man's side. She bore the children, kept the home fires burning, kept things clean and organized and gave the family a sense of stability and security.

Linné gave me so much, but I gave him that. And during this time of high stress, it was what he needed most. It was worth the sacrifice of Bardvilla. It felt like what I was born to do.

It was real romance.

CHAPTER 4

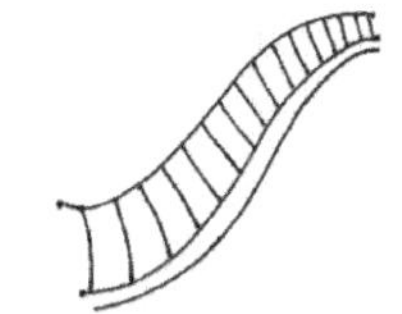

A Cannery Widow

Ed hates anything that keeps him from going to the movies every night. I guess I'm what's called a Garbo Widow.

—character in "Dinner at Eight," 1933

Chatham Cannery
Sitkoh Bay, Alaska
July 10, 1963

I took a second look around the kitchen the next day and my eye fell on the oil stove, and it reminded me of the ones we'd had aboard the *Estella* and *Alma*. The oil stove is well known in Alaska, mainly for use aboard boats but also in buildings. The heat was fairly well distributed on the shiny, flat surface, but you could always find a spot that was best for whatever you were cooking.

On the downside, if you spilled something on it the smell was awful. Especially coffee. I did that once when I was pregnant with Dori. I couldn't drink coffee after that for years. Like all stoves, it had to be cleaned fairly often. You had to turn off the fuel before scrubbing it with a wet pumice stone (as long as it was wet it wouldn't ruin the enamel) then you wiped it clean with a rag and turned the fuel back on.

Of course, I wouldn't have to have much to do with it since all of our meals would be provided for us.

My first concern of the day was to tackle the dirty laundry from last night. I advanced warily on the wringer washing machine. To my jaundiced eye it looked like a relative of the rotund robot on sci-fi movie posters that carried off the scantily clad lady screaming for her male co-star to save her.

Nobody was going to save me, I had to conquer this monster on my own.

This model had claimed victims in the past, according to urban legend. One gruesome story that stuck in one's mind was of a housewife who reached into the wringer as it was in operation and got her fingers caught and pulled in. Her skin was peeled back from her whole arm.

Housewives, I thought grimly, deserved danger pay.

The real question was if I'd have enough water to wash the soiled bedding, pajamas, and towels. I was happily surprised to discover that because the cannery had shut down last night around three a.m. due to a short closure on the grounds, I had plenty of water—and hot water at that.

That was the end of the good news. I soon discovered that if I plugged the washing machine into the only available and inconveniently placed outlet—more on that in a minute—the hose wouldn't reach the drain. If the hose reached the drain, it wouldn't reach the faucet. If the hose reached the faucet, it wouldn't plug in.

So in order to shift from one stage to the other I had to climb on a chair to unplug the washing machine. Remember the only available outlet? Well, I had to plug into the ceiling receptacle which was hot and required a potholder to handle. Then I climbed down and tugged and pulled the machine to the next position to attach hoses for filling or emptying. Each position required wrestling mightily with the machine to move it, which was usually full of water.

After figuring this out, I began to fill the machine with hot water. Blaine, having interestedly observed my labors, offered to help. I handed him the hose to direct into the machine while I got the soap out of the cupboard. In his enthusiasm to be of assistance, he pulled a wee bit too hard, and the hose detached from the spigot.

It sprayed us and when I grabbed for it I dropped the detergent.

In seconds we were slipping and sliding on the soapy linoleum.

By the time I'd cleaned the kitchen up, I had even more laundry to do, including Blaine's only outfit since it was his suitcase the airlines had misplaced. The gaping maw of the machine hungrily swallowed it all.

Linné had promised to take the kids and me on a tour of the cannery, but before that, and directly after breakfast, we wandered the length of the boardwalk to get the lay of the land. The first thing we did was troop past the cannery buildings to reach the post office on the dock.

Across from it, in the company store, we bought matching black sweatshirts. They had *Chatham, Alaska* printed on them in white with a leaping salmon between the two words. After seeing so many other people wearing them, it made us feel a real part of the cannery already. Plus the extra shirt would help stretch Blaine's threadbare wardrobe.

Inside the cool and shadowed store, the man behind the counter got anything down from the shelves that we wanted (the kids asked for a six pack of marshmallows with intentions of toasting them on the oil stove up at the house). The store was stocked with everything an isolated population would need: besides a full line of groceries and frozen meats, there were rain clothes, boots, fishing gear, batteries, light bulbs, baby nursing bottles, cosmetics, engine parts, greeting cards, hardware—both marine and land-based—medicine, house and boat paint, and more.

Of course, there was the usual paperback book and magazine exchange: shelves filled with well-thumbed books with spines cracked by innumerable fishermen as they borrowed and returned, free of charge.

Lined up at the front counter were five or six Native children with teeth showing signs of early decay. They stood raptly in front of the candy display clutching a dollar bill in their fists and drinking Shasta soda pop, the store's biggest seller.

The storekeeper, who also turned out to be Chatham's first aid man, since there was no doctor, was busy making out boat orders in boxes on the wooden floor. Boats radioed in, sending lists of groceries they wanted so they could stay out on the fishing grounds for a week or two at a time. Very little money was exchanged. Most things were charged.

Once we got that out of our system, we emerged outside again into the water-reflected light, so bright it made us squint. Massive flocks of sea gulls screeched loud enough to be heard over the cannery's processing machinery and the rumble of the boats coming and going. I arranged to have a photo taken of us in our new Chatham sweatshirts.

Then we bypassed the huge cannery complex built out over the water on pilings with its maze of wooden alleys. Linné planned to give us a guided tour of it when he had a free moment.

Past it was a huge stack of lumber and a large wooden water pipe (called by all "the Penstock") that ran the length of the boardwalk below the sagging power lines.

The 10-inch water pipe was made of Penstock redwood staves wrapped with wire. All the way down the boardwalk, from one end to the other little orange-red fire stations (different from the chili pepper red of the buildings) with fire hoses coiled inside their small, peaked roofs were tapped into the waterline. Catastrophic fires were unfortunately common to wooden canneries in Southeast Alaska, so it was best to be able to combat it every so many yards.

We followed the water line, and one fire station after another, all the way down to the Filipino bunkhouse and their oriental mess hall.

Then we crossed a bridge and came to the Standard Oil dock. Innumerable steel drums were stacked on it and kids clambered about on them like they were a playground feature. The dock was bedecked from one end to the other with drying laundry.

Beyond it was the firewood-cutter's open-air shack, and then the laundry/bathhouse in which wringer washing machines menaced the unwary and showers refreshed the weary.

Finally, we reached the Upper and Lower Native Village.

It was inhabited mostly by people from Angoon. The cannery would send a barge or two over to Angoon to pick up workers and bring them across Chatham Strait to Sitkoh Bay. They were accompanied by children, grandparents, dogs, washing machines, you name it: whatever workers would need to get through the salmon season.

Those families from Angoon looked forward every summer to returning to Chatham while their husbands were fishing, or maybe working in the cannery too. The dogs loved it, the children loved it, and the grandmothers loved it. It was the family's chance to work and get out of debt again.

Native laborers were on their own for food (which never seemed right to either my husband as superintendent, or me, but that was the cast-iron tradition). The Natives worked just as hard as anyone else, and then had to go back to take care of their families. Most village houses had racks of salmon drying outside to make so-called "squaw candy."

Sun drying salmon.

When Chatham Cannery had first operated at the tail end of the nineteenth century (as one of the first canneries in Alaska), the workers used to live outdoors in tents and cook over open fires. I found it hard to imagine because of how rainy and cold a typical Southeast Alaska summer was. It must have been difficult to keep up the pace of the cannery back then.

During my family's tenure there in the 1960s, the Native workers at Chatham (mostly Tlingit Indians and the occasional woman of any descent) lived in wooden shacks, all painted barn red with white trim like the main cannery buildings.

The houses were simple rectangles. Some of them had only one room, with paned windows that slanted out, open at the top, for ventilation. But most of the houses had a living room and at least one bedroom. Some of the better homes, we found, had showers and a few even had toilets inside. For the rest there were twin saltwater outdoor latrines known as "Ma" and "Pa."

The walkway between the houses was built on pilings and had a quaint, old-fashioned air with its narrow wooden pathways, handrails and steps descending from each house. The endless forest loomed over it all, marching way up into the mountains. Disorderly foliage encroached on the boardwalk and village: pushki (wild celery), skunk cabbage, goose tongue, Devil's Club and acres of salmonberry bushes. Many Natives gathered and dried plants for food and medicine, such as the leaves of the Labrador tea plant to replace the expense of Lipton's tea at the company store.

Children hung out on house steps. The oldest ones, often not yet teens, were babysitting their younger siblings, including toddlers, while their parents worked.

Friendships on a porch - Dori and Joanne Jacobs.

Right before the Native village, I spied an open barge tied to the float at the end of the segmented dock that consisted of floats that were tied together and went dry when the tide was out. Only the airplane float, with an airplane ramp on one side on the very end, stayed floating all the time.

There were many beached wooden dories hiding in the tall beach grass below the skirts of the evergreens and the children sat inside them, having imaginary adventures, or played in the tide pools. Dori would soon enjoy a game of catch-and-release with the bullheads in those pools, using a tin can to capture them. Blaine and Rolf preferred to fish for tanner crabs with fishing poles. They'd tease them with a weight and the crabs would pinch the weight and get reeled in.

Kids in a dory.

I soaked it all in. Buildings made of wood have a rustic, close to nature feel, as if they could almost speak and interact with us as living things. Despite the constant hum of modern machinery, it was easy to lose track of the modern world. The wooden buildings could have been from any era. All of Chatham bore the imprint of the builder, of the men who sawed the boards and nailed them in place. None of it was cookie-cutter perfection. Quirks and dents abounded providing a much more personal and human ambience.

I wanted to capture it all with my paintbrush. At the time, I only painted *en plein air* (on location), and I only painted scenes with buildings in them, the older the better. I liked capturing history with my hands. As I looked around, I murmured under my breath, "If they only could speak for themselves, the stories they could tell." And I kicked myself again for not bringing my paints.

In our boardwalk investigation we met every nationality it seemed, including Negro, Japanese, Filipino, Tlingit, and Whites from various countries. Everyone took a moment to chat with us. Even though they were all dog tired, they maintained a cheerful attitude. The Filipinos were particularly courteous and invited the kids to partake of the coffee break cart with its yummy, glazed donuts.

Filipino handouts for children.

Years later, Blaine would say that it wasn't until he'd long been an adult that he realized how privileged he and his siblings were. Not only as the superintendent's children, but as White children. Every summer my kids would run toward the Filipinos' break cart whenever it was brought out and were welcome to partake of it, but the Native children would hang back.

Filipino mug up cart.

"The Filipinos treated us differently," Blaine stated. "We had a certain level of privilege that they didn't have. We didn't think about it then."

Dori remembered it too, looking back, as extremely class oriented. "Dad as superintendent was king." There was even an Upper Native Village and Lower Native Village. Inside them, as inside Native Villages throughout Southeast Alaska, Elders wielded more authority than State Troopers. And at the very top tier was the superintendent's house up on the hill that everyone had to look up at.

Blaine said, "I've always been proud that my dad was the most liberated person I know, but he was in charge of the most sexist, racist, arrangement there is. We had the white man bunk house, the Native Village, the Filipino bunkhouse. At all of these we were allowed privileges. You know my Native friends couldn't go over to the white bunkhouse or the mess hall."

Looking back, I've thought how it must have been intimidating to the workers, gazing up at the nice house on the hill, setting in place the hierarchy of how everyone was seen by each other, what their station in life at Chatham was. Now we can hardly wrap our minds around it, but at the time none of us thought anything of it. We were products of our time and accepted what was around us, and the privilege granted us, as normal.

When the cannery lunch whistle blew that day and I met Linné in the Mess Hall he said he'd have to postpone the tour of the cannery. I understood with how busy everything was.

The men around Linné teased me—as they would at every meal, morning, noon, and night—asking if I'd seen my first bear yet. They spoke with all the confidence and near-ennui of the bear sophisticate, apparently having seen so many they could no longer become excited at the prospect. They looked with amused pity upon the bear neophyte in their midst, namely me.

It was time I took seating arrangements into my own hands, and I found a seat for myself at the superintendent's table. I was going to be part of the adult conversation, no matter how much Marla shook her head and muttered under her breath about interfering superintendent's wives.

The roomy White Mess Hall had four main rooms, the galley, the mug-up room, the cook's living quarters, and the dining room which sat about 30 people, 3 rows—ten to a table. The beach gang, store crew, and office crew ate with us. The Japanese were given the option of eating in the White Mess Hall, but they liked the type of food found in the Filipino Bunkhouse better.

The children sat at the far end of the second row of the picnic style tables and benches. I got them squared away in front of their upside down thick white plates with a mug on top and then joined Linné so I could not only be part of the cannery conversation but also be next to my husband. Three meals a day… it might be all the waking time I got to spend with him, so I was going to make the most of it.

Our children at the Mess Hall.

The noon meal consisted of sides of salads, soups, French fries and bread and rolls. The entrees were hot and cold sandwiches, burgers, and pizzas, plus a dessert. The workers, who had taken the time to wash their hands and faces and change out of their stained overalls, preferred food that could be quickly eaten. They hoped to have time to catch a nap before they had to go back to work. They left in streams while those at the head table continued to eat, nurse their coffee, and discuss matters of the day.

It was true that Southeast Alaska was enjoying a record season for salmon, but Linné and the other men discussed how Bristol Bay up north was completely failing, bringing in fewer salmon than the rock-bottom season in 1958. The state fisheries experts before the season opened had predicted a total return of a 15 million fish harvest in Bristol Bay, but now they were saying it was likely to be less than three million.

"It's those Japanese drift nets catching them before the salmon can make it back to Bristol," someone said.

"They're crossing into Alaska illegally to do it. Something needs to be done about it."

The men got plenty heated on the subject. Going by what they said, if they'd been fishing in the area, there might have been "an international incident" that could have led to a war. From there I heard stories about fishermen in this area exchanging shots when one boat "set down" another— that is ran over and cut off someone's gear.

In 1963, Alaska was still very much the wild and woolly frontier.

While glasses clinked, silverware clanked, and dishes were scraped, everyone's voices criss-crossing over each other, Linné found a moment to ask about the kids. I told him we'd enjoyed visiting the Native Village. The Native children had followed us back and explored every nook and cranny of the house.

"You'll have to do something about that," Linné said. While he ate, he carefully sniffed his food, a habit he had that drove me nuts. His mother told me he'd always done it, so I gave up the notion that he suspected me of poisoning him. I'm sure Marla thought I put him up to it just to aggravate her.

"What do you mean?" I asked. "It's fun to see how interested the village kids are in everything."

"It will just build. You won't have a free moment to yourself. They'll pretty much move in and be underfoot all day long."

It seemed a shame to banish the kids, but I saw the wisdom in what he was saying. I decided I'd let my kids bring up any friends they made in more manageable numbers, say a couple at a time.

I was hoping that Dori would make lots of friends. She was our boat baby and loved every carefree minute of our back-to-nature summers in Bardvilla on San Juan Island. But in Seattle, Dori had been extremely shy and hadn't found much in common with the city kids. Hopefully she and the kids here would hit it off.

"By the way," Linné said casually as everyone at our table started getting up, "we're going to be having a guest stay at the house tonight."

"You mean—sleep there? Overnight?"

Linné nodded. "He used to work for NEFCO but now he visits one cannery after another picking up salmon eggs. He processes them for bait."

I was less interested in what he did and more interested in where I'd put him. "We only have the two bedrooms. Where is he going to sleep?"

"I don't know. Reason and deduct."

I should have known he'd say that. It was a phrase he'd picked up from his math teacher in high school and was his favorite answer whenever the kids or I asked him how to do something. It translated to *figure it out.*

He was dragged away on the surge of humanity returning to the cannery at the imperative summons of the steam whistle.

I marched back up the 79 steps, shooed the curious village kids away, and took stock of the house, going over it from top to bottom. I climbed the narrow staircase to the attic and was once again impressed by how spacious it was. It struck me that it would make a perfect dormitory and playroom for the kids.

"Which will leave the other bedroom downstairs free for unexpected guests."

"What did you say, Mommy?" Dori asked, having followed me upstairs.

"How would you like to move up here with your brothers? You could use the little rooms under the slant of the roof as a theater. I'll put up drapes to make it dark. What do you say?"

Seven-year-old Dori was creative like me and loved dress up and staging shows. To my relief, she was immediately won over and didn't press for more details than I had, since I was winging it. Although shy with kids her own age, she was independent minded around adults and always wanted answers and would keep questioning until she got them. She and Linné had some lively discussions, but like my own mom, I tended to steer clear of argumentative scenes.

Back then, Blaine was the most adventurous, active one of the kids, who never turned down a challenge, even when he should have. When he got involved in something he shouldn't, his little brother Rolf was always on hand to let everyone know about it. Not that Blaine minded since he enjoyed the attention however it came.

Thinking of Dori's brothers, I added, "We could make a real rainy day playground up here: draw hopscotch squares on the floor, hang rings to swing through, even put in a fireman's pole."

And that's exactly what we did. We put three plain, steel frame bunkhouse beds at one end, the playground at the other, and the theater rooms under the eaves. Dori even had a Barbie Doll house set up to play with.

As it turned out, the kids didn't spend the majority of their time up there, preferring to run around outside all hours of the day. Somehow I always managed to get them in the tub for a bubble bath and dressed in nice clothes before dinner. (Rolf would later express astonishment about that and note how frustrating it must have been for me when they traipsed home coated in creosote from playing on loose pilings in the bay. *Indeed.*)

Chatham bubble bath.

During our household maneuvers, the kids unearthed a folded American flag. When we unfolded it, we found that it had only 49 stars. Considering Alaska was granted statehood as the forty-ninth state in January 1959 and Hawaii became the fiftieth state in August of 1959, there couldn't have been too many flags made with only 49 stars on them. It was quite a collector's item.

The most charming place in the house for me was the living room where I had a desk singled out for my use and already set up with a typewriter loaded with paper so that I could jot down things as I thought of them. The typewriter had been my parents' graduation present from high school and in the end, I'd wind up documenting our entire Chatham adventure in letters to my parents on that typewriter, on official NEFCO stationery. Mom would then re-type them with several pieces of carbon paper sandwiched in so she could share my Alaskan adventures with her friends.

On nice days I preferred to don a T-shirt and shorts and take the typewriter outside. I'd place it on an empty rope spool at the bottom of the front steps with another spool used as a small table to hold my pencil and a drink, put a pillow on the first step, sit myself down and type away in the sunshine.

Empty rope spools could be had by the dozen, and I deployed them liberally as occasional tables on the broad and breezy veranda with its large white square columns.

Writing letters to my parents.

While I was busy with these things, Linné was dealing with the loss of his head bookkeeper, who had to be flown out to Seattle. The bookkeeper's history involved his love affair with booze. Apparently, his idea of how to cope with the stress of his job had been to exist on a liquid diet consisting of alcohol and more alcohol. He began drinking right from the beginning of the big run of fish. He hadn't eaten in a week and was just wasting away.

Linné hated to see him go because he'd been with the company for many years and knew his job backwards and forwards. But the office was in disarray, and we couldn't continue like that, especially in the busiest fish season we'd ever had. Poor Linné was desperate.

In the wake of his loss, the office was even worse off, in a complete shambles. I remembered that Jay Gage had talked about how the office had a high turnover of bookkeepers. Poor Linné somehow had to figure out a fix for that as well as everything else.

It was nearly impossible to keep up with the amount of fish coming in, even with some of the fish being sent to Petersburg, nearly a hundred miles away. The fishermen were loud in their anger at not being able to unload quickly so they could go back out and catch and sell as much as they were allowed.

I realized at the end of our second day that I'd have to learn to not wait up for Linné. That night he climbed the golden stairs sometime between midnight and 3 a.m., and that would be his schedule for the foreseeable future.

He and our guest stayed up, chatting in the living room over a beer. It was a good thing there was a corner sink in our bedroom, so I didn't have to go traipsing through their conversation to brush my teeth and complete the rest of my nighttime ablutions.

By the time Linné got into bed, he was too tired to talk, but he did promise once again to give us a tour of the cannery. He lit up when he said it, he was so proud of the place even if it was working him into the ground.

I'd heard of "Garbo Widows" back in my parents' day, women who'd lost their husband's attention due to a fascination with Greta Garbo as they spent all their free hours at the theater watching her movies.

Apparently, I was a Cannery Widow.

CHAPTER 5

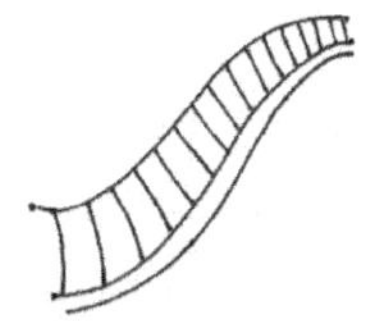

Those Tender Days

*When Julius Caesar, about 56 B.C., led his legions into
Gaul… he found silver salmon leaping amid the swift
current of the river Garonne. The Romans named this
fish salmo meaning "to leap."*

—*NEFCO: From Sea to World Markets:
The Story of New England Fish Co.* by Harry R. Beard

**Chatham Cannery
Sitkoh Bay, Alaska
July 11, 1963**

Linné pounded his chest. "Um Gawa!"

I laughed, waking up to his morning Tarzan greeting. He gave me a quick massage with his big hands, "Boogily Woogily" to use his phrase. He was gone in the next moment, after informing me that the promised tour probably wouldn't come off until that evening.

I got the kids up and dressed for breakfast and had to face Marla's surly complaints about the children being messy and scraps of food winding up on the floor under their table. She insisted that they needed adult supervision and that *she* couldn't be expected to watch them. "I'm not getting paid to babysit!"

I could have said she *was* getting paid to keep a clean kitchen. However, I managed to bite my tongue. I didn't need to start a feud with any of the staff and have them complain to Linné making his job harder. I'd already heard that the kitchen staff was bemoaning the extra Mug-Ups and meals they were called on to provide with the cannery going all hours.

Marla may have complained privately to me about the children, but in public she treated them as special. It was one way that she could maintain control and deny the adults some craved food items while being able to hold the high moral ground. For instance, she wouldn't let anyone but the children have the good boxed milk. "It is for the children," she'd say loftily when an adult asked for it.

I dismissed her from my mind, determined to enjoy my morning time with my husband.

At the superintendent's table, the conversation that morning centered on a "laundry catastrophe." I stiffened in my seat. Was my sudsy calamity of yesterday now common knowledge? Even, apparently, the talk of the mess hall?

Then someone mentioned a chicken coming off the worse for it in the laundry, and I was perplexed, to say the least, until the facts came to light.

Apparently, two trolling boats, one named *Chicken*, had collided near Elfin Cove, a small, charming community on the opposite tip of Chichagof Island from Sitkoh Bay. The boats had been fishing a narrow channel called "The Laundry" because of how agitated and fast running the water was. The trollers had been so busy hauling in the abundant cohos that they hadn't realized how close they were until they'd rammed each other. One boat broke a trolling pole, their gear got entangled, and some caught fish returned to the briny deep.

After the meal, I made sure the children scraped their plates into the large garbage can under the stainless steel kitchen table and put their silverware in a bucket of water and their plates on the sink counter. It looked like some dishes had been sitting there for a week, but again I held my tongue.

Outside, the kids and I were drawn to the colorful boat scene. The fishermen tugged Dori's brown braids and teased the boys. One told Blaine he was falling behind—a seven-year-old boy had, back in April, caught a king salmon that weighed in at 36 pounds and 11 ounces. The fish had won a derby contest down on Prince of Wales Island to the south of us.

Blaine was more than ready to take up the challenge…as soon as Linné had some free time to take him out fishing.

Eventually Blaine became quite the fisherman.

Other fishermen shook their heads and talked about the dangerous ways of boys. Two small boys had recently wandered into the empty wheelhouse of one of Alaska's new state ferries, the *Taku*, as it was tied to the Petersburg terminal with its engines idling. They curiously pushed the wrong lever and the vessel surged forward. It twisted and broke two 75-foot steel counterbalance towers, tore out part of the dock, and dropped the 180-foot loading ramp into the drink. At least no one was on the ramp at the time.

A crew member managed to stop the ferry from ramming into the shore, but it sustained about $4,000-worth of damage, while the dock's repairs were expected to run around $100,000.

"And that, my lads," the fishermen said, "is one of the reasons why kids, especially boys, aren't allowed in some areas of the cannery."

I soaked it in and reveled in being surrounded by the familiar sights, scents and sounds of the fishing industry.

After my short hiatus away, raising three small children in Seattle, I was happy to be back in the business of fish. That was the way Linné and I had started out—two weeks after the wedding when we took up our wedded life onboard a fish tender in the wilds of Alaska. My parents were still amazed by the opposite path I'd chosen from having been raised in New York to be "a lady."

The *Alma's* new crew member.

Once I was aboard the tender *Estella*, I never looked back. Later, on our new boat the *Alma,* I would have happily remained on board indefinitely but for our baby daughter's need to crawl, putting an end to offshore life. Eighty degrees on the ceiling and 40 degrees on the floor didn't make for a stable platform for a baby learning the ways of self-locomotion.

Linné's daytime job back when we first returned to shore was at a Texaco service station, checking oil, washing windshields, pumping gas. It was at the gas station where he accidentally left his wedding band in the men's room sink. I had made it with the help of a professional jeweler. Gone forever, much to my heartache.

It was a hard time, and I was basically raising the children alone…

that was *my* job.

And here I was, back with the fish, but still raising the kids basically alone… at least for now, while the cannery was slammed with salmon.

Besides sitting beside him at breakfast and lunch, I only saw Linné again before evening one time in the first few days. I stopped in the post office, which was also his strictly utilitarian office, and heard him on the ship to shore radio.

Back then two-way radios were the only way to communicate with far-flung vessels. The radios were powered by hot, bulky and fragile vacuum tubes that needed to warm up before they could function. They used too much electricity to be kept on all the time, so twice daily schedules were kept.

Linné, seated in front of the green square radio that dwarfed him despite his size, wore his usual cardigan over a polo shirt, plus Dockers pants. This was his uniform, more or less, since he never bothered to carry many clothes with him.

"This is KWF57 *Chatham* calling KWF65 the *Hetta*. Calling KWF65

Do you read…? Over.

the *Hetta*. Calling KWF65 the *Hetta*. Do you read, over?" he said into the mike, hailing one of the cannery's tenders.

A moment later the reply came with the sound of an engine rumbling in the background, "This is KWF65 the *Hetta* back to KWF57 *Chatham*. You're coming in loud and clear, over."

"KWF57 *Chatham* back, how's it going? Over?

"*Hetta* back, oh, we've got about 10,000 pinks aboard, Linné. Shall I come to the cannery now, over?"

"Roger, roger, roger. We'll see you at six o'clock, over."

As soon as he was done with that call, another boat called, and another after that, or he called a boat. I didn't get a chance to even catch his eye, let alone have a quick chat with him.

The kids and I, having no desire to spend the hours indoors, spent considerable time that afternoon on the cannery wharf. It was made of rough boards, but the kids for some reason never got splinters despite going barefoot practically from day one.

The air smelled strongly of fish and the iodine scent of the low tide beach. Many of the fishermen wore black floppy rain hats as the sun dodged in and out between threatening cloud banks. The cannery, perched way up and away from shore, would one moment be in shade and the next its buildings shimmered a vibrant red, the shingled roofs glowed with its green moss, and its multi-paned windows flashed blindingly. Seagulls wheeled and shrieked and strutted about, pooping where they pleased.

Everyone was busy, and the machinery kept up a growling, grinding, and hissing cacophony with few reductions in the noise level. Steam vented constantly. It was hard to believe, standing there in the midst of so much modern industrial productivity, that we were only a tiny human outpost surrounded by vast tracts of uninhabited and untraversable silent wilderness that covered entire mountain ranges, bounded by endless, intricate waterways.

**Dot paying a fisherman
on the *Alma*.**

We found a position from which we could observe a buyer unloading his fish. I couldn't help but get nostalgic as I watched the pinks (also called humpies) flop from one elevator to another.

I looked back at myself and Linné a few years ago when we were buying fish to take to a cannery. My job had been to pay the fishermen in cash, add up the fish slips, cook for our crew, buy groceries and do laundry whenever we were in town. I had been something of an oddity in a male oriented occupation and some of the time pregnant.

Linné's job was to navigate the boat. His other jobs included keeping the engine oiled and maintained and taking radio schedules with the fishermen to find out where they were and how much "catch" they had aboard, to transfer salmon from their boats to ours, to deliver the fish to a cannery or cold storage, take on ice, then wash down the boat, and return to the fishing grounds as quickly as possible.

We shared four-hour wheel watches. "Step aside," he'd say peremptorily when he'd take the wheel. It offended me the first time he said it, I thought it was disrespectful. But I got used to it, which was good since he later adopted it during his reign as bathroom bully on shore.

On one of my watches, Linné grabbed the wheel out of my hands without a word. I had been on wheel watch in the middle of the night while Linné slept. Sensing danger, he started awake and came charging into the pilot house and grabbed the wheel.

When I protested in surprise, he flicked on the overhead masthead spotlight.

The blood drained out of my head, leaving me white and faint. I had been warned about the dangers of icebergs which could slice through a wooden hull like ours and sink us within minutes. There was a huge one sliding past, right where the boat would have been if he hadn't grabbed the wheel and spun it.

Without a word, Linné turned on the back deck light to observe our wake. The light caught the last glimpse of the berg slipping away, exactly in the path of where the *Estella* had been.

It was scary enough at the time, but later Linné made the most of it. He never let facts get in the way of telling a great tale, and he liked to exaggerate when he told the story: "The biggest iceberg I'd ever seen!" You'd have thought I was the captain of the *Titanic* by the time he was done telling it.

The close encounter with the berg was exactly the sort of thing Dad had been concerned about knowing his fashionable daughter would be aboard as a responsible crewmember. Being a mariner by profession, he knew the dangers. I was simply in love, doing the best I could to please the skipper.

Standing there with the kids, watching the raingear-covered crew in the tender's hold wading in and sliding on a massive catch of salmon as they unloaded, I could visualize the stack of fish slips which surely had just been sent to the company office for re-cap (during which, in my first time as fish-tender bookkeeper using a hand-cranked adding machine, several mistakes would be discovered).

I thought about the cook standing in the doorway planning his congratulatory dinner of steak for the crew, or going over his list of necessities from the company store and hoping the skipper would remember to take on water. No one on the boats in front of us had an inkling that the superintendent's wife had been in their shoes just a few years earlier.

And how could I have known during those tender days as a newlywed that I'd one day be wife of the superintendent—the so-called First Lady—of Chatham cannery?

Back then I had been a part of the fishing action. In a way I missed that, but I wouldn't give up being a mother for anything. Also, I was good at homemaking and being the kind of support Linné needed right now, someone who could make him glad he was home, however little time he had to enjoy it after working all hours of the day to support the family. I took pride in that.

The entire cannery, and a major share of the fishing industry, depended on Linné and he was encouraged and invigorated by our uncomplaining, enthusiastic presence. I still had an integral part to play in the fish business, even if my hands were free of fish scales and fishermen's cash. And I, unlike Linné, could get a full night's sleep between shifts.

That night, after dinner, the kids and I were finally given the promised tour of the cannery.

CHAPTER 6

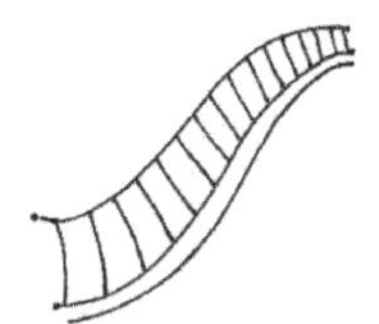

Till Fish Do Us Part

The can's distinguished history began in 1795 when the French government, led by Napoleon, offered a prize of 12,000 francs to anyone who could invent a method of preserving food for its army and navy.

—"History of the Can," by Danil Zhiltsov

Chatham Cannery
Sitkoh Bay, Alaska
July 11, 1963 (Evening)

Linné was eager to show us everything "on the tour." He did it with pride and it made me look at all of the strictly practical machinery through rose-tinted glasses. I was ready to be as enthused about everything as he was. This, after all, was *our* cannery as much as it was his.

As Linné showed us around, he held my hand, pointing things out with his free one. An affectionate but not demonstrative man, this touched me, even though I suspected he did it to slow me down. I tended to walk faster than him, always eager to get to the next thing. He would say, tongue in cheek, "Slow down. Don't you know a woman's proper place is several steps behind her husband?"

(He liked to sound like a male chauvinist but actually he'd already told me he thought women were the superior sex. He was always ready to help a woman whenever she came to him for advice, or even money. He loved to flirt with every woman in sight; they all fell for him, but then men were charmed by him too.)

We were brought to watch crews unload fish by elevator, and neither the kids nor I stole Linné's thunder as he described its workings in detail by telling him we'd already seen our fill of this aspect of the cannery earlier in the day.

A favorite pastime: watching a boat tie up at the dock.

The interior of the cannery was completely open and all wood except for the line of windows facing the bay that bathed the line of working women in a trenchant golden light of an Alaskan evening. The bars of the windowpanes crossed them as they stood, hands busy at their gory business, as they looked up for my camera.

A cannery tour was a satisfying experience for someone who was as obsessed with order as I was. I was one of those people who couldn't resist straightening every crooked picture frame I came across, even when it was in someone else's house. It drove Linné crazy.

Here all of the equipment and the various areas were carefully placed after much forethought and learned experience. The design was meticulous, making everything flow with efficiency and precision.

On the downside, there weren't a lot of safety devices as you'd see today. Pulleys and conveyer belts were not contained, making them a danger to which we were naively oblivious.

The fish came in on a conveyor belt where they were guided into an Iron Chink. This machine handled whole fish at the rate of about 75 every minute, removing head, fins, tail, scales and entrails, while washing away the blood along the backbone. The Iron Chink was the goriest sight I'd ever seen—fish slime and blood flying in every direction landing ankle deep around the workers who were unperturbed by it all. ("Iron Chink" because when the machine was invented it replaced the labor of Chinese workers. The Chinese of course felt that "chink" was a derogatory word, so at some point the industry found another term to define the machine that did all that work.)

Next, we saw the headless, stomach-less fish slimed by hand by women wielding sharp knives under running water gushing from floppy black hoses hanging above the tables. Then the fish were cut by machine into can size chunks and put into the cans by a fast-moving machine that filled them at the rate of 240 per minute. The machinery threw water in every direction, but it didn't bother the workers because they were protected by raingear.

The cans, called 1-pound Talls, were filled next (at some point a pellet of salt dropped into each filled can) and were weighed on a tiny scale showing the weight with an oscillating marker like rapidly moving hands on a clock. Cans were kicked out by the scale if they were short on weight. Four women would inspect each rapidly passing can to see if they were filled enough and deftly grab the cans that needed to be patched, adding a little salmon flesh to bring them up to the required weight.

This was called "patching."

The cans passed between inspectors who removed off-grade cans and any showing defects in workmanship. The second were repacked, the first were placed in a separate lot. (We wound up with many of these cans of salmon from the discard lot, taking them with us to Seattle to fill out our pantry. They really helped with the food bill in winter.)

From the inspection tables, the cans passed through closing machines that clapped covers on the cans and sealed them under high vacuum at the rate of 240 per minute. (This number continually makes an appearance—the cans were packed and sealed at 240 cans per minute and were cooked in the retorts at 240 degrees Fahrenheit.)

The women, who were like living extensions of the machinery with their quick, repetitive motions, all had curlers in their hair with hair nets over them as if they were preparing for a special event. But I was to discover that they wore their hair this way every day, even when there *was* a special event like the 4th of July. The goal, of course, was to end up with a fashionable beehive hairdo. (Even Dori tried to put her hair in curlers to get it to pile into a beehive, but sadly she didn't know how to tease her hair and certainly I didn't know either.)

Once the women had patched the cans and the lids were put on the cans by a machine, the finished product arranged itself in a neat square in metal trays or "coolers" stacked on long-handled trolleys that were run into the retorts.

The retort was a long tubular cooker which handled many cases of salmon at once. It cooked the cans at 240 degrees for 90 minutes with "live" steam. This sterilized the contents of the cans and softened the bones so that they were edible.

The finished cans were run through a cooling bath in the warehouse and then stacked on pallets. Forklifts carried them to a cooling room where they cooled overnight, pinging and popping in a never ending cacophony that could have driven a person mad if they were trapped in there with them.

The stacks of cooled cans journeyed onward to be labeled.

We found the labeling machine particularly intriguing, and the kids asked how the lady could pick out unlabeled cans so quickly as they rolled past. She was a "spotter" and had what Linné said was the hardest, most tedious job in the cannery, for she could not let one can go by that was missing a label. Then the cans were collected in boxes and sent down another conveyor belt to the warehouse. Eventually they would be shipped out on a freighter to markets in the Lower 48 and across the world.

Both lines were going even at that time of the day, emphasizing just how busy the cannery was and why we saw so little of Linné.

It was impressive to see it firsthand and to know my husband was in charge of every last detail, from ordering supplies to the fish elevator to the slime line to the end, boxed product, and to getting it shipped out to feed hundreds of thousands of Americans in the Lower 48 and to other peoples abroad.

Dot was still counting fish at 7 am.

Sometimes it seemed like the entire world revolved around fish. At any rate, my world *had* often revolved around fish, sometimes to my dismay.

When I lived and worked on tenders with Linné, for a time I even developed a dislike of fish because we never seemed able to get away from the subject.

I mean, we were on the boat all the time, constantly running from one cove to the next, listening to the radio and the engine, preparing meals, cleaning up, buying fish, or unloading the boat, plus the innumerable other little jobs that were routine such as washing clothes or chipping paint. And the one constant was fish, fish, more fish…oh, and did I mention—*FISH*.

I was a newlywed, deeply in love, and would have liked to have discussed more romantic topics: love, art, music, books, our future children, food, laundry, plumbing… any subject, any subject at all in fact, that didn't have scales on it.

But there was scarcely a word to be found about our married life in the short, frenzied salmon season. It was always about FISH.

And here I was again, almost a decade later, standing beside my husband as he orated eloquently on that gilled subject. A decade hence it would be the same.

I have often thought, in fact, that my marriage vows should have more accurately included, "Till fish do us part."

CHAPTER 7

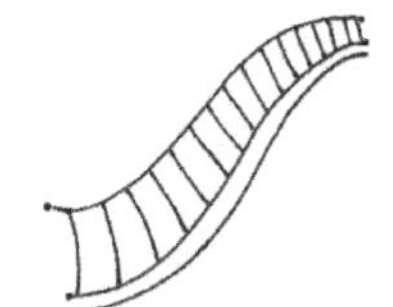

The Disease

Anyone who commits themselves to a creative practice, be it visual art, writing or music, likely has an obsessive streak. A person capable of eschewing social contact in favour of perfecting their craft, is often committed to a pathological degree.

—"Obsession or Therapy? The Art of Repetition"
by Marianne Eloise

Chatham Cannery
Sitkoh Bay, Alaska
July 12, 1963

Art is a disease. Once you have it, there is no escape.

I had to do it. That was my all-time hobby, even as a small child. Even when I got into a lot of trouble in school doing drawings instead of listening to the teacher, I still persisted, despite being a generally compliant (if outspoken) child with good grades.

My best friend in grade school, junior high, and high school was a fabulous artist. We'd sit for hours drawing paper dolls with clothing designs we'd seen in movies. They were imitations of Varga Girls, very sexy. We both made banners for school events.

The disease ran in my family. My mother was a crafter. Her sister went to art school at Columbia University. My grandmother was pretty good with oils. My Dad was an engineer and could reproduce anything on paper accurately including self-portraits, pastels, and of course the film he developed himself in his own personal dark room.

The disease bled over into other areas of my life. It insisted on turning chaotic nature into aesthetic order. This latent instinct (as a teenager I was normally messy) was triggered and trained by my introduction, via marriage, into a Swedish tradition of orderliness.

I took it to the next level. Things had to look "right," no mismatched dishes, mismatched towels, clothes, etc. I was always straightening pictures on the walls (other peoples' too, in doctors' offices, wherever) even the way we parked cars, planted a tree, painted the house. I couldn't stand bad signs. I was critical of cluttered yards, you name it. The disease was an exacting taskmaster.

Linné was much more relaxed and his idea of housekeeping and being tidy (although he was part Swedish and had helped trigger my latent obsession with orderliness). He was extraordinarily tidy on a boat. One has to be, lest nature rearranges everything during an unanticipated storm. One has to be ready to prevent upheaval. On land he was less organized. Between trips on the boat or working in the garage, there seemed to me to be no rhyme or reason to the clutter of tools seemingly flung helter skelter. How could he find anything? I dared not look.

Still, he had no choice but to tolerate my disease. It was always present in me. Even when I wasn't actually painting, I was studying a scene and imagining how I would make the first stroke with pen or brush and how I would add water to make colors blend or run, an effect I was always painting in my mind if not on paper. I was always asking myself how I would show roundness or make someone think there was something going on around the corner, even if they couldn't see it.

The disease had nearly overcome me upon my first glimpse of the tantalizingly picturesque Native Village in Chatham. I'd been itching to break out my sketching materials, since I hadn't—much to my growing dismay—brought along my watercolors. I'd have to settle for sketching, rather than painting, but it was better than nothing.

Finally, the day arrived!

But before I could get to that, I had to make sure my home was as tidy as it could be—the disease demanded that as much as it urged me to deploy my sketching pencils.

So I girded myself for the Battle of the Bulging Cupboards. There was over twenty years' worth of the accumulated flotsam and jetsam of bygone superintendents and their families. Most of it was rubbish, but I did find an old iron, a relic of Rosie the Riveter days.

It weighed enough to be used as a door stop. I gingerly plugged in the detachable cloth cord and kept checking it with a wetted fingertip. After three minutes it warmed to the touch. So I asserted my command over the Bakelite handle and made certain my family would appear wrinkle-free at dinners.

My mother would be so proud, and I was pleased that I'd be able to casually insert in my next letter home that I was ironing away in the Last Frontier and keeping up appearances despite living in the back end of beyond.

As I communed with the iron, I simultaneously sorted out the kids' various problems—Blaine and Rolf couldn't go a couple of hours without getting into a pitched battle. I never could understand what they were fighting about. They'd be playing together peacefully and all of a sudden something would set them off and there would be a ruckus.

When I'd settled them, I tended to their other demands as they slammed in and out of the house and explored everything within my view. I was still too concerned about the bears to let them explore very far.

The internal imperative for tidiness having been satisfied, I gladly turned my focus to my itch to create art. Even though it would be extremely difficult to break away from all that was required in my standards for being a good parent, the urge to sketch gnawed at me.

Unfortunately, I couldn't buy painting supplies at the company store, and we didn't have art supply catalogues in those days. It would be hard to tell my mother what to buy and even harder for her to wrap watercolor paper (22 x 33 inches) for shipping to a remote cannery. It made me realize how important it would be for me to bring all my painting supplies the following year.

I felt marooned away from my watercolor supplies, but drawing, I hoped, would help to satisfy the immediate urge to capture children and old cannery buildings on paper. I just had to fit it in between my duties as a mom and being hostess to unexpected guests at a high functioning cannery in a year swamped with fish.

I gathered up my sketching materials, reminding myself that sketching was maybe the most important part of being an artist. After all, if you can't draw, you can't paint. I realized I was missing my 3B and 4B soft drawing pencils and dashed into the living room to type up a request to my parents to slip a couple of them into an envelope and mail them to me. Those, at least, were art supplies they could easily mail to me.

Finally, I had everything I needed in a bag. With a heart full of anticipation, I put my hand on the knob to step outside and call the kids when there was a knock on the other side. The glow in my heart suffered a dimming, but after a quick breath, I opened the door with a smile.

A man stood there. The new bookkeeper, it turned out, making a duty call on "the first lady," i.e., the supe's wife. I knew the bookkeeper situation was dire, and it was in Linné's best interests to make sure the new one was happy. So I set down the bag near the door and invited him in, widening my smile. He accepted my offer of refreshments.

He glanced at the bag of art supplies and clearly saw I was in the middle of something. He even inquired about it, but he kept talking about how he'd worked in Chatham previously but had been in Ketchikan for a while and was glad to be back.

He was a nice man, but even the nicest of men took it for granted that a woman would set aside her own interests to gladly pay attention to him. He was brought up in a culture that made it normal to expect that, and I was brought up in the same culture that made me go along with it without a second thought.

Unfortunately, he stayed so long that by the time he left, the kids had stormed inside, pointing out that they'd heard the Mess Hall lunch bell, and they were "starved!"

So down to the Mess Hall we traipsed. When I discovered that Linné wasn't there, after the kids were settled with their food, I went looking for him and found him in the office being yelled at over the radio.

In order for the cannery, even running two lines, to keep up with the record season, Linné had placed a limit on how much fish Chatham could buy from each boat—300 fish per man, per day. But that day he'd learned from the Department of Fisheries that fishing would be closed all weekend instead of open as usual. That meant he'd have more time to can fish.

So he immediately lifted the limit by publicly announcing it over the airwaves.

The fisherman he was talking to when I stepped into the office was not happy, to put it mildly. I found it almost comical that for the most part, no matter how heated the conversation became, neither of them forgot radio protocol.

"What do you mean you're lifting the limit, without even a hint that you'd do that?" The fisherman bellowed. "How on that, over!"

"I don't set the closures. Over," Linné reminded the man, who, it transpired, was beyond listening to reason.

"Do you realize that I just cut loose from a boat I gave my surplus to? Over!"

"Roger that. Over."

"2,000 fish! Do you hear? I just gave away 2,000 fish! That's real money! Who do you think you are, God? That's food out of my kids' mouths! Over!!"

While he continued to scream blue murder over the airwaves, I discreetly withdrew.

If that was how Linné's day was going, I had nothing to complain about. I went back to the Mess Hall and made a plate for Linné and, disregarding Marla's scowl, took it to him before returning to dig in myself.

The kids finished before me and when I came out from chow, I noticed two Native girls standing with them. I asked their names and chatted with them. They were Rose and Patsy and seemed older, by maybe a couple years, than Dori. Although I was itching to get back to the house and take up my sketching plans, I felt that my first job was being a parent. I took the boys out on the dock to see if any boats were unloading pinks, for there was nothing that fascinated them more.

As there were no boats, we returned right away and noticed that the girls were gone. I climbed the golden stairs and much to my astonishment Dori and the two girls were comfortably ensconced in the living room, nattering away like boon companions from way back.

As they all disappeared upstairs, I could hear Dori, transformed, waxing eloquently and exposing the girls to the charms of her Chatty Cathy doll. With a gleeful smile I went into the living room and typed onto the paper rolled into the typewriter all that had happened and added: *Lo and behold if our shy violet hasn't made a couple of friends.* My parents, I knew, would be as tickled as I was.

While I was typing, I could hear all of the kids in one of the downstairs rooms. It seemed a shame to disturb them, especially Dori who was so thoroughly coming out of her shell. I decided to give them a little time for the girls to feel at home (so they'd feel free to come again), before setting off to sketch.

I preplanned which houses I would sketch in the Native Village. Next year when we returned, and I brought all of my art supplies, I could paint the same buildings. Some might think I could have painted from the sketches when I returned to Seattle, but that wasn't so. I was an "on location" (technically *en plein air*) painter.

It all began in my second year at Lasell College. I was majoring in fashion design and later in advertising art. But one day the professor took the class out on a field trip to broaden our experience and found a vantage point from which his class could paint. I had my paints, brushes, pencil, and a 20" X 30" piece of 140# watercolor stretched onto a drawing board. Some students painted small. I liked painting big from the get-go with bigger brushes. After I made that first *plein air* painting, I was hooked. In fact, I thought—for a long time—that was the only way to make a watercolor.

That first painting at Lasell was of a service station. (I wish I knew what happened to that painting. I really liked it. I think when my folks moved from Seattle to the Coast Guard Yard in Curtis Bay, Maryland, some of my personal stuff got lost in the household goods. Either that or Dad disposed of them, thinking: *Dot won't want these. One has a tear in it and the perspective was off in the other one.*)

I liked the idea of sitting outside and putting down on paper, brush stroke by brush stroke, my interpretation of the scene: leaving out things in it that would not contribute to its success, concentrating on things that would tell the story of the scene.

Yet, people's comments about my *plein airs* talked about "so much detail" so apparently I was looking for and picking up on the slightest crack in the wall, or texture, what was in the window, anything that would exaggerate the history of an old building (and I liked doing old buildings from the very start). My paintings in the 1960s were historic, pretty realistic, and popular. I had no trouble selling them, sometimes right off the board where I was still painting the scene. Sometimes people had to wait for me to finish it.

My dad taught me perspective, which I exaggerated a little. That was invaluable. Later on I'd see so many nice paintings from artists who did not have this training, with the perspective being all wrong, and I found it annoying.

The study of perspective is very interesting, based on the vanishing point. Dad drummed the rules into me. This, combined with my college-learned understanding of contrast, cool and warm colors and how they interact with each other, how they can make things go back or come forward in a painting, and other tricks of the trade, increasingly enabled me to be fairly successful early on in my career at presenting a believable story.

And every painting had a story.

Thinking about painting heightened my creative urge, making me all the more eager to head out and get busy sketching, especially since the day was getting on. I called to the kids, but as I reached the door… a knock sounded on the other side.

For a second, I stared at it in disbelief. Then I braced my shoulders, retrieved the "cannery first lady" smile, and opened the door.

"Hello, you're Mrs. Bardarson?" A man breezed inside. He had some light luggage with him. This man, it appeared, wasn't here for light refreshment and then would be on his way. He was here for the duration.

"Hello, yes, I'm Mrs. Bardarson. Please call me Dot," I said automatically.

"Glad to meet you, Dot. I'm Kemper Freeman. Linné said I'd be staying here tonight. I'm a member of the board of directors for New England Fish Company here to cast an eye over the operation. I've already made a circuit of the Northern canneries. They're hurting up there, don't know if you've heard. A record low of fish, unlike here where it's the opposite."

I briefly introduced the kids and then shooed them away, much to their delight. I watched wistfully as they scampered off to freedom.

Then I turned back to my visitor and tried to say something inviting but didn't have to bother. He kept right on talking as I directed him to the room, the kids' former room, where he'd be staying and where he could park his luggage. We had three beds made up, ever at the ready, for visiting dignitaries.

All the while he got me up to date on who he was…the whole background. It was pretty interesting, I'd give him that, even as the urge to sketch became an ever-growing ache inside me.

He used to run the helicopter flights from the top of the Food Circus during the Seattle World's Fair last year, he shared, and gave a rundown on the history of world fairs. I attempted to mention my own modest contributions to the Fair, but he had already moved on. He, I soon discovered, owned half of the Bellevue Shopping Center and two radio stations and knew more about the history of radio stations than I thought was humanly possible.

Later I wrote to my parents: *He is one of those people who knows a lot about a lot of things. I could have been talking with Dad for all the information I gleaned on any conceivable subject. It appears that this man enjoys imparting his knowledge.*

He accepted a mug of coffee and talked and talked until it was empty, and so was the second one I poured him. Just as he seemed to be winding down, I made the mistake of mentioning that a common topic at the Mess Hall was the upcoming eclipse and I asked if he was looking forward to seeing it.

"Of course! This is a total eclipse of the sun, which is rare. On the average there are three solar eclipses to two lunar ones, but at any one point on earth a total eclipse of the sun is observable only about three times in 1,000 years."

"That does sound rare," I said meekly.

"Because of its rarity, the total solar eclipse of July 20 of this year is of particular interest. We're fortunate that we're in the path of totality which commences at dawn in northern Japan, sweeps northeastward to Alaska, eastward across Alaska and the Yukon, then southeastward across Canada and northern Maine, concluding at sunset in the mid-Atlantic. It will occur at noon near the eastern boundary of the Yukon, where the duration is greatest." He added a few more details about the upcoming celestial event, but then his expression darkened. "Less fortunately, the weather probabilities for this eclipse are, generally speaking, not good."

"Oh, I hope we have good weather for it. My kids and the workers will be so disappointed if—"

He was off on weather probabilities and the finer details of weather forecasting.

Finally, he said regretfully that he had to get on about his job and was gone. I took a moment to recover, feeling like I'd tangled with a walking encyclopedia.

He had talked for so long that by then I had to admit it was too late to do any sketching. I had to get the kids into the bathtub and into their nice dinner clothes and send Rose and Patsy back home.

There was always tomorrow… weather, as Kemper Freman could have lengthily explained, permitting.

CHAPTER 8

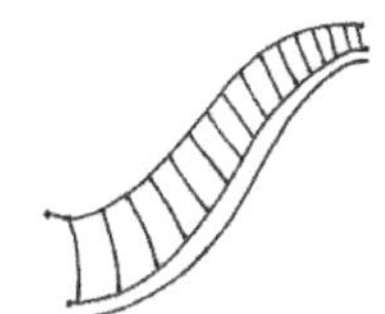

Plotting a Heist

Interestingly, academic studies that discuss the historical significance of the canned salmon industry rarely mention the role of the mess hall. They tend to focus on economics, technology, even ethnic and environmental perspectives. But if we listen carefully to the interviews and stories told by people who worked at Alaska canneries, we can conclude that what they ate was important to them and seems to be a common denominator that in many ways, bonded people together.

—"MUG-UP: The Role of the Mess Hall
in Cannery Life" by Katherine Ringsmuth

Chatham Cannery
Sitkoh Bay, Alaska
July 15, 1963

We woke to a grey day, with a fine, saturating mist that obscured the buildings and laid a gloss on everything. It was one of Southeast Alaska's most infamous weather patterns in its meteorological bag of tricks. Within minutes of being outside in that gossamer mist, you were as wet as if you'd jumped in the bay. It created a chill that reached right to the bones.

Sketching in it was out of the question.

Although disappointed to run up against another obstacle to capturing the Native Village on paper, I was thankful we'd created the upstairs playroom for the kids. One of our favorite things to do, after wearing off energy with hopscotch and gymnastic rings (the boys making a life or death rivalry out of it no matter how much I remonstrated with them to get along), was for me to read aloud from one of the books we'd gotten from the library in Juneau.

The kids sprawled on the rugs and listened in the cozy warmth of the attic, with the mist dripping from the eaves and the cannery rumbling in the distance, to hear me read yet another book I'd gotten from the library, like *Treasure Island, Old Yeller,* or *Robinson Crusoe.*

I loved these moments. From the start, I'd taken parenting very seriously. I saw it as my career, and I'd tried to understand each child's personality to be able to adapt my parenting style to their needs. My goal was to not just bring up my children in love, but to make sure they'd grow up to be considerate, hardworking people who would contribute to society. I'd always made sure, no matter where I lived, to find stay-at-home moms with the same mindset and goals.

As I read, I took the time to enjoy being with my children, marveling as always at their distinct personalities and their thirst for discovery.

Chatty Cathy went everywhere with Dori.

Dori: She was my sidekick and wanted to do art like me—I taught her silk screen when she was ten. She had a mind of her own and was independent, and just now at Chatham was emerging from her shyness. (She'd been bullied by a co-Girl Scout in Seattle which had helped to drive her into her shell.) Dori loved Chatty Cathy (we sent the doll to the hospital to get a new voice when the first one wore out). At age seven she was compliant—it wasn't until she was about 11 that she began to argue with me.

I liked that she did not take sides with the boys, never favoring one over the other. She liked to read after going to bed, under the sheets if she thought I'd try to stop her. (She didn't have her own bedroom in Seattle until she was nine. All three kids slept in the same room. We finally enclosed a tiny space in the half basement. She loved being alone in her room with her canary.) She loved animals at an early age and wanted a horse. She'd have to wait a while before that dream came true.

Blaine: He was always cheerful, tractable, somewhat dyslexic. He liked to be next to Dad. One year, like most boys his age in America, he desperately wanted a Daniel Boon hat. I finally built him one from things at Goodwill. He showed early signs of wanting to hike or go out and find adventure. He absolutely adored his paternal grandmother (Blaine was Amma's—as the kids called Gertrude—favorite grandchild and everyone knew it) and maternal grandfather. One of his favorite things was to work in Grampa's carpenter shop.

Blaine was very verbal. To my concern (I blamed myself and my inadequate teaching skills), he had trouble learning to read and repeated first grade. I took him to a tutor once a week during school times. He could charm the socks out of his tutor, teachers, grandmother, anyone. He loved being read to, as all the kids did. But, unlike the other kids, he did not like to sing with the family or even listen to it (although he did have a favorite song: "I Wish I was Single Again.")

He was very happy to do any job that Linné assigned

Blaine caught this Dungeness crab that we ate for dinner.

him. His grades in school were pretty average, but he showed leadership qualities from a young age. To my eye he was the tormentor in sibling rivalry with his brother, though other accounts put the blame on Rolf for provoking his older brother. Whatever the case, Blaine would say, "Rolf has peanut butter on his breath," and the fight would be on.

Rolf: He was so sweet, so earnest when he would tell a story, especially if he felt victimized. An easy child, he learned to talk later than the other two but once he started speaking, he never stopped. He liked things orderly: he would line up his trucks and cars in a curving row. He carried his stuffed doggie around and called it Puppy. I found him easy to discipline. He understood pretty much anything I wished to get across without more than talking to him. Like the others, he loved to be read to. He learned to read normally but was a C student.

Rolf hiding in the fire box.

One of Rolf's quirks was picking up miscellaneous information and then repeating it back to whomever would listen—shades of my father. He liked to chew his food interminably and was sneaky about disposing of peas at the dinner table. One of the things he enjoyed was finding places to hide so that I'd have a hard time finding him (he was so small he could tuck himself into the open wood pillar under the firehouse of the numerous small fire stations around the cannery). Rolf was diligent in tattling on Blaine.

My chosen parenting style was, in those days, known

as "permissive." I wanted them to develop naturally according to their own personalities, and they most certainly did. However, while we encouraged them to express themselves, Linné would not tolerate disrespect or lying, even more so than I.

Physically, Linné and I liked to allow the kids enough freedom to explore without injuring themselves. Of course, they did end up with some stitches, but who hadn't in childhood.

To me, their childhood was our responsibility along with our entertainment. It was so much fun. I loved every age. They were so cute! I would sometimes actually say aloud, "Oh, I don't want this stage to end."

Linné, on the other hand, wasn't interested in babies. He didn't understand them at all and kept his distance. It used to bother me, but when we talked about it, he'd say, "I like middle-aged children. You wait and see." And it was true. Once the kids headed into school age, he became totally involved with them.

Then the next stage would come along and of course I'd feel the same, like now, watching them absorb the classic story they were listening to—it was all brand new to them and they reacted to it with exclamations and questions which I answered to the best of my ability.

They made me stretch myself in ways I'd never imagined I could stretch, and I often felt that I was growing along with them. I wanted to hang onto every memory and had the urge to write them down—but if I did that, I'd miss out on something.

I carried a camera everywhere but was judicious with taking photos because they were expensive to have developed, and two weeks out. I got some good ones, though, and 8-mm movies (no sound—how I wish I had their dear little voices on record, but I only had them in my head).

I was into educating them—not formally but giving them experiences that would enable them to build their knowledge. I tried to teach them how to read before going to kindergarten, but that was a complete failure. I didn't know how to do it, and they were resistant. I think they wanted to play, and

I didn't present teaching reading in a playful way. That was disappointing to me.

Of course, I thought my children were exceptional. What parent didn't? But teaching them to read was off limits. They did fine in school, nothing exceptional.

We read a lot of books wherever we were. As they got older, I read to them books from the library. We would go together. Also there was a Bookmobile that stopped on our street every week, which was great when we only owned one car and Linné had it.

We couldn't afford a TV and didn't generally miss it. But sometimes we would rent one for a month ($10). Or occasionally Linné and I would take them to outdoor movies. The kids loved that. They'd fall asleep in the back seat. One of Linné's favorite memories was carrying each one from the car into their bedroom when we returned from the Drive-in.

In Seattle our backyard was full of kids. I built a jungle gym out of two by twos, two by fours, and through-bolts. A picnic table enabled me to serve snacks, or for the kids to play at. Our side yard was full of big trees and plenty of dirt for making forts. I did not pay much attention to that. It was their space, with shovels.

One winter I built an ice skating rink in the back yard with a huge tarp to contain two inches of water. The children and I all went regularly to the ice skating rink in North Seattle and Dori even got lessons.

On Seattle jungle gym.

In Chatham we didn't have that backyard, but the converted attic was a nice alternative, especially on a day with rainy weather when we could hear the patter on the roof. It was a fun place.

After lunch there was a break in the mist and the kids and I took to the stairs and the boardwalk. The sky threatened to resume its wet ways at any moment, so we enjoyed being outdoors for as long as we could. How I would have loved to have captured the shiny gloss on everything, the vivid red and white reflections of the buildings captured in the hollows of the boardwalk's planks, the colorfulness of fishermen in their rain gear.

But of course, I didn't have my paints—and I couldn't have painted under that threatening sky even if I did.

The kids and I loitered at the rail of the main dock and watched a Grumman Goose take off. Its belly skipped along the waves, and it seemed far too heavy and cumbersome to ever take off, but then suddenly it was airborne and full of grace.

I bumped into Linné about 2:30 p.m. and he casually mentioned that he had just returned from a flight to the Sitka on "that plane that just took off."

You never knew where Linné was going to be next.

When the dinner bell rang that evening, the mist had thickened to actual rain and we donned our rain gear and boots to troop down the 79 steps.

It might have been more practical to keep the kids home and feed them myself on a day like that since we had the luxury of a stocked refrigerator (I can only imagine how they got the fridge up the hill, along with the washing machine and other modern conveniences). Linné had stocked it before we came including a case of boxed milk for the kids. I supplemented it with food from the store to make meals for Linné, since he often didn't make it to the Mess Hall.

The truth was, the most we saw of Linné was at the Mess Hall, when he could make it, and I didn't want the kids or me to lose the opportunity to be with him.

On guard for his health, I made sure Linné had access to real (if boxed) milk, not the watery stuff Marla tried to force the adults to drink. But Linné was a purist and saw the Real Fresh boxed milk as medicine. I felt bad for the men who craved it. Every time they tried to help themselves to the milk that hadn't been watered down, Marla would fly out of the kitchen and yell at them, smugly saying the good milk was only for the children.

As soon as she stomped back to the kitchen, I told the men they should go ahead and sneak it. The kids got plenty of milk at home. Dori was like her father and didn't like it, but the boys (and I) actually kind of liked the boxed milk, though it did have that caramelized taste. The boys and I knew the trick of it: just pretend it was some beverage other than milk.

I was delighted to see that Linné was at the table that evening, but a muted groan went up from everyone when we saw that it was so-called "steak" night. We prodded the grey slabs on our plates, poking hopefully as if the meat would suddenly become transformed to a more appetizing hue.

"I think she piles them on each other and cooks them in the oven," Linné surmised after doing a postmortem on his cadaver—I mean, steak.

The sad part was we had steaks three times a week. This should have been something to anticipate and celebrate, but when the result looked like weathered wood and tasted about the same, our hearts sank.

It was too bad. The men, working those long, monotonous, strenuous and slimy hours, lived for their meals. They woke up for the 7 a.m. breakfast whistle, and by 10 a.m. were more than ready for the first mug-up whistle to blow so they could gulp coffee and gobble doughnuts and other pastries provided by the Filipino Mess Hall in the cannery. Then lunch at noon, and the three o'clock mug-up in the White Mess Hall.

But it was dinner that meant the most to them when they were not yet so exhausted that they ate simply as a break from the work, such as at the nine o'clock mug-up and the even later midnight meal when the work was at fever pitch.

Dinner was when they needed not only nutrients to sustain them, but a certain amount of hominess and camaraderie to encourage them and make them feel like we were all family united in a single purpose. There was nothing homey about Marla's Mess Hall.

We had all, by then, given up the pretense of Marla being only an assistant cook. The head cook was too cowed by her, or too lazy, to try to assert his authority. It was useless going to him to change anything.

Linné told me he had constant complaints from the men on the one hand, and on the other hand from the cooks who felt themselves overworked and underappreciated. But until other cooks could be found, we were stuck with Marla.

Mom, in one of her letters, suggested I assist the cooks to help the situation along tactfully. After all, she said, besides having been a cook on fish tenders, I'd had experience in a catering business.

She was referring to how, during our first year of marriage (after the fishing season was over in Alaska), we took over Linné's mother's food business in Seattle while she started a new one in Oklahoma. The Chatham cooks, mom wrote, would surely respect my experience in the food industry and be eager to have my help. I had to break it to her that there was no hope of that happening.

"I ordered some charcoal briquettes," Linné said in a low voice to me, under the laborious sawing of meat and criss-cross of melancholy conversation around us. "We'll see if we can get steaks from the Mess Hall freezer."

I was on his wavelength instantly. "We can cook our own steaks in the fireplace." I thought it a brilliant plan. I only wished we had a real barbecue, like the one I remembered from my childhood, so all of the men could have shared in the joy of grilled steak.

For a moment, as I chewed arduously, I thought wistfully of bygone times and much better-prepared beef. As a pre-teen when we lived in Linthicum, Maryland, Dad—who was always building something—built a swimming pool in the backyard with a foot bath, outdoor shower, surrounded by a wonderful outdoor barbecue. I loved it when Mom and Dad had warm evening parties out there with hamburgers in buns dipped in Worcestershire Sauce and butter, served with Mint Juleps. My mouth watered just thinking about it.

That was what Chatham needed, I thought. A large barbecue like that where the entire neighborhood—or, in this case, cannery workers—could gather and enjoy *real* food and fellowship.

Until such a barbecue could be had, the fireplace would have to suffice.

The only problem was trying to outguess when Marla would serve steaks, so that I could get our fair share from the meat locker. She didn't keep to a regular schedule and trying to pin her down was impossible. She liked the control she wielded and refused to be "dictated to by the superintendent's wife" and told when she could or could not serve something.

I could only imagine the hullaballoo and hurt feelings that would ensue if I outright asked for the meat to cook for Linné and myself. More complaints from Marla was the last thing Linné needed to deal with right now with this bumper year of salmon.

I spent the rest of the unsatisfying meal plotting a raid on the meat locker. It would be difficult to do it without getting caught. Both cooks lived on the premises, in the cook's quarters attached to the galley/kitchen.

While we were still working our way through the leather steaks, the children came rushing into the Mess Hall (they'd already finished eating and weren't allowed back into the hall after they'd left) with enormous, wide eyes. "Bears! Bears! We saw bears out there!"

All conversation stopped as we heard all about it. Someone had invited the kids into the bunkhouse to see three bears that were standing just below. I guess it was like watching the wild rabbits at San Juan Island. The guys poked fun at me, saying they couldn't believe I still hadn't seen a bear, even though my children had.

After dinner was over, when I went in to scrape our plates, I lingered. Usually I did it quickly and departed before any chance of a conversation could arise between Marla and me. That evening, I risked it in order to "case the joint."

Or at any rate, check out how easily accessible the meat locker was. Not that I was doing anything wrong. It wasn't like I was going to heist more than our fair share, I only wanted to appropriate our allotted meat.

Marla caught me with my hand on the handle of the locker. Her eye immediately acquired a suspicious glitter. "What are you doing? Are you *checking up on us?*"

"Checking up—?"

"You think we're stealing from the cannery!"

"What? I never—"

Her harsh voice rose. "You think as the superintendent's wife that you can slander us like this, but I won't have it! First your husband tries to work us to the bone, now this! It's going too far. Where would your precious husband be if we walked out when the cannery is this busy? After this, we just might! Just think about that, why don't you, Mrs. Superintendent!"

She had the upper hand there, and I quickly beat a retreat, though not without another good look around to see the best way to conduct the meat heist. Not that I could do it any time soon: the briquettes that Linné had ordered from Juneau hadn't even arrived yet.

But maybe that was just as well; it would give Marla time to calm down and not be on high alert. And then, I plotted, the meat heist would commence.

At least it was a diversion that took my mind off not being able to do my art.

CHAPTER 9

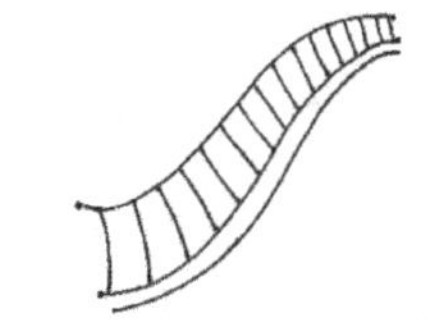

A Letter Home

A particular value of Emily's letters is that they are impressions of events described as they are happening. Because the details were immediately fresh in her mind, it is possible to gain insights into life at frontier posts that may be clearer or more accurate than views from memoirs, which may have been written through a nostalgic haze.

—Joan I. Biddle, Foreword to An Army Doctor's Wife on the Frontier: The Letters of Emily McCorkle Fitzgerald from Alaska and the Far West, 1874-78

Chatham Cannery
Sitkoh Bay, Alaska
July 16-22, 1963

I plopped down on a pillow on the porch steps, my legs stretched on either side of a rope spool with the typewriter on top of it and banged out:

Life goes on and I don't know how. The pinks still pour in. Fishing is every other day now and Linne has raised the limit to 500 fish per man. The cannery can just keep up with the constant flow by working a 16 hour day. The foreman, Tom Anderson, is frantic because the machinery never shuts down long enough to make repairs. Last night he was working on the elevator until 5am. Then he was flown to Juneau, very sick. He suffers from ulcers (I don't wonder). But he was back just hours later, much to Linne's relief.

It annoyed me that I couldn't get the accent over Linné's name. I supposed I could do it manually with a pen later. It was a pet peeve of mine that Linné's mother hadn't just spelled his name Linnae, without the need for the accent. I almost laughed out loud, catching myself being irked over something so minor when Linné was dealing with so much.

His foreman getting sick had been particularly worrying. Linné was already doing more than his superintendent position required (or his employers wanted him to do). But that wasn't what stressed him. It was the part he was required to do—the office work—that stressed him the most.

One of the things that New England Fish Co. had an issue with Linné about was that he loved being "on the floor," so to speak. He'd been hired by them to be in the office. Instead, he spent a lot of time in the cannery checking on things, demonstrating how to do a job, or talking with the mechanics. That's where he loved to be most.

When the cannery was understaffed because of long hours or an emergency, Linné would jump in and pretty much do anyone's job. He especially was good on the forklift, without ever dumping a load. He could also work on the machinery. He showed his labor force how to work fast, safely, efficiently, and with an awareness of everything else that was going on. He loved to demonstrate that he was the fastest worker on the dock— that no job was too small or large for him, that he was good at everything, and by golly, they'd need to measure up! At the same time, he mingled with them and got them laughing. He kept the morale high.

Linné was accustomed to hard physical labor, not just in his youth, but in making it all the way up the fish industry ladder. He'd worked his way up in the field, from fishing, skiff man on a seiner, captaining fish tenders (with me as his deckhand), assistant superintendent of Chatham Cannery to now the superintendent (and one day, in the future, he'd become the manager of Seward Fisheries and finally his own boss with a successful fish transport company, American Viking Lines. But that was a ways in the future yet).

Of course, he did have to be in the office a lot, to take radio schedules and be on hand for problems that came up. Often, someone would have to go find him.

One of the few times I had the chance to talk with Linné he said, after NEFCO got on his case again about being on the floor instead of the office, "Dot, you know me. I love work, actual *work*. Pushing papers is not my thing."

"I know," I'd said sympathetically. Making reports and keeping the Seattle office informed truly was a waste of his skills and energy.

"I knew what I was in for when I became superintendent," he said. "I knew there'd be a lot of paperwork."

Knowing is one thing. Dealing with it is another, I thought. He was an audio, meaning that if you told him something he'd remember it and act on it. (Whereas I was a visual…I had to see it written.) Dealing with written reports was alien to his nature but a necessary part of his job.

"Well, I'll do it. But I'll keep on helping out on the floor too."

That much I was sure of, especially during this crisis. He thrived on emergencies all his life, jumping out of bed in the middle of the night to tend to one. I would have hated that. He also had the social ability to talk with the fishermen because he had himself spent a season doing just that and understood their concerns. I don't think anyone ever thought he was condescending. He liked being in the thick of things, and actually accomplishing something, rather than reporting about it.

That was one of the reasons why most people loved Linné. Of course, there were a few that probably didn't, but he could pretty much turn anyone around. (I had those skills too.)

He was, at heart, a problem solver—and very good at it. There wasn't a man I admired or respected more. Or loved, with all my heart.

I sighed and typed to my parents: *Linne figures another 4 weeks of this.*

Would I finally get my husband, then? It was so strange being near him for some meals, seeing him at a distance, sleeping beside him but feeling as lonely and missing him as much as I ever did when we spent summers apart. Now I was continually teased by his presence without ever really having much of his time or attention.

It wasn't just a physical thing, though of course that had always been a healthy aspect of our relationship. I missed being surprised by him. Linné was sensitive to other people's feelings, sentimental, and kind. He'd bring me up short if he felt I had overstepped someone. He was full of surprises. Just when I thought I had him figured out, he'd do something that was off the grid.

We laughed so much together, too. I missed that.

I frowned as I looked at the words I'd typed: *Linne figures another 4 weeks of this*. This was how it had to be, and I was determined to make the best of it without complaint, though I wasn't sure I could bottle it up forever. I had, after all, been known to break down into uncontrollable laughter in the most inappropriate places, like church or the library. Something about the solemnity and quiet brought it out of me, I supposed, especially if I was under any kind of stress.

The beach gang repairs the boardwalk.

I continued educating my parents about a working cannery, knowing Dad in particular would want all the details. I had no doubt he'd take delight in lecturing some poor captive soul about them at some point.

No cannery, I typed, *can do without the beach gang. There are about ten men on ours. Their job is maintenance and they are always finding places to repair. They work as a team.*

The carpenter shack was the domain of the beach gang and one of my favorite places… the smell of shaved wood penetrated the outdoors too. Boardwalks were made from raw, fresh-cut lumber. They were constantly falling apart, rotting, or overgrown with moss. Planks had to be replaced.

**Blaine and Dori watch the beach gang
rebuild the top of the stairs.**

Pilings too, underneath the foundation for every building and boardwalk, had to be dealt with as they eventually deteriorated or were damaged by storm-tossed logs. The lead paint, on the other hand, held up well under the assault of sun, salt, and incessant rain.

The beach gang is also responsible for maintenance on the house. I never know when 3 men might be up here working on a window, hauling out trash, or putting in a new foundation.

One particular favorite among the beach gang not just for me but for the entire cannery was Harold "Smokey" Hansen, who was also the winter watchman. He looked after the remote, shutdown cannery with his wife, Elizabeth, and their three kids during the long, dark winter months of storms, and had few interactions with the outside world. Later on, he and his family would play a much bigger role at the cannery and in our lives.

The beach gang's most impressive job was when they replaced a huge, rusted tank that was leaking with a brand new one. I watched in fascination trying to guess how they would move such a monstrosity from a barge, uphill, to a place on the other side of the boardwalk where it would permanently reside.

Like a bunch of ancient Egyptians, they managed to get rollers underneath so they could inch it up with a block and tackle, painfully and slowly without losing a log, which would mean doing the hard part all over again. Finally, they had to skid the giant tank into place, using their own skid grease consisting of a mixture of beef tallow and used lubricating oil thinned with kerosene.

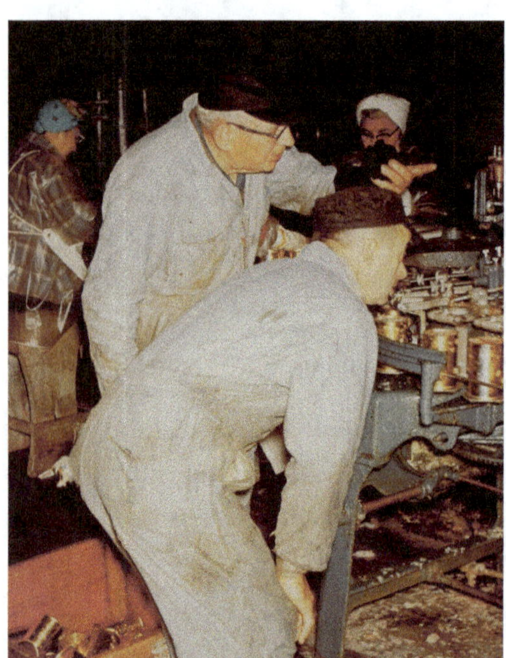

Tom Anderson and Marvin Remlinger waste no time fixing a problem on the cannery line.

I couldn't imagine how a cannery would continue in good health without the diligent ministrations of the beach gang.

Then there were the machinists. I typed: *They have their own shop and are in charge of fixing canning machines. Often they have to tool their own parts to make a repair.*

Talk about inventive— they couldn't just go to the hardware store. If they did buy something from Juneau, it would have to be flown out in a chartered plane. Time was of the essence. Linné couldn't have workers standing around doing nothing who were being paid by the hour, so when the cannery was forced to shut down, there was a lot of scurrying about to find the right person and tools to do the job quickly, even if the repair had to be jury-rigged until a more permanent repair was possible.

Linné was not a carpenter, but he understood machinery, anything metal, and was often seen consulting with the machinists for the quickest analysis of the problem and helping invent something.

Great minds at work! Nothing seemed impossible for them. I doubted those brilliant minds had college educations, but they were valuable blue-collar workers who understood logic and urgency. They had marketable skills, and they were captive, sort of, at an outlying cannery in Alaska. I hoped they were paid well. Most of them returned to Chatham year after year, so they must have liked the challenge.

I tapped my chin, considering who I could focus on to write about to my parents.

There were many characters that stood out, even though I hadn't met everyone yet. There were the Ebonas, for example. I tackled the typewriter keys:

Martin Ebona, our bull cook, is a dear little man, tireless, hard-working, silent, and always looking out for our comfort. He is rather squat with snaggle teeth and glazed eyes, a man who waits for you to speak first and who lights up if he finds your words pleasant. He is the salt of the earth Filipino, and an institution at Chatham cannery.

I added, knowing Dad would want definitions, *The term bull cook applies to the leader of the bull gang whose job it is to care for the needs of the people working here.*

"Bull cook" was a logging term for all around handyman, and Martin was the official assistant for the Filipino Mess Hall. But Martin also made himself useful on the docks, checking and counting salmon as they were delivered by fish elevator.

Martin's daughter, Mary, who was the village queen at 15, and his son Augie, didn't seem very attentive to their father, at least to my mind, as they ran with the younger crowd.

My parents, of course, would be more interested in my family and what happened to us. I typed:

Linne played a small part in an Alaska drama the other day. A radio call came through from Waterfall Cannery which was trying to reach Ketchikan with an emergency call, while Linne was transmitting. The superintendent of the other cannery was desperately looking for not one doctor, but several, since his wife was having a severe asthma attack. For the next 20 minutes the air was filled with attempts to get help and then someone cut in and said, "Cancel the call; the superintendent's wife died."

I stopped typing. I was still moved by the sympathy in the voice of the person who took the ensuing telegram and the people in our office who didn't even know either the man or his wife. Alaska was a small place, really, with everyone tied in with each other in some sort of kinship. Our only communication was the radio. We were all involved just by listening.

Seated on the house's front steps, I was high above the entire cannery complex with a warm breeze rustling through the endless forest. I felt viscerally that I was alive, all of my senses soaking in the beauty of the Alaskan wilderness while I did something as ordinary as write a letter home.

Just that quickly another superintendent's wife, at another cannery, was dead. It brought home how remote and cut off from the social safety net and taken-for-granted medical services we were out here in the wilderness. But I never let that get me down and always focused on the positive in life no matter where we lived.

I went back to hammering the keys:

When I checked the post office, there was a box from grandma for the kids with all sorts of fun do-dads, but their favorite was the used sparklers you sent. We receive mail on Tuesday, Thursday and Saturday. You'll never know what it means at Chatham.

The postmaster (Linne) says that stamps and cigarettes are the 2 fastest moving commodities. This afternoon Linne, although he's been acting as the post master, was finally sworn in and fingerprinted as the official Chatham postmaster. He had to fill out so many forms. An inspector came out to examine the books and handle the ceremony. Linne listed Dad as a personal reference.

At the post office, besides the box from Mom, I'd found a letter from Alaska Coastal Airlines. I thought I'd enclose it for my parents. It said:

Dear Mrs. Bardarson; We have found your four coats and are on flite [sic] this date. However we have not been able to find your green suitcase yet, we have sent tracers to all our stations plus Pan American, we should be hearing on it soon, and will send to Chatham as soon as located. Sincerely, Juneau Traffic, R.F. Angell

I'd actually been hoping the suitcase would stay lost—it was insured for $100. I could use that to buy a new set of luggage. (It wasn't long after this that it was found and sent to Chatham.)

Enough with the mundane. Time to share my most exciting moment of the week. *I saw my first bear. I was thrilled to see him right on our beach looking for 3-day old fish, oblivious of the bank of eyes viewing him. The sluggish beast was very busy.*

I had been teased at every meal about not having seen a bear yet. But when everyone rushed to watch the bruin—Native children, the office crew, fishermen, cooks, men from the bunkhouse—I realized that seeing a bear close was, after all, an occasion, not a daily routine, as I had been led to believe.

But bear stories continued to scare me.

Only the other day in the Mess Hall the men were talking about bone fragments, a plastic helmet, and a rifle being found on Chichagof Island—the island our cannery was on. The evidence indicated that the man was killed by a bear. Dental records proved that it was a businessman who had gone missing two years ago on a hunting trip. Despite an intensive search, he wasn't found until his scanty remains turned up this year.

I shuddered and added: *We have seen quite a few bears roaming the beach. We watch from the safety of the bunkhouse while the bears root for old fish. Linne says that as more fish heads are deposited into the bay the number of bears will increase and so will their bravery.*

To get my mind off it, I focused on the total solar eclipse that Kemper Freeman had told me about in so much detail. It occurred on July 20, 1963 and lasted for 1 minute and 40 seconds. Since it was a rare event, most of the country was keyed up to watch it including my parents.

Wasn't it perfect weather for the eclipse? I typed. *Everyone was staring at the sun through negatives, smoked glass, welder hoods, etc. I kept the kids indoors to protect their eyes, and later wished I had made a pinhole viewer.*

I took a sip of water and flexed my hands. Pounding on the typewriter for so long was hard on the fingers. I could hear the kids' high voices as they played nearby and added:

It is wonderful to be available to the children completely. We have read the novel "Black Beauty" and "Toby Tyler" and innumerable other stories. Now we are on "The Bobbsey Twins." Blaine has been able to learn several words to the point where I can't confuse him on them.

I didn't just read to the kids. I was also getting caught up on my own reading. I'd read two books so far and had just picked up *Hawaii* by James Michener. But I grew embarrassed at the realization that I was probably the only one in camp who had time to read, so I offered my so-called accounting services at the company store.

Unfortunately, that meant that the children would practically live there, so I brought the grocery bills up to the house along with an adding machine. Everything was by credit at the store, so every candy bar and soda pop was itemized by hand. The largest bill so far was $485. They were so far behind in the store as in every other department, I told my parents, that I was sure I could be of some help if I didn't make too many mistakes. *Adding machines and I have never gotten along,* I ruefully typed.

As I was adding up store receipts, I couldn't help but chuckle at one. They were supposed to be initialed by the customer, but the clerk had written in "Too drunk to sign." I knew my parents would get a chuckle out of that.

We'd had more overnight guests which added to the laundry. I typed: *My linens haven't been picked up yet and there is quite a pile, though I have laundered some myself. The infernal washing machine still outsmarts me.*

I frowned as I included something that continued to bother me: *Yesterday, I caught all 3 kids rolling cigarettes underneath the tall oil tank. They were making them out of band aids and teabags and lighting them. The thought still haunts me of the possibility of an ensuing holocaust of the entire cannery.*

(As it happened, there were later consequences for Dori from this. She'd become particular friends with a little Native girl named Dorcas Paul. Our next summer after the kids smoked under the oil tank, Dori went eagerly down to the Native Village to renew her friendship. But Dorcas' mother took her aside and wouldn't let Dori play with her daughter until Dori assured her that she did not smoke. She didn't want her Dorcas to be

Dori and Blaine with Dorcas Paul.

friends with a hard-boiled eight-year-old smoker. "That ended my career as a smoker," Dori would later say.)

I suddenly realized how late it was. The dinner bell would soon be rung, and I needed to get the kids into a bath and dress them in nice clothes. I packed up the typewriter, pillow, and spools and rounded up the kids.

Later, before going to bed, I slipped into the living room to finish the letter home, typing: *Tonight, the conversation at the Mess Hall revolved around the Liston/Patterson fight.*

Linné wasn't usually interested in boxing despite having learned to box during his YMCA days when he was 13. His sport was basketball. As an adult at six foot seven inches, he was a natural for the sport, and he played for the University of Washington in college. (During the Gold Medal Tournament in Juneau, he complained to the refs that the other team was ganging up on him, trying to prevent him from making a basket. "Can't you see what's going on? They're all over me." "What difference does it make?" the refs responded. "You're making them anyway.")

So he wasn't naturally invested in the fight, but the other men in the Mess Hall were very much so. I gathered this fight was something out of the way, for the heavyweight champion title. It was apparently an epic match—or, rather, re-match—between good (Floyd Patterson, the "Gentleman Boxer") and evil (Sonny Liston, an ex-con with mafia ties). Or so the media's narrative ran.

Patterson—an Olympic gold medalist—was widely expected to win the revenge bout, despite having last time been knocked out in the first round, third fastest in history. Once again, Patterson was knocked out in the first round, lasting only 4 seconds longer than the original match. Reportedly the crowd booed, and the men at our table got heated over whether Patterson had thrown the fight.

My focus during dinner had been on the meal I pushed around my plate. The food continued to disappoint, to put it mildly. Marla was clearly suspicious of my every move and watched me like a hawk whenever I was in the kitchen/galley. So far I hadn't had a chance to put the steak heist into action, although the briquettes had come and were burning a metaphorical hole in my metaphorical pocket.

I sat at the desk in the quiet house, the kids long since asleep, and listened to the constant rumble of the cannery that would continue after I went to sleep. I might not even be awake when Linné came back home.

I was surrounded by my family, and my husband was technically present. I understood and appreciated perfectly why he couldn't spend more time with me…but there were times, especially since I couldn't do my art, when I was lonely.

I finished my letter to my parents: *I could use a female friend about now.*

134

CHAPTER 10

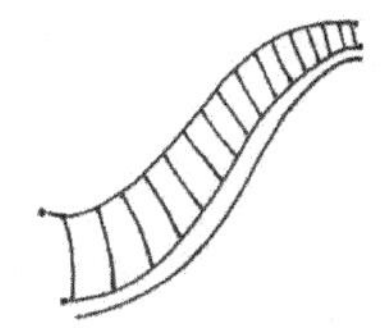

High Noon in the Mess Hall

In those days the mess hall was literally at the center of cannery life… I always remember my father, Gary Johnson, who was superintendent at the South Naknek cannery, saying that his cook was one of his most important employees. He understood the cannery workers' trip to the mess hall was "the social event of the day." In fact, he would say he hired (and fired) his baker depending on how well he or she made maple bars. And indeed, my dad was not the only cannery superintendent that felt this way.

—"MUG-UP: The Role of the Mess Hall
in Cannery Life" by Katherine Ringsmuth

**Chatham Cannery
Sitkoh Bay, Alaska
July 23-25, 1963**

Linné, with his storytelling flare, told me about it so vividly that I felt like I was there.

It started with an actual phone being installed at the office. Hoonah and Pelican, distant villages that shared our huge island (Chichagof), had enjoyed the luxury of having phones installed two years ago. This summer it was Angoon's turn to have a phone system installed…actual dial phones in a variety of decorator colors! Southeast Alaska was joining the modern world, it seemed.

Since we were just across the strait, they did Chatham at the same time—though we only got the one phone reserved primarily for the superintendent for cannery business. It made a huge difference for Linné to have direct, private communication with the Seattle office. Previously, if the "supe" didn't want other people listening in, he'd had to take a floatplane to Sitka (40 miles away over a high mountain range) to make a sensitive phone call to the home office.

All the equipment necessary, including Alaska Communication Systems (ACS) microwave equipment, was installed and tested in specially built vans in Seattle and shipped north by boat. Just the tower was built on location. Chatham, however, didn't have a tower—it had a cable that ran underwater from Angoon.

Practically the first thing Linné did when he had access to a phone was call for a new, interim cook, which would give him time to find more permanent ones without the threat of Marla and the head cook quitting at any moment and leaving the cannery in the lurch.

The new cook, Harry, arrived from the Pederson Point cannery on Bristol Bay which was also run by the New England Fish Company. With the dire fishing season, they were having up there, it only made sense to send that plant's cook to Chatham where he was more needed.

After meeting Harry's plane, Linné promptly took him to the Mess Hall's galley.

"You'll be happy to know," Linné informed the head cook without preamble, "that your complaints about being overworked have been heard. Harry will take over immediately, leaving you free to find a job more suited to your needs."

All sounds in the galley ceased, except the hissing of steam from water boiling in a huge three-gallon kettle on the stove being readied for the mid-afternoon mug up. The head cook looked from Linné to the new cook and didn't say anything. But then, he rarely did.

It was always Marla who did the talking, and she didn't disappoint this time either. With a bull walrus charge, she faced off with Linné and planted her hands on her hips. In her usual rasping voice she screamed,

"Now let's get down to business here. I want to know 'why'! No don't tell me, I already know. I know why we are being let go. It's because your wife doesn't like me. That's it, isn't it?"

Linné, slightly flabbergasted, said, "My wife doesn't have a darn thing to say about how this cannery operates."

"Likely story!" Marla's face was contorted and red with rage. "I know she has it in for me. I've seen her snooping around here, looking for things to get mad about and report back to you! As if we don't have enough on our hands, what with feeding everyone all hours of the day and night!"

"It would seem, with all that you've had to deal with here, that you should be tickled to death to be released from your misery," Linné said.

"That's not—" she stopped, baffled by his reasonable tone and calm demeanor.

"You're already tired and with no end in sight of fish, the rest of this season will no doubt continue at its present pace and be too much for you."

Her self-righteous wrath wilted. It was hard to be screamingly furious when someone was being reasonable and concerned about your welfare. She didn't pursue the "whys" further, and I thought, when Linné told me about it later, that she was probably afraid he would tell her.

So although Marla scowled and stamped about, muttering under her breath, she nonetheless gathered up her belongings.

I was present for the denouement. I even felt kind of sorry for the cooks as they made their long walk down the boardwalk to the plane with their suitcases under a lowering sky, misty entrails streaming down from the clouds. No one waved them on, or joked with them, or wished them well in their next venture.

The red cannery buildings continued to hum under the overcast light, even while workers came outside to find out what had happened to the always anticipated mug-up. The news of Linné's rout of the cooks spread like wildfire, and the workers flocked to the scene of the cooks' defeat.

Trolling bells rang, tolling a fitting taps for Marla's reign, as fishermen stepped off their boats. Sea gulls strutted and gloated over the warped decking, but no one paid any attention to them. Everyone was silent as they lined the railings and watched Marla the Dictator board the plane to Elba, or at any rate to eternal exile from Chatham.

A cheer went up as the plane roared, freed itself of the water's grasp, and lifted into the sky, taking Marla away to harass future quarry in unknown places.

The new cook, Harry, and I got along much better from the outset. He was more than willing to accept any help I had to offer, which would please Mom enormously, I knew. He took over even before his predecessors left in disgrace. He was planning to serve what he termed "the usual Saturday night steak," but when he saw the condition of the band saw used to cut meat, he balked, and changed the menu to fresh salmon.

Nobody was upset with his first big, culinary decision.

A fresh salmon dinner, something usually reserved for the wealthiest and most privileged strata of society? Who would say no to that? *Such is our life,* I joked to my parents in my next letter to them.

After the cooks left, several fellows and I turned our hands to making the kitchen ship-shape. What I loved about the interior of cannery buildings was the rich, warm color of the woodwork that contrasted with white walls. It was time to bring out the best points of the much-abused kitchen/galley.

The mess hall galley had a huge, eight-foot iron stove with brass-hinged doors on its side-by-side double oven. Above it hung an enormous metal hood. The chimney was on the left and a brick heat guard rose from the floor to the ceiling behind it. Next to it was the tall boiler.

The deep sink was opposite, its wood counter lined with double-hung, 12-paned windows that opened inward on top to vent steam and allow air circulation. Floor-to-ceiling open shelves held the dishes on the top shelves and the pots, pans and kettles on the bottom shelves—or that's how it was, once order was established.

I took over the mug-up room. Marla's mug-up usually consisted of bread, cold cereal, coffee, juices and leftovers from previous meals. Marla had scraped the serving dishes into a mess and tossed it on the mug-up table.

I cleared the entire table, scrubbed the cheesecloth with scouring powder, dried it to a gloss and refurbished it with cups lined up in rows, dishes arranged, and a glass of fresh wildflowers given pride of place. It was amazing to me how much those little things meant to the men, who made pilgrimages to the scene to pay their respects and gaze in deep appreciation at the charming setup. Perhaps, rough as they lived their lives now, it reminded them of a gentler time when Mother kept house and tended to all their childhood needs.

There was much clatter, scraping, scrubbing and banter, and the strong scents of various cleansing agents as we all set to with a will to sweep and wash away all trace of the previous cooks.

I climbed onto the counter and went to work on the little panes of windows above the sink and counter which were so encrusted with grease, dirt, and the desiccated remains of bugs that they seemed like etched glass. The men were most amazed to not only see through them but to see themselves in them. Comments to me included: "Is this what you expected to be doing as the superintendent's wife before you came, Dot?"

It was a very simple meal, really, that evening—nothing to rave about—but you should have heard those men. The comments were hilarious. It was one of the nicest meals I've shared, with much back slapping, congratulations, and mimicking of Marla, the dictator. The men indulged themselves in as much of the good milk as they liked, lifting their full glasses that glinted under the bare light bulbs suspended above the picnic-style tables, to toast the fall and exile of Mad Marla.

The next morning when I showed up for galley detail, two men were cleaning the meat house. The bandsaw was encrusted with decaying meat, the cabinets were disorganized, and the floor was filthy. By using up all the hot water, the place soon gleamed. I imagined the bacteria, which had been living the life of Riley, meeting their doom under the agitated bearers of scrub brushes and mops.

Head-shaking and muttering continued in the kitchen. I tackled the baking room. When I wrote about it to my parents later, I typed: *I hesitate to describe it, for you may not have had your lunch yet. I bet we have the strongest antibodies in Alaska.*

Aside from the thick layer of grease on everything and the complete chaos, there was a huge pile of stale bread being saved for bread pudding and stuffing. It had been dumped on an already dirty pie crust rolling area. While I was shoveling this into boxes to dump into the bay, my eye fell on several expired flies, bees, and daddy longlegs—waiting, I supposed, to be included in the next meal's dessert.

After several hours with hands in ammonia and water, the room began to look like it could support the baking of a few cakes for that night's dinner. I planned to march on the pantry next, and after that the freezer, causeway, etc.

The cook, meanwhile, was dealing with the stove, which required a deep clean, but he couldn't let it cool long enough to clean it as thoroughly as he'd like when he had to use it to cook the four major meals and snacks that were part of the routine.

Once, when he joined me as I made war on the bacteria in the pantry, he said, "If I'd known what I'd be facing taking on this job, I probably wouldn't have come."

"I'm glad for all our sakes that you did," I said as I scraped at an indeterminate hill of gunk glued to a shelf. "And we'll make sure you get all the help you need to hold up to the pace while the cannery is going at all hours like this."

He still looked doubtful and mentioned how different the terrain was from the wide open tundra he was used to up north. Apparently, he felt that Chatham was claustrophobically closed in by the endless forests, mountains, and the narrow slough that fed into the strait. Homesickness in addition to being faced with the squalor and chaos he'd been thrown into clearly didn't endear Chatham to our new cook.

I hoped Linné had plans to find a more permanent solution to cooking duties. Harry was only the interim, after all, and it looked like he didn't plan on sticking around any longer than absolutely necessary.

Luxuriating in my better relationship with the cook, I didn't hesitate to ask for a couple steaks to cook at home. Harry flung open the meat locker's doors and let me have full access to all within. What a difference! There was no further need of a heist.

It took several trips up the 79 steps to prepare dinner, freely borrowing whatever I needed from the galley. I used the briquettes Linné had ordered weeks ago to finally make a perfect steak dinner in the fireplace.

It was worth the exertion of all the steps. While the kids got to eat in the Mess Hall without parental oversight (Harry agreed to keep an eye on them), Linné enjoyed eating quietly in his home and I loved feeding him.

We sat in the classic, dark paneled dining room. I set Aladdin kerosene lamps, with their tall, slender glass chimneys and delicate mantles, on the table and lit them for a romantic, golden glow. After I caught him up on what the kids and I had been doing and reading, he gave me the story of the High Noon showdown in the Mess Hall.

I couldn't help but be impressed with how he'd handled Marla. And all in that devastatingly agreeable tone that had completely undercut her fury. It had long been my opinion, after seeing him in action in all sorts of circumstances with a variety of personalities, that Linné was a masterful psychological strategist.

How he got around a raging Mess Hall Tyrant so easily was proof positive.

He was called away before we got to dessert, but at least we had a few husband and wife minutes together and a delicious steak dinner first. That was something.

CHAPTER 11

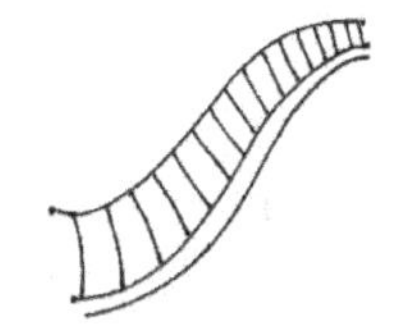

Cracking Up

*The act of sign-paining is extremely technical: ensuring that
a design works for the space, getting the right equipment,
adjusting the plan and strategy depending on the condition
of the wall, inclement weather or tight timelines... and
finally, the art and design aspect: the embellishments and
stylized forms that are so essential to typographic design
and hand-lettering.*

—"Venerable Vintages: History of Sign Painting"
by Catherine Monahan

**Chatham Cannery
Sitkoh Bay, Alaska
July 26-28, 1963**

Dad impressed on all of us kids, "Always leave things better than you found them."

Once, when we were visiting Grandma and Grampa in Dad's hometown of Twin Falls, Idaho where he'd grown up a poor boy on a dairy farm, he took us to the ice cave where he'd spent much of his childhood exploring.

Although he grew up without a lot of material things (his mother was a clever seamstress and could alter and repair hand-me-downs for her three sons), he did have a beautiful bay horse named Prince to carry him on his adventures. I'd seen an old sepia-tinted photo of him in a flat cap and rolled up pants standing on Prince's hind quarters while the glossy horse looked quizzically at the camera.

We drove out of town onto the broad, arid Snake River plains of southern Idaho that seemed like a desert to me. It was intensely hot, even with the windows rolled down, with a dusty furnace blast of a breeze blowing in my face. I imagined Dad riding his horse through this desert-like country as a boy.

An impressive canyon bisected the plain and in the side of one of its rock walls there was a hole. It was a cave, with hand-placed steps to get down into it.

While crouching, we made our way inside out of the blistering sunshine and oh, what a relief! It was cold in there. Dad showed us the interior with his flashlight. With all the dark nooks and crannies, and the slithering shadows caused by the light in Dad's hand, it was spooky—but so much fun. Mom, who was basically an indoor person, ventured into these adventures with Dad as a good sport but was always glad to get back on familiar turf. As we emerged from the mysteries of the ice cave, Mom headed for the car (even hotter now, from having been parked in the burning sun).

Not Dad. He had to stop and find some large flat rocks to make another step into the cave, enjoying himself thoroughly as he worked to make a sturdy support for the next people who discovered the secret cave.

Mom sat in the car with her latest *Reader's Digest* while we four kids offered smaller rocks to tuck under the big ones to make the step secure. We listened respectfully to Dad telling us we should always "leave things better than the way we found them." It was the first time (though certainly not the last) I'd heard him say it and it made a deep impression on me.

Sitting around at Chatham, reading books and watching the kids while everyone else was desperately busy, I couldn't help thinking about what Dad had said and the ways I could use my unique skills to contribute to the cannery.

With that in mind, I said to Linné over a much improved breakfast at the Mess Hall, "I brought my lettering brush." I didn't know how it had wound up in my luggage when I'd left all my other painting supplies behind, but I was glad now that it had.

It doubled as my watercolor flat brush, but I'd made a little money on San Juan Island painting signs with it and teaching others oil painting. I had also helped decorate floats for the County Fair parade by doing the signage for them in calligraphy. And, of course, my kids got to ride on floats, which was always fun.

"Why don't we put up some little signs to identify the various buildings on the boardwalk?" I suggested.

"Good idea," Linné said promptly, and I warmed with gratification at his enthusiasm and support. "Go talk to Gilbert in the Carpenter Shop. Get him to cut boards for the signs."

Brimming with eagerness, I immediately descended upon the carpenter shack with its barn-like red double doors to talk with the guys about wood for the signs. The shop was aromatic with the carroty scent of fresh cut cedar shavings and peppery fir. It was an open space lined with paned windows, and below them 12-foot built-in workbenches resided. Two large tables were strategically placed, and a variety of tools were ready to use including several large vises.

The beach gang, including the personable and much-liked Smokey Hansen, although busy about their various projects, stopped what they were doing to listen interestedly to my plans. They quickly compiled scraps of wood that I could use for the small signs, like the one for the mess hall.

They supplied me with sawhorses, primer, and oil-based, exterior lead paint (we, of course, were unaware of its dangers back then) that would stand the test of time. I used my watercolor brush, being careful to clean it well with paint thinner, soap, and warm water.

I applied my calligraphy skills with my flat white bristle brush. Admittedly, it was kind of fancy for a cannery, but the reactions were worth it. Everyone thought the signs dressed up the buildings, and they seemed to appreciate my efforts. Cook Harry, still homesick for Up North, nonetheless admired the mess hall sign, even admitting that they didn't have anything that nice at Pederson Point.

That was all the thanks I needed to expand into bigger signs. Next was the area over the door to the company store. That turned out so well that I was finally ready to broach the giant New England Company sign. I was thrilled when the beach gang put a nice frame around the wood for this main sign that would be put on the big warehouse facing Sitkoh Bay. Every visiting boat and plane would see it.

I had taken lettering at the University of Washington so understood about spacing and the importance of making the lettering big enough to see from a distance. I gave the big sign board three coats of primer and two coats of semi-gloss.

While it dried, I designed the lettering on tracing paper. When the paint dried, I transferred the letters to the sign with carbon paper on the back side. (I would normally rub a soft pencil like 4B to transfer a drawing onto paper to do a watercolor painting. But carbon paper worked best on a hard surface like a painted board.)

Thankful for a sunny day, I painted outside the shop at the foot of the stairs, in front of the carpenter's shack next to a big pile of bricks that looked like they'd resided there for a quarter of a century.

Doing my part to contribute to the Chatham Cannery.

The big boards were spread out to make a 24-foot-long sign and carefully balanced on three sawhorses. All around me were the familiar sounds of a busy cannery—machinery humming, steam venting, boats rumbling in and their engines acquiring a higher timbre when they reversed into place at the docks, boots clumping as the beach gang came and went with lots of hammering and sawing inside the shack. Every time they passed me, often carrying lumber, they paused to admire my work.

In addition to the cannery sounds, bees were droning and bumbling about in the foliage pressing up against the boardwalk, and the kids shrieked and laughed as they played, barefoot, within eyesight of where I worked.

I stood back to inspect my paint job and sighed in enjoyment. I felt like a working and respected member of the cannery. Finally, I was doing my part, and with a skill unique to me that was of value. Sign painting, after all, was a well-respected trade at the time.

Dot painting the big sign for the warehouse.

During that time sign painters went to a trade school to learn their profession and then would apprentice for a few years, but that wasn't the end of their learning. The next step was working in a union and handling ropes, ladders, and scaffolding with maybe three dozen other beginning sign painters in a big city like Seattle, Chicago, or Boston.

The profession's rules demanded that students (typically all male) had to master specific techniques required to transfer small drawings onto the sides of very large buildings before they were allowed to do a sign on their own and then were granted the designation "sign painter." An experienced sign painter could make enough to raise a family and buy a really nice home in the suburbs.

I, of course, wouldn't charge what a professional sign painter could. I carefully filled in the tracing with black paint, feeling a sense of satisfaction as the paintbrush glided on the boards making sharp, clear lines. I decided, since I had no idea what the current wage would be for a sign painting job like this, that I would charge the same amount that a cannery worker was paid: $2.50 an hour.

I really liked that sign. Once it was mounted on the main building, it made Chatham Cannery feel instantly much more "on the map." Alaska's history was a story of booms and busts, and most communities had a temporary feel. Many, many communities were lost to time, gobbled up by the ever-encroaching forest and surging tide. My sign proclaimed that New England Fish Company was here to stay in Sitkoh Bay, just off Chatham Strait.

And, wonderfully, I'd gotten to paint. It might not have fully satisfied the creative urge—only doing one of my watercolor paintings would assuage that—but it made me feel productive and helpful. Best of all, I knew I'd lived up to Dad's mantra to always leave a place better than I'd found it.

With a very real sense of accomplishment and belonging, I smiled as I presented Linné with the bill for my services. I'd kept careful track of my time, and I explained that I wouldn't feel comfortable accepting more than what the average cannery worker received.

Linné was busy in the office, signing the papers the bookkeeper had just dropped off that needed to get in the mail. "The signs look nice," he said distractedly as he went to put his signature on another paper, but it was the bill I'd laid in front of him.

He held it up with a quizzical glance at me. "What's this?"

I repeated what I'd said, not surprised he hadn't heard me the first time with all that was on his mind. I probably could have saved it to give him at the house, but often I never got a chance to really talk to him. Plus, this *was* cannery business.

"You can see that I wrote down my hours rather than charge by the sign, which is to the company's advantage—"

He held up his hand, stopping me. "We can't charge the company for your sign paintings, Dot." He shook his head at me.

I gaze back, surprised. "What do you mean?"

"The company has made it possible for my family to stay with me this summer at the cannery—they've provided you and the kids with bed and board and all of your meals. I can't ask them to pay for my wife's hobby, too."

I stood there without speaking.

He handed back the paper I'd given him. "I don't want you to submit a bill to New England Fish Co. The signs are a nice way to show appreciation for having my family here at Chatham."

He turned back to what he was doing. I'm not sure how long I stood there before I finally left. I went through the motions of getting the kids in the bathtub and ready for dinner.

It wasn't until years later that I found the words for an argument: that we didn't owe the company anything for feeding us and boarding us. Every superintendent's family previously had enjoyed the same privileges as a matter of course. My painting skills should have been properly and professionally compensated.

And, years later, Linné agreed with me. But at the time he'd seen it through the eyes of a culture that didn't value a woman's work as it deserved, on its own merits. In addition, when I could see it more clearly in hindsight, I recognized Linné's characteristically moral desire not to take advantage of his position.

For example, at the end of that year in 1963 when we were back in Seattle, after Linné had been the superintendent of Chatham Cannery for one season, he got a call from the cannery's equipment suppliers.

Linné had been responsible for ordering cannery equipment which included the mess hall's needs. They wanted him to come down to their warehouse and pick out premium gifts for his own personal use to thank him for putting in such nice orders. The selection of "gifts" had to do with pots and pans.

We were struggling financially at the time. A new set of pots and pans would have really helped. But Linné said, "That isn't right. I was just doing my job for New England Fish Co. I can't accept their offer."

So he went down to NEFCO and talked with his boss about this, and was laughed right out of the office. In the end, we did choose some nice new cookware—Revere Ware with the copper bottoms, all the rage in the Sixties—which served us well for many years. But he often mumbled, "It's not right."

I understood much later how this strong desire in him to not take advantage might have come into play when he refused to allow me to be paid for my work on the signs, but at the time it knocked my feet right out from under me.

I clamped down on my feelings as usual and went back to reading to the kids and watching from a distance as the cannery bustled and hummed with exhausted workers.

The kids were my saving grace. I could lose myself in their experiences and development.

Dori and Blaine fishing at Chatham.

Dori was close friends with a six-year-old Native girl named Dorcas Paul. She was a darling and was Dori's constant companion in the afternoon and after dinner. (The Native children didn't get up before noon due to the evening activity on the boardwalk sometimes as late as midnight, which was still daylight.)

I loved to listen to their conversations as they played with Dori's beloved Chatty Cathy doll. It was a relief and warmed my heart to see Dori blossom and leave her shyness behind.

Typing up the modest events of the day and keeping my parents informed on what cannery life was like also helped keep me occupied. I typed: *The clipping you sent by regular mail was postmarked July 23 and arrived here July 25. But Linne says, "Better stick to airmail anyway. Every once in a while the post office teaches people a lesson by sending letters on a steamer."*

Dori with floating piling.

Since the grandparents wanted to know what the kids were up to, I also wrote:

On hot sunny days the kids have taken to fishing and swimming off the dock down by the Native Village. Curiously, the Native children at first didn't participate and seemed to find the superintendent's children strange for doing so. But soon enough they had joined Dori, Blaine and Rolf in the splashing and shrieking fun.

That civilized experience of swimming in a well-regulated pool was a far cry from what my children were experiencing as they jumped off the dock where floatplanes docked, with sea gulls shrieking from the tops of nearby pilings and bald eagles swooping overhead.

At lunch, a couple days after the big sign was put up that I hadn't been paid for, everything started off normally enough. But during the course of passing the plate of wieners to Linné, one slid off directly into my glass. The phallic symbol of the wiener reached into my inner, pent-up desires.

A laugh slipped past my lips. *Uh-oh.*

I felt the pressure building in my chest as it used to as a child when I was stifling feelings about something. Not only was I sexually repressed, but I was suppressing feelings of emotional loneliness, frustrated creativity, and being undervalued. I was ripe for explosion.

Another laugh rolled out and I couldn't stop. Without making a sound, and with much effort to stifle myself and a few tears, I finally got control, and stared directly into my coffee cup. But the instinct for release could not be dammed. I succumbed and found the need again of a huge napkin to wipe my eyes.

By then Linné and others at the table had caught the spirit and were duly snickering, so knowing I was licked, and in great agony, I left the Mess Hall.

Regaining my composure in the cool air and dabbing my tear-streaked cheeks, I returned to resume my meal in dignity. But alas, there was my plate completely covered with a napkin and sticking up very high, and I knew before I lifted the napkin that I was doomed.

There was the glass and the offending wiener, and by now, several "great big kids" were waiting for the resulting breakdown. I didn't disappoint them, and they were engulfed themselves in bellows of laughter. We could hear the next table making comments such as "Don't stare." That didn't help.

I wrote to my parents: *I think I am cracking up.*

CHAPTER 12

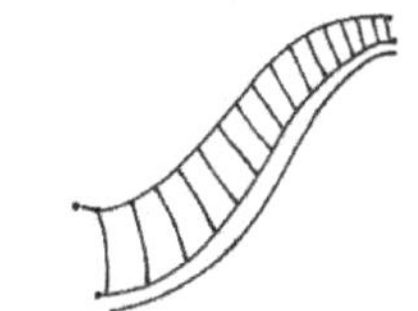

For His Mother

The cannery store sold food and sundries, not just the snack foods that the cannery workers favored, but also the milk, eggs and other staples purchased by the fishermen. The store being on the main dock by the business office [the storekeeper] had her ear to the source of important cannery gossip.

—Land of Bear and Eagle: A Home in the Kodiak Wilderness by Tanyo Ravicz

Chatham Cannery
Sitkoh Bay, Alaska
July 29-August 7, 1963

During my occasional visits to the store, I'd hidden more than a few flinches at how disorganized it was. How they managed to work in there was a mystery to me. It seemed obvious that the store needed somebody who did no selling. Someone who was responsible for nothing but housekeeping.

As it was, the office/stockroom was behind in book work, the floor was littered with paper, half-empty boxes, egg crates, you name it. You could hardly walk back there.

The problem was that the two men—Clint and Duane—in charge of selling to Chatham customers and boxing up orders for fishing boats, hardly had enough time to take a breather. Boats called in continuously and foot customers were lined up three deep practically every hour the store was open—and even when it wasn't. They got constant calls to open the store for someone with a late night craving.

In my eternal quest for productive contribution (despite having tried doing book work at the store previously and it not working out), I decided to make cleaning the store a project. The inefficiency of a messy store was unbelievable and, to my mind, indefensible. All it took was some elbow grease, method, and someone dedicated to the task.

Later, Bill Anderson was our storekeeper.

My kids ran in and out, the bell at the top of the door jangling constantly and made nuisances of themselves until we made it a game for them to take boxes to the dock and dump them in the fire pile and then race back for more. There was always more.

Satisfying my internal itch for orderliness, I made an attempt to sort and label the merchandise so that instead of taking a half hour to find something, anyone could immediately see whether it was in stock or not. But the trouble was that even when neat and orderly, it only took an afternoon of very busy selling to discombobulate everything.

I was only in the store a couple hours at a time, and during my shift, candy seemed to be the fastest moving commodity. Prior to my arrival in the store, Duane had been completely out of candy. So when news reached the village that a new shipment had arrived, the kids came in clamoring droves clutching dollar bills and fifty cent pieces in their hot little fists.

The whole time I was taking their money, I lectured them on the evils of candy. This didn't deter them in the least, of course. They would return time and time again during the following days before we ran out again.

So Duane ordered 48 boxes, containing 24 bars each. As each child left with his assorted teeth-rotters, I would remark, "See you at the dentist's."

The irony was, of course, that most of them had never even met a dentist.

One boy *had* visited a dentist, however. He rebutted my warnings with a laconic: "Candy doesn't bother me anymore. I had all my teeth pulled."

With this, he opened his mouth wide for my inspection and sure enough, all his molars were gone and waiting for the second teeth to come in.

"You do realize your relentless consumption of candy will rot your second, permanent teeth too?" I pointed out.

"I don't care," he said, and shoved half a candy bar in his mouth.

One evening after dinner we were so far behind in boat orders that I grabbed my kids and locked the store door and worked at catching up. Several customers came banging at the door and if they were insistent enough, we'd open it a crack to see how urgent the request was. We allowed a couple of fishermen in to pick up orders or buy something off the shelves. But that was it. The store was simply closed.

One youngster wouldn't be denied, however, and pounded on the door until he got a response.

Clint opened the door a crack. "Is it important?"

The little boy shoved his foot in the door like an experienced door-to-door salesman and shouted, "Yes! Very important. I have to get it for my mother. I have to get in the store."

"What is it your mother needs so desperately that she can't wait until morning?"

"Candy! My mother's gotta have candy!"

Clint rolled his eyes at me and told our little would-be customer that the store would be open in the morning and he could come back for "his mother's" candy then.

"NO! MY MOTHER NEEDS IT NOW!!!" the boy roared and rained

fists on the door, foot firmly wedged in the crack.

I lost it, just like I had over the wiener in the glass. I laughed until I cried as Clint tried to convince the boy that his mother would survive without candy for one more night. He finally managed to extricate the little foot from the door though the ranting and pounding on the other side continued for quite a while making me helpless with laughter.

In the end, I had to stop working in the store again. It just wasn't going to work out at all. After the first three days, the kids stopped hanging around and went instead to the Native village to play which would have been all right except that there was no adult supervision there at all.

So we returned to the enjoyable routine of reading stories. I had fond memories of reading as a kid, and I wanted my kids to have the same.

Although my main focus even as a child was on art, plus crafts and piano, my friend Rosalie who drew paper dolls with me also joined me in reading Nancy Drew mysteries. I loved English in school and working for the school newspapers, both writing articles and drawing, and I also wrote poetry—which perhaps led to songwriting with Linné. But more on that later.

At Chatham when I had more time on my hands than I wanted, I got in quite a bit of reading, managing to get through James Michener's massive saga *Hawaii.* As I read it, I thought how much Dad would have been interested in the geological history Michener described in dramatic detail. The characters were true to life and had the kinds of ups and downs that kept a reader hooked. I enthused about it as I read it so much that eventually Linné read it too, when he had the time, and we had an enjoyable time discussing it.

At Chatham, I liked to read outside on the veranda where I could keep an eye on the kids, and they could easily find me. More often than not, though, if the kids saw me reading to myself, they would crowd around and cuddle close, demanding that I read to them.

Together we read *Alice in Wonderland, Tom Sawyer* and many stories in the *Humpty Dumpty Magazine.*

I wrote to my parents: *Blaine has a reading vocabulary of 17 words so far. Dori went through her first set of Easy Readers so fast that I ordered more at Price Mart. We are amassing quite a library.*

Typically, during less frenetic seasons, reel-to-reel movies would be shown in the mess hall, but there was no time for such relaxing entertainment during that summer. However, a short film was sent out to Linné in which he had a great interest.

There was no opportunity to show it in the mess hall, but he managed to carve out an hour one night to show it up at the house. He carried the heavy projector and an unwieldy, rolled screen up the 79 steps, and after setting everything up, he invited a few people to see it with us.

On the flickering screen in the darkened dining room, the only sound the sibilant rattling of the reel-to-reel projector, we saw the title: "Valley of the Kings."

It had been shot back in 1954 in Taku Inlet, a beautiful fjord with the Taku Glacier emptying into it, not that far from Chatham. It was filmed by famous *National Geographic* photographer, writer, filmmaker, explorer (and alleged secret agent) Amos Burg. His travels and adventures captured the public's imagination, and his work was critically acclaimed, earning him an Academy Award nomination for one of his documentaries.

He'd pioneered the use of inflatable rubber rafts on white-water rivers in 1939 and had made film documentaries in the wildernesses of Central and South America, Europe, Asia, the American west, and Alaska.

In 1941 he used a recording machine borrowed from the Library of Congress to record narratives, songs, and interviews throughout isolated areas of Alaska, including the songs and anecdotes of a storyteller named Lonesome Pete who lived off the land in the tiny, cut-off fishing village of Meyers Chuck about 40 miles northwest of Ketchikan.

"Valley of the Kings" was about king salmon gillnet fishing on Taku Inlet, near Juneau. It followed the process of fishermen catching and then selling the harvest and then followed the fish up the Taku River into Canada to their spawning grounds in the Nakina River.

As the kids and our visitors watched familiar scenes of wet, glinting salmon being unloaded from fishing boats onto a tender, there were gasps of surprise and excitement. For who was it captaining and deck-handing the tender up there on the screen?

None other than Linné and myself.

There was much excitement and many questions that we fielded as we watched the rest of the film.

I'm not sure if Linné approached Amos, or Amos contacted Linné. Whatever the case, Amos spent a lot of time aboard the *Alma* with us. A slim man with a deep, slightly accented voice, and warm smile, he looked a bit like Woodrow Wilson minus the *pince nez*. He packed around a big movie camera with lots of 16-mm film and kept copious notes to key with the frames in the movies that he would edit when he was back in Juneau.

At the time, we had aboard Doug Graef, an intellectual who spoke English like a cross between Shakespeare and a researcher. He got along really well with Amos, who was known to be somewhat shy, but was well-read and didn't talk like a fisherman.

We found ourselves very much enjoying Amos' company when he ate with us on the *Alma*. We listened intently to his adventures when there was a break in the evening— adventures such as his solo trip around Cape Horn in a small boat. While we talked, we played cribbage, drank coffee or tea while cigarette smoke

Amos Burg filming "Valley of the Kings."

crept along the ceiling and created a halo around a bare light bulb above us while the water licked and splashed against our hull and the anchor chain grated as the boat swung in an arc.

It was fun to take a break from the concerns of Chatham for an hour watching the film and reminiscing about those *Alma* days, but all too soon Linné was called back to work.

CHAPTER 13

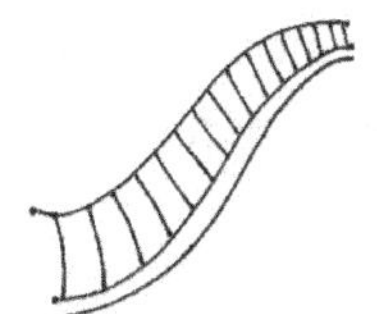

The Spirit of Chatham

Because the entire operations of the canned salmon industry are carried on at tidewater levels... the most economical movement of the pack is obtained by shipping the Alaska portion by steamer [such as the Southport]... NEFCO's Alaska pack is brought to Seattle where it is warehoused pending movement to its final markets, either by rail or by ocean steamer.

—NEFCO: From Sea to World Markets.
The Story of New England Fish Co. by Harry R. Beard

Chatham Cannery
Sitkoh Bay, Alaska
August 1963

To my delight, I finally got the chance to carry my art materials down to the village and take my time communing with soft pencils and a sketch pad.

It was a wonderful relief to expend the dammed up creative energy that had been building up pressure inside me. As I sketched, I visualized myself next summer being able to paint right there on the boardwalk or the cannery dock.

As I sketched and the kids played on the beach below the boardwalk, I thought I might still be lonely with no special confidant to share experiences and thoughts with, I might still only see my much-loved husband occasionally, but at least I had the joy of seeing my experience of my surroundings take shape on the paper in front of me.

I no longer felt quite so stifled. Sketching opened up my mental and emotional horizons, and I was able to look around at the Chatham experience with new eyes and see how special it was.

With a fresh outlook, re-energized and re-charged after being able to immerse myself in my art, I embraced what social opportunities there were to be had at Chatham.

One of them was rather prestigious: Linné and I were invited to partake of a first class meal aboard the 422-foot Liberty Ship, the *Southport*, which was docked at Chatham to take on every case we had of the labeled and canned product.

The *Southport* was an impressive sight out in the remote wilderness. It was built by New England Shipbuilding Co. in 1945 and was 7,216 tons. It had one obsolete but rugged triple expansion steam engine, single shaft with one screw producing 2,500 hp, allowing the ship to travel at 11 knots.

Liberty ships were built quickly (shipwrights used welding instead of the slower riveting) and cheaply but with a reliable design. They had a range of 17,000 miles and had five cargo holds, three forward of the engine room and two aft, in the rear portion of the ship. Each could carry 10,800 deadweight tons (the weight of cargo a ship could carry) or 4,380 net tons (the amount of space available for cargo and passengers).

The docking process at Chatham was quite harrowing for a ship of that size.

The problem was that the ship was too long to fit in the space available at the dock, so they had to secure one end of the ship to the dock and keep the other end out in the bay with fishing boats continually pushing on the bow acting as tugboats holding the *Southport* at an angle to the dock.

Coming in to dock, the steel steamship looked more than a little out of its element as its enormous hull with its propeller half out of the water maneuvered into position in the limited space. It dropped its anchor and swung its stern in an arc which prepared the ship for a landing.

I chuckled as Linné, the former skipper of our 95-foot cannery tender, muttered comments to himself and worried like a mother hen about the ship tearing out his fish elevator.

But as the operation slowly progressed, he had to admit he was impressed by the calculated gentleness with which the skipper eased the ship in to a landing.

In retrospect, although clever, it did seem hazardous. Wouldn't Linné have been horrified if the dock had collapsed under the sheer force of a huge ship crashing into it? But the captain was skilled in unusual landings, and he and Linné had discussed it before the *Southport's* arrival.

Outsized manila lines were deftly handled. Salmon cases were slung aboard.

Our already tired crew worked all night, longshoring. Linné was grateful to climb into bed at five a.m. only to be awakened at six for breakfast aboard the *Southport*.

The men grabbed cat naps here and there as the day wore on, then the night again, nonstop. At night, with all of its lights on, the giant ship lit up the entire cannery. Looking out from the house and down on the bay it looked to me as if a small city had tied itself to the dock. Its lights glimmered in wiggly streaks on the dark water while all around the vast wilderness slept in deep shadow.

Linné needed a counterbalance.

After midnight, Linné searched all over for someone who would know how to run a forklift, having run out of drivers. He found one who tried, but the poor man wound up dumping the whole load. So of course, Linné climbed into the seat himself and that's where he spent the night.

During this two-day period, he had a two-hour nap in the daytime and one at night. He napped on the daybed in the dining room. This was his usual napping area, and usually the kids and I kept on as usual, unworried about waking him. But this time his sleep was so necessary that I kept the kids quiet upstairs or occupied outside.

Everybody's eyes were bloodshot as they worked all night under the unnatural glare of electric lights, but somehow they managed to keep going on the good food which was now served in the Mess Hall.

Nobody complained except me. I went around offering sympathy and making everyone laugh by insisting they grab some sleep. "You're always good for a laugh, Dot," Linné said with a tired chuckle. The more I clucked the more stoic they became.

In the midst of all this, Captain Burns invited Linné and I aboard the *Southport* for dinner. When he issued the invitation, he told us that he knew Linné's mother, Gertrude Bardarson. (It wasn't surprising that he remembered her, since she was a strikingly regal woman in appearance and always made an impression on people. He'd probably met her in Seattle at some event.)

I got the kids cleaned up and sent them alone to the mess hall before Linné and I branched off toward the wharf.

Stepping aboard the massive steel ship with Linné, I felt familiar with it for having been aboard the Coast Guard Cutter *Ingham* (327-feet long with a 41-foot beam), the ship that Dad had commanded. So much metal. So many narrow, steep mesh stairs and tight spaces. That and the protocol, with the combination of blue collar workers and white collar management, was very much the same as how a Coast Guard ship operated.

Not having foreseen such a grand social event when I was packing for a summer at a remote Alaskan cannery, you might think I'd not have anything to wear appropriate for the occasion. But even though it was a time when women were transitioning from skirts and nylons to long pants, when I went out for dinner in Seattle or anywhere, I wore a skirt and nylons— even at Chatham. I had nothing to feel embarrassed about as I was led to the impressive scene, neat and trim in a skirt and nylons.

We ate in the Captain's quarters in his formal dining room with his uniformed officers. What always impressed me in situations like this were the linens, always pristine white, heavy duty, and freshly ironed. So it was on the *Southport,* along with crystal glasses and fine silverware glinting under the overhead lights and orderlies standing by to tend to our every wish with a uniformed Negro steward meticulously overseeing the occasion.

Linné and the captain spoke with each other about guess what? Fish! And the process of loading the ship with palettes of canned salmon. I was pretty much honored as "the wife" or so-called "first lady" of the cannery. Except for initial courtesies, I was seen and not heard, a gracious listener at these events.

Fortunately, I was comfortable with formal dining etiquette. During a formal dinner you had to know the order with which to select your utensils in order to not fumble—of course, we wanted to make a good impression.

Just because we had worked on fish boats didn't mean we had lost all sense of correctness in formal dining. Both Linné and I had been schooled in it, so understood working from the outside in towards the plate. We also knew that if we were in doubt, to follow the captain's lead. Even if his etiquette wasn't perfect, by doing this, we would show respect.

We made our dinner selections from a menu. Although it was so very formal, we found it enjoyable as we rediscovered the delights of fresh green vegetables, prime rib *au jus*, real milk, fresh strawberries and ice cream.

We didn't linger unnecessarily since there was still so much work to do. But before we could leave the chef made an appearance holding a lemon meringue pie and to my surprise and delight, he said: "Please give this to your children with my compliments, Mrs. Bardarson."

It was the finishing touch to a memorable dining experience in the Alaskan wilderness.

Back on shore, normal life resumed. If you could call the extremes Linné and his workers were experiencing "normal." Aggravating to the lack of hands and desperately long hours, was the first real rain we'd had all summer combined with a cold and erratic wind. The hatch men worked under tents and the salmon on the dock was covered with Visqueen tarps. The longshoremen bundled themselves up in oilskins.

Meanwhile the cannery operated one line and tenders continued to deliver salmon. But the steamer was so long that it hung way out past the dock right where the elevator took on fish.

Although the ship was at an angle to the dock and the tenders fitted into the wedge shape between the ship and dock, each time a tender needed to come or go they had to drop the bow line. At the same time a tender acting as a tugboat pushed the steamer bow to keep the ship from being pushed out by the wind, which would have caused the stern to crush the loading dock. It was quite an operation and caused Linné endless stress.

Finally, the *Southport* disembarked with 55,000 cases of Chatham salmon.

Linné fully intended to get to bed early Saturday night, but the Filipinos had practically bribed the fish slimers to work faster to enable the cannery to be finished early in the evening so they could throw one of their famous dances. The superintendent and his wife were expected to attend, I was informed.

I was faced with the eternal female question: What to wear?

Since it was a much less formal occasion than dinner aboard the *Southport*, I figured pants would be acceptable. Mom would have been appalled, but I'd started wearing long pants when I was on the *Estella* in 1954. I went Up Town in Juneau and bought my first pair of men's black work pants and never looked back.

In addition to being the capital of Alaska, Juneau was a fishing town in the 1950s. It had several stores dedicated to the fishing industry, everything you could possibly need to work on a boat including work pants for men. I chose black. I also wore a pair of overalls, which I thought looked adorable on me, and totally practical. In these, I could peugh fish or work all night counting salmon varieties. I'm sure Mom cringed at photos of her daughter in these men's outfits. They made perfect sense to me in that environment.

Back in Seattle, I returned to dresses or skirts. But on the *Alma* in 1956 it was back to work pants. By this time the fashion world had Capri slacks for women, which were mid-calf pants, buttoning on the side, in colors or multi-colored designs. They were feminine and I enjoyed wearing them on the boat. Gradually skirts for me and other women across the nation remained in the closet.

Women experienced such an emancipation from fashion norms during the 60s. I loved it when women's pants eventually zippered in the front! I'd have loved it even more if they'd made women's pants with deep pockets.

Linné always wore his white halibut hat, I guess to keep fish slime off his hair. He looked handsome in one. It was part of his uniform, as was a grey boiled wool work jacket over a white T-shirt. That was his standard outfit, and he wore it to the Filipino dance.

His only comment on my attire was a protective warning for me to not wear my favorite bright red lipstick. He felt the vivid lipstick might invite improprieties brought on by little sleep and too much black market alcohol.

So, fortifying himself with a powerful stay-awake capsule donated to the cause by a visiting dignitary, and some bourbon, Linné took me to the dance. As we made our way down the boardwalk under the high latitude evening light to the Filipino House, he said, "It might be best if you temporarily store some of your usual exuberance."

"But it's a dance. Exuberance is called for, surely."

"I think you'll find being a little more, shall we say, *reserved* will serve you better."

"Why is that?"

"I'm pretty sure the party is going to be on the wild side. They're going to party at least as hard as they've worked."

I considered that. "I see your point." So with Linné as a bulwark of protection, the reserved Mrs. Bardarson was introduced to the Filipino House.

We entered the dance hall (a revamped Mess Hall) and were immediately greeted by the second boss who told us that Buddy Elession (the Filipino boss) wanted to meet with us in his room. We were ceremoniously ushered into the small room where we perched with as much dignity as possible on beds.

Someone had the honor of carrying in a bottle of whiskey which Buddy Elession solemnly poured into small glasses. Along with it we were served roast pork in thin slices, dipped in hot mustard and sesame seeds. He was solicitous and polite towards Linné and very respectful to me. The men did all the talking about, guess what? Fish! Of course.

This was the first part of a well-orchestrated schedule of any cannery dance.

Eventually we were ushered back into the mess hall which had been transformed into a dance hall. It was the first room as you entered from a middle door on the cannery boardwalk, a big room with wooden floor planks. I never got to see it as a mess hall. But when I went there to a Filipino dance, the walls were lined with backless, unpainted, wooden benches where people sat waiting to dance. There was always live dance music, from jitterbug to close dancing.

We were offered Dungeness crab with drawn butter and white sticky rice and assorted other delicacies. We were surrounded by Natives and Filipinos who were already enjoying the newfound freedom from the cannery and some black-market booze. I was whisked onto the dance floor by a Native worker.

The band was composed of local talent wielding two saxophones, a steel string guitar, and a washtub rigged with a sturdy string, which when plucked would emit a bass rhythm, all depending on how far back you pulled the post, to mimic a standing string bass. The music was lively and continuous. One year there was a corrugated, metal washboard and a hillbilly saw. Drumming, of course, could be done on anything. It was really quite effective. I loved it when the Filipinos all sang together in their language, usually spontaneously.

Everyone had a wonderful time. All adult residents of Chatham had been invited. Linné towered over everyone there at six-foot seven inches. But that didn't keep him from dancing with the shortest cannery worker there while I was whisked away by a fisherman or worker to do the fox trot.

Those were the days (eventually to be replaced by expressive, individual dancing) when everyone had been taught dancing lessons in schools and at the YMCA, so everyone knew the various steps depending on the timing of the music—4/4 time, fox trot or 3/4 time, which was a waltz.

While I danced with 5-foot 2-inch Filipino cannery workers, a Negro mechanic, our entire office crew, and the Native contingency enjoying varying degrees of equilibrium (or enebrium), Linné worked out with their female counterparts.

Eventually, Linné and I did an exhibition Jitterbug while everyone stood around and cheered. In Seattle we had won any number of awards for our athletic version. We were both good ballroom dance partners. He was a good leader, I, a good follower. With slow dancing, he liked to do "dips."

Those who weren't dancing were sitting on benches along the four walls. Native children raced in and out. One Native worker was asleep in a sitting up position. Linné and I received a perpetual line of people waiting to pay respects or dance.

The center support of our bench collapsed under the dead weight of one 300-pound slimer who spent the evening interrupting conversations to deliriously regale us with how she began working on the sliming table when she was 12, before child labor laws were implemented.

Finally, we were introduced to the assembly during a singular break in the music, and invited to give speeches, in which we praised the workers for their fine support of the record salmon pack.

There was a big cake commemorating someone's anniversary. There was not a trace of liquor in sight (but plenty hidden) and for the most part everyone was well behaved. The speechmaking was an important part of the evening. The Filipinos excelled at it.

How Linné staggered through his duties, official and social, I'll never know, because bright and early the next morning he was on the job again. After a three-day closure of the fishing grounds, and two days during which the cannery did not can, but was enjoying some maintenance, the new and vigorous week began with over 90,000 fish to can.

There certainly was no letup. But then, Linné was inspired by the urge to beat 1961's total pack of 146,000 cases. There was to be a celebration of some sort when we reached 150,000 sometime in the coming week.

Although we had already bought way in excess of 1961's pinks, the case count was not as good. In 1961 a total of 16 fish comprised a case. This year the fish were smaller, so the case count was running 21 to 23 per case.

Everyone continued to work hard, refreshed by the community warmth engendered by the dance. That night after the dance when Linné and I had trooped up the 79 stairs on throbbing, tired feet, but with the music and laughter still tingling in my veins, I realized that I hadn't really caught the spirit of Chatham before I'd been to a Chatham dance.

CHAPTER 14

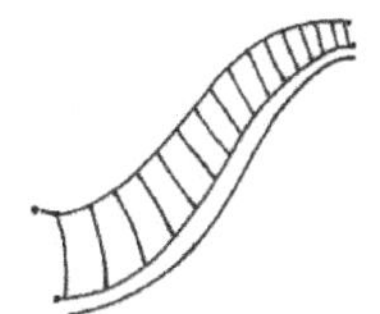

A Mason Jar of Holy Water

During stormy fall days, we'd often hide in a sheltered bay with a bevy of boats rafted up to us. Then everyone would gather in the galley of the [fish tender] Savage, for steaming cups of coffee, food, and good conversation... Those were truly gatherings to be thankful for, safe at harbor away from the brutal weather and waves of the fishing grounds.

—The Fishes & Dishes Cookbook
by Kiyo and Tomi Marsh and Laura Cooper

**Chatham Cannery
Sitkoh Bay, Alaska
August 10-19, 1963**

While I was sketching on another sunny day, a familiar voice hailed me. When I looked up, my mind fully immersed in the art in front of me, it took me a moment to recognize Bob Thorstenson grinning at me.

"Why hello, Bob! Where did you come from?"

I suppose I shouldn't have been surprised he'd show up in a fishing industry hot spot.

Linné's fraternity days at the University of Washington led to life-long friends, one of whom was Bob Thorstenson. Linné got Bob his first job in Alaska, tendering for a cannery in Petersburg. Fifteen years later, Bob was a titan in the fish industry.

He would eventually commission me to do a full-size watercolor of the main cannery building, which when framed he hung over the mantle of his living-room fireplace in Seattle. That day when he interrupted my sketching, he was visiting Chatham with other members of Pacific American Fisheries. (In two years, he would help found Icicle Seafoods, originally named Petersburg Fisheries, Inc., one of Alaska's largest and longest-lived seafood companies.)

We chatted for a bit about fishing industry experiences before he continued on his way. Meeting Bob got me to remembering again those wonderful newlywed days with Linné, when I first experienced Alaska. Back then I couldn't have pictured myself the mother of three children, the wife of a cannery superintendent, sitting on the boardwalk sketching a piece of Alaskan history.

I soaked it in, feeling my heart and mind expand.

During the following week, I had lots of time to spend on my art since the kids were invited to join a Sunday School traveling mission.

The *Anna Jackman* was a missionary boat built in Jackson, FL, and launched in 1958. It was designed by the Seattle naval architect Edwin Monk, who was known for his streamlined, practical Pacific Northwest workboats.

I thought it looked like a big river yacht from the 1950s with the hull long and rounded at the turn of the bilges, unusual in a steel-hulled vessel. The compound curved hull plates needed to be pre-bent to an exact shape with no two plates (except the opposite side's section) being the same. It was pleasing to look at, especially to someone with an artistic mindset.

Although the *Anna Jackman* was built for Presbyterian Church Missions of New York, it was used to proselytize to small coastal Native Alaskan villages. It could accommodate 26 kids, sometimes three in a bunk with the girls in the forward sleeping section and the boys the aft separated by a heavy steel watertight doorway.

The hull had a deep draft with a displacement of 60 tons. Because it was constructed of such thick steel, it was ideal for surviving contact with

Alaska's many uncharted shoals. One rock in Gastineau Channel outside Juneau left a permanent dent in her bottom—there was photo of the *Anna Jackman* balanced atop it.

Every summer the *Anna Jackman* tied up at the float at Chatham cannery to bring "the word of the Lord" to children in the Native Village. Its skipper was Capt. Ed Cade and there were usually several young missionaries aboard. They'd stay here a week offering "fun time" at 10 a.m. and Bible class from 1 to 3 p.m. each day.

The children looked forward to it because they knew they would have a week of fun, with games, stories, entertainment, snacks, and they might even be invited aboard the boat. If the children somehow got advance notice that the boat was coming, they would eagerly scan Sitkoh Bay for signs of its arrival and be down at the float during tie-up. Excitement was keen as they jumped up and down, frantically waving in welcome.

Anna Jackmen Sunday school.

The boat was welcome in Chatham by everyone. It kept the children busy all the while teaching them some important attitudes and beliefs. At the time, I wasn't into religion and leery of the "Christ is Coming" fervor and what affect it might have on the kids, especially on Dori who was at an impressionable age. But I did appreciate what else they brought to the kids.

There was little in Chatham that was kid-oriented, and that was what the missionary boat excelled at. The college age missionaries would take up temporary residence on an old, beached scow with its red-painted boards looking for all the world like a floating cattle pen, and they'd pin up photos of Jesus before inviting the children aboard.

As the clamoring horde of children scrambled aboard, they gathered around to listen to the first story of the day. A canvas dust sheet was laid down on the floor of the scow for the kids to sit on and look at the pictures pinned to the scow's walls surrounded by fresh air, forest and water, and the big sky overhead as they listened raptly to the missionaries.

In addition to parables, crayon drawing, and singing, they had plenty of beach games. Blaine responded quickly to competition. That was, when he could be bothered to attend. That first year he'd just caught five good sized fish with a friend (without bait even) including two Dolly Varden trout and declined the invitation and spent the rest of the day fishing near me while I sketched.

Blaine chases another kid in a missionary game.

But Dori and Rolf never missed Bible school along with about 30 other children. Rolf's group met on a scow where a lady told a flannel board story. Dori's group met first on the beach for some ring-around-the-rosy type games, then went aboard the *Anna Jackman*.

Berry, the storekeeper's wife, and I were invited aboard the 65-foot vessel. My impression was of a craft that was well-designed, clean, and fully equipped (radar, huge freezer, lovely galley, comfortable accommodations, double mattresses in all eight bunks, even a piano). The crew of six included a skipper, ordained minister, a deckhand, and three girls to teach lessons.

It was a more romantic image of mission life than I'd ever heard about.

While the *Anna Jackman* was still docked, the *Southport* arrived again to clean out our warehouse on its way to Anacortes. I hoped the crew wouldn't work all night again.

We were able to repay the skipper for his wonderful, formal dinner by inviting him up to the house for the evening meal.

I took the entire afternoon, while the kids were with the missionaries, to prepare food. I wanted to make it as nice as I could, running a veritable marathon up and down the stairs and in and out of the Mess Hall's galley for food and dishes. In between I did battle with the wringer-washer. And somehow I managed to fit in a huge box of grocery books to be totaled for the store sometime during the day.

Fortunately, I pulled off the dinner with much appreciated compliments from the captain. We first shared a drink and chatting in the living room with its bay windows overlooking Sitkoh Bay and the captain's ship tied to the cannery pier. Then we moved on to the dining room with its elegant hardwood paneling and ceiling, with a brass candle chandelier hanging over the circular table (that I'd lengthened to make oval) with its carved legs. I might not have had crystal, damask tablecloths, and stewards waiting on us, but I wasn't embarrassed by the results as we sat down to the meal.

Despite the insanely hectic pace of the season and multiple machinery and labor breakdowns, Chatham made it almost to the very end of the season without a major medical emergency.

And then it happened, impacting all of us, but in particular, the Filipino community.

The extremely close-knit Filipino community had its roots in Alaska as early as the late 1920s during the onset of the Great Depression, when Filipinos from Seattle were contracted to work in Alaskan canneries. They offered summer work for students (one of the groups hit hardest by the Great Depression) to pay for their studies. They came to proudly call themselves "Alaskaroos," eventually numbering more than 4,000.

Right away Filipinos had a strong presence in Alaska, dominating the work force through their union led by fierce activists since the 1930s. Two were assassinated when they fought back against the tradition of cannery labor contractors requiring a bribe in order to be hired as well as other exploitative tactics, such as the contractors selling them items that were supposed to be compensated to the workers including food, work supplies, bedding and lodging.

One historical source notes that: "Sometimes, the contractors would take off without paying Filipino laborers their wages at the end of the season, leaving them without any money, and with no way to leave." Fighting against these practices wasn't the end of their struggles. In the 1950s the government attempted to break up the union by labeling them "Communists" and trying to deport them, but the Filipino community held strong.

The Alaskaroos benefited from that strong sense of community in the Filipino culture and were able to rely on their traditional system of mutual aid to help get them through even the roughest of hard times.

There was such a sense of familial closeness in the community that Filipino workers didn't feel like they had to get in touch between seasons because they knew they would go the next season and catch up. That was part of the reason why they kept returning…for that sense of camaraderie that was especially cemented around the mug-up cart during the midday coffee break.

Hearing the mug-up bell rung revived everyone. It gave cannery workers a 15-minute reprieve from the deadly monotony of slime line work and the din of the canning machines. They could all chat around the

Cushman cart, as it was called, enjoying fresh made pastries among other treats, and laugh, and catch up on each other's news from back home, and grow closer to each other.

The Filipino Mess Hall, next to the bunkhouse, not only was the center for the Filipino community at a cannery, but as I'd found out after attending a dance they put on, it functioned as a center for the entire cannery community, drawing everyone together from every ethnic group and stratum of society.

Martin Ebona was a salt of the earth Filipino bull cook (whom I'd written to my parents about earlier) and was an absolute institution at Chatham cannery.

As he was making his rounds, he walked up the same steps he had been mounting for 22 years when he was suddenly snatched by the revolving shaft which drove the fish elevator.

A quick-thinking passerby saw Martin's dilemma and leaped to turn off the machinery, but Martin made at least two full revolutions before he was spun off to land on the dock twelve feet below, unconscious, and completely stripped of his clothes, leaving him in only his socks.

The first-aid man was summoned from his duties at the store, and Linné quickly got on the radio to find an airplane. He tried calling Juneau first, since they had the most advanced hospital care in the vicinity. But the response came back that no plane could be sent from Juneau due to dense fog.

That was one of the drawbacks of living in remote Alaska, where the only fast travel for emergencies was reliant entirely on the weather. Against the Ebona family's wishes, Linné decided to radio Sitka, hoping a plane could make it from there.

Besides Juneau being the capitol with better medical care, it was the Ebonas' offseason home and the home of their Catholic priest (in case last rites were needed), and they wanted Martin to go there. In fact, they insisted on it. This was when the Filipino culture of tight community worked against them.

"Listen," Linné replied, "in matters of life or death, destination doesn't matter. The important thing is to get him advanced medical care as quickly as possible."

As it turned out, we didn't get our mail until 8 days later because air traffic around Juneau was curtailed. Martin would likely have died if Linné had waited for a plane from Juneau.

Sitka said they wouldn't be able to send the plane until the following day, so everyone in the entire cannery community focused on willing Martin to hang in there.

Martin's daughter, Mary, and his son Augie, not usually attentive to their father, realized how quickly they could lose him and became distraught with worry. In the middle of the night at around 1:30 the first-aid man was called from his bunk to do what he could to calm down Mary, and finally the brother was sent for on a boat. It went round the cannery that Augie bawled her out and told her to stop carrying on and grow up.

Fortunately, the plane from Sitka made it through the mountain passes without incident and landed in Sitkoh Bay, taxiing to the main cannery dock.

The crew did what it could for Martin, and he revived long enough to ask what happened, and with a typical Alaskan spirit insisted he could walk to the plane. It didn't take much to convince him to ride on the stretcher.

The Ebona family and friends gathered for a prayer meeting. They insisted that the plane could not depart until holy water could ride passenger with Martin, to look over him. Finally, holy water, sloshing about in a Mason jar, was rounded up and sent with Martin in the plane.

We all waited anxiously to hear what the outcome was for Martin, but it wasn't till the next day that we finally got word. He'd been sent on to Anchorage and the doctors there declined to give much information other than that his leg and ribs were broken, and he was on the critical list.

It was a sad way to end one of the most productive seasons ever, but at least by the time we all left Chatham we got word that Martin would recover. It was a bittersweet ending to Linné's first season as superintendent of Chatham cannery.

The final pack was 167,000 cases plus 60,000 that were packed in Petersburg and Excursion Inlet.

I looked out the floatplane windows after we boarded it to fly to Juneau and from there catch a jet back to Seattle.

How little I'd realized, when I'd first gone to Fran to convince me that I would survive a season without Bardvilla to live at a remote cannery in Alaska, that choosing Chatham would turn out so positive, that the cannery would work its way into my heart and become home.

Gazing at the picturesque, bright red cannery buildings perched on the water with the endless jewel green forest behind them I thought:

Next year. Next year I will paint you.

PART II: 1964-1967

CHAPTER 15

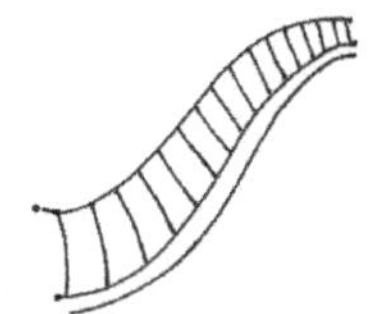

Adventures in Flying and First Days Back

In its heyday the [canning] industry caught and canned enough salmon to feed four pounds of salmon a year to every man, woman, and child in America. Lined up end to end, these one pound tins could have circled the globe.

—"Canned: The NN Cannery Project"
by Katherine Ringsmuth

Four seasoned travelers, the kids and myself (and one beginner—Nugget, the cat), arrived in Juneau, Alaska about 1:30 p.m. after an uneventful flight. The children were so good that the only time their presence was felt in the jet was during a landing when the cat crunchies went chasing down the aisle and bounced against the pilot door like buckshot.

A lot had happened since we'd last been in Alaska. President Kennedy was assassinated, shocking the world. We were insulated from it by not having TV. The kids were exposed to it more in school, where the teachers sometimes gave way to tears.

Regionally, the news was bad as well that winter. Although Southeast Alaska in general and Chatham in particular had experienced an unprecedented boom in the salmon catch, up north suffered a catastrophic salmon run.

The Bristol Bay area was hit so hard that food relief had to be sent in. We read that the State of Alaska ordered 125 tons of food to be distributed to Bristol Bay area residents. That was in addition to the 19 tons sent directly after the disastrous salmon run. The first shipment to leave Seattle was enough to meet the needs of 1,400 people for a quarter of the year. It included flour, corn meal, dried eggs, dry milk, dry beans, rice, rolled wheat, lard, butter, processed cheese, canned meats and peanut butter.

This summer the salmon season would prove to be more balanced for the entire state.

The four-and-a-half-hour wait in Juneau was tiring. We visited the museum and saw an excellent display of Indian artifacts, mastodon bones, dog sleds, ivory carvings, totem poles, and a stuffed moose. One of the highlights of the exhibit was an eardrum from a whale. There was also a man's pelvic bone with an arrowhead stuck in it which the children contemplated. Rock carvings inspired Blaine to decide he'd make his own petroglyphs at Chatham. Sadly, we didn't find out until the writing of this book that there were already petroglyphs at Chatham!

The famous anthropologist and ethnologist Frederica de Laguna wrote about them in her book *The Story of A Tlingit Community* published by the Smithsonian Institution. She visited Sitkoh Bay in 1949 and wrote:

> The bay is still an important area for the Angoon people, since a number of them work and fish at the New England Fish Company cannery at Chatham, halfway up the southeast side of the bay, and some also buy their winter supplies from the cannery store when prices are reduced at the end of the fishing season. The cannery is about 4 miles above Point Craven....

> About three-fourths mile above the cannery is the site of the former Ganaxadi village, sit'qo [Sitkoh] (possibly sit'xo, "Among the Glaciers"). Our friends, the Reverend and Mrs. Cyrus Peck, took us to see the many petroglyphs at this site. The village was on a terraced knoll, just south of the mouth of Sitkoh River, a sockeye salmon stream which drains Sitkoh Lake some 4 miles inland....

> At the base of the rocks which form the southeastern edge of the knoll are carved a number of petroglyphs, some on the deep slope of the bedrock, some on the joint planes, and a few on

fallen slabs. A native who was with us at the site reported that there used to be a spring which bubbled out of the rocks along the shore between the site and the stream near the cannery. Below the spring was a deep pool, and on the rocks above was carved a face.

Among the images carved into the rocks by ancient artists, according to de Laguna, were concentric circles (one with arms), a spiral, a frog, a "devilfish" and more. How the kids and I would have loved to have seen those petroglyphs if only we'd known they were there at the time!

This year, and all the following years that we flew out to Chatham, we went with a freelance pilot named Dean Goodwin who didn't fly for any airlines. He had a straight face, but a belying twinkle in his eyes. Little did I know at that first meeting that one day, Dean would have me design and silk screen his Christmas cards for two years. The second year, he used a poem I wrote to go along with it. I also designed Christmas cards and verses for the cannery from 1963 through 1966 (see Appendix C, Dot's Christmas Cards and Christmas Verses from Chatham, 1963-1966).

Christmas card I designed and silk screened for Dean Goodwin.

On that second season trip to Chatham when he saw my 8-mm hand-held movie camera, he said I should sit in the copilot seat up front to get the best view.

It was a regular 8, I hadn't yet graduated to the much better Super 8. The movie camera had two reels inside, one was the "take-up reel" and the other I bought and inserted on the post inside. The film on this had to be threaded onto the take-up reel that would store the shot film.

Once we were in the air and on our way, I craned to get the shots below the pontoons, trying futilely to capture the breathtaking grandeur of snowcapped mountain ranges, striated glaciers, and rocky, rugged passes. The camera had to be wound between scenes. There was no way to review what I had taken, which was a bother, but I felt very much a part of the modern twentieth century as I documented our trip.

Filming had become big a part of my life as a photographer, and I was determined to document everything I could at Chatham.

When a reel was full, the camera would stop working. Somewhere in the dark, I'd take the now full take-up reel out and send it to be developed. It would come back two weeks later on a flatter, different reel in a yellow box. The movie was only three minutes long. My dad had instructed me to count to seven when I was filming. He said that holding on a specific sight beyond seven seconds was usually redundant, and the viewer would become bored (Today's videos can be longer with sound, yet even so, I notice that after 20-plus seconds, people stop watching and want to talk about the situation being shown, no matter how interesting it might be... true even with professional videos.).

Of course, the movies I shot didn't have sound. Once I got the film back, it needed editing. The scene might be too long, redundant, or there might have been a jam inside that caused the scene to jump around until it self-corrected.

You couldn't open the camera, of course, because any light at all would expose the film, ruining all the movies you'd taken. At home, I had a little editing device. I'd cut out the part to dispose of, feed the end of the good part onto sprockets that fit the tiny rectangular holes. Then feed the next good scene onto the other side in the same way. Now came the special fast-drying glue with a tiny brush that I used to paint one end of the film that would overlap the other, for a clean transition to the next frame. It was a labor of love, and I enjoyed doing it as a hobby.

To watch the movie meant getting out the projector, setting up a portable viewing screen with a light-gathering surface, and calling the family and friends to come and watch. The finished reels, arriving in metal cases, were twenty minutes long, each film having to be carefully threaded onto the projector. If all went well, we'd turn out the lights and watch the next canister. If not, much cursing and fumbling went on with other people (usually men) trying to help and much discussion. This was all right though; it gave the audience time to visit.

Dean Goodwin in the cockpit.

Dean flew us over Mendenhall Glacier for a close look at glacial lakes, before heading south to the cannery. If he saw something interesting on the way, he diverted a little to share the scene with us and I filmed it all. He seemed to like children… maybe not so much when the boys were having a barfing contest in the back seats of the plane.

Dori later said: "We loved Dean Goodwin. We would load down his little Cessna 180 and head out. Our favorite part was when we could get him to go up and down. Mom hated it, but when he'd drop that plane and our stomachs would stay up in the air, we loved it."

During another trip out to Chatham, Dori was in the co-pilot seat when she asked Dean Goodwin what to do with a banana peel. He told her to open the little window on her right side and wait for his command.

Dean then pushed the yoke forward and swooped down. I glanced around and saw that my boys were wide-eyed. *What was he doing?* As he circled over a seine boat, he gave Dori the high sign and she let go.

Bombs away! The banana peels dropped onto the deck where the men were making a set. They shook their fists at him as he flew away. Bananas were considered bad luck on boats by superstitious fishermen. Dean laughed heartily at his prank—apparently, he'd done this before. He came to be known as the Banana Bombardier!

This year's arrival was in sharp contrast to that of last summer. We were met by Linné at the airplane float. Someone else handled our bags, all eleven of them, and carried them up the 79 steps to the house.

There was one slight mishap on the float when my art paper was knocked into the bay. All of last season flashed before my eyes, lonely and unable to express myself in paint. I wasn't about to let that happen again. I lunged for it, perilously balanced on the plane's pontoon, and grabbed its string just as it was starting to go under for the first time.

Linné later remarked, "You would have risked your life to save that art paper."

I couldn't deny it. I made quick work to un-wrap it and thankfully managed to get it out still dry.

As soon as we were all settled in and the weather cooperated, I intended to set up outside and start capturing Chatham on paper.

In preparation, I got out my art bag and put in a soft pencil (no eraser—you didn't ever want to disturb the perfect textured finish of watercolor paper), testing paper (to test the moisture of your brush with pigment), Q-tips, paper towels, painting water, drinking water, Reynolds Wrap (for texturing), an empty slide (for viewing the subject), a towel, black garbage bag to store the finished painting, tape, an old cut mat, eye dropper, ruler, favorite flat and round brushes, tube pigments, fresh Masquoid (a resist) with a bar of soap and masque cleaner, spray bottle with water, bug dope, sun screen, a piece of cheese and dark chocolate.

I made sure to bring all my art supplies on the plane with us to Chatham this time and every year after. I liked to paint big, so most of my watercolors were on paper that was 20 x 30 inches. Watercolor paper had to be pristine clean, no creases. I put stiffener on both sides. In those days I painted on D'Arches 140.

It was the thing to do back then to immerse the paper in warm water in the bathtub, then place it on a piece of plywood and tape it down, so that when the paper dried it would be stretched. The wide tape had to be the kind that you licked (that's the best way) to dampen it.

Then you could think about painting. It was a darn nuisance. On occasion, the paper would snap in two from the stretch and you'd have to start all over.

Once I had a painting, I had to be very careful to get it back to Seattle in one piece where it could be framed. Traveling in Alaska with three children and a cat on a small plane with lots of baggage maybe coming in two trips, was not conducive to arriving home with unblemished watercolors.

Every season after that first hectic one, we spent considerable time with Linné upon arrival. After dinner we'd don boots from the cannery and go fishing at a nearby creek where Linné would catch several trout and keep the biggest. By the time the kids had exhausted the poor flipping fish, they would be covered with fish slime which meant I was doomed to spend another traumatic session with the wringer washing ma-

Our kids loved those boat rides.

chine. Other times, Linné would take us for a spin in the outboard so we could see the cannery from the water.

The morning of our second season Linné showed me the cannery again, which was being readied for the coming season and wasn't busy like the first time I'd seen it. The fish house was getting a new deck and an extension for another piece of equipment.

He took me up to the net loft, a big open warehouse type room with tarred web hanging from the rafters and other web, cork and lead lines in huge piles on the floor. Linné told me how every cannery had a net loft and in the spring a crew came up early to make up new nets and go over the old ones to get them into shape for the fishing season. Racks were used to repair and dry nets, and they were washed in tanks containing a solution of bluestone, an acid that would destroy marine growth (Fishermen used it to bathe their fishing clothes in before storing them for winter; it acted as an early type of bleach.).

A salmon seine, I was informed, was about 200 fathoms (1,200 feet)-long made from cotton netting, mostly for-inch mesh, "stretched measure." It was 250 to 430 meshes deep, depending on the area to be fished, giving a depth when hung of 10 to 15 fathoms (60 to 90 feet). The complete weight was around 5,200 pounds, roughly the weight of an adult male rhinoceros. (Today's seiners make 10 to 15 sets a day. In the earlier part of the 20th century, they made two, three or four at the most. There were more fish and fewer boats, and they just didn't waste their effort.)

Linné added that one of the main interests of NEFCO's Research Department was to study the preservation of the linen and cotton of the nets during fishing and storage. "They've invented their own preservative that works better than most you find on the market," he said.

While I was always interested in being told the inner details of a working cannery, something else snagged my attention: I spied some seine rings. Being Dad's daughter, I hinted strongly that we scrounge a couple for our children to swing on. In no time, Linné had spliced the rings on some black synthetic line and hung them from the ceiling in the attic for the kids to play on.

The cannery workers had not yet arrived for the season, and it was disconcertingly quiet, especially around the cannery buildings and dock. With the Native Village silent without the sound of shrieking kids and barking dogs, my kids had to find things to occupy themselves.

Blaine didn't waste a second setting out to go fishing with his new reel. Dori, of course, spent most of her time reading, and Rolf went off in another direction with a ball. The rest of the time the kids had to make do with playing with each other until everyone arrived.

Our cat Nugget immediately found a friend: a black short-hair tiger bobtail who hadn't seen another cat since last summer. His name was Joseph. Respect for each other was about even. To begin with, all they did was sniff noses and keep each other within a few feet.

The bobtail talked continually in a throaty closed mouth rumble and occasionally batted at Nugget. I wrote to my parents:

Suddenly there was a flurry of fur and loud meowing but it was all over in a few seconds. Then they sat and eyed each other for another half hour. Curiosity was keen but they were so tense they didn't take time to clean themselves during the lull. They were in and out of the house at will. And the next night the bobtail spent the night on our back porch waiting for Nugget.

From then on, they were inseparable companions.

We had a furry visitor our first night back who upset the garbage can on our back porch, strewing our garbage all over the yard and then rolling the can around for fun. So in the morning, I had Matt, the bull cook, come up and empty the can and thoroughly disinfect it and turn it upside down on the porch. I decided we'd store our garbage inside until the bear got discouraged.

I couldn't get used to how different the cannery felt with no people around. It was almost unnervingly silent, a veritable ghost town. We could hardly wait for the entire population of the Native Village to be barged in from across the strait from Angoon.

Although mostly unknown now, the ancient Tlingit stronghold called Angoon, on Admiralty Island, directly across Chatham Strait from us, had a tragic history. It became nationally known by an infamous incident in the fall of 1882.

On a nearby island, the village of Killisnoo was created by the Northwest Trading Company which established a whaling station and the first fish processing plant in the U.S. Territory of Alaska. It was the only one of its kind for forty years and employed many Kootznoowoo Tlingits from Angoon.

Our old friend Amos Berg was the one who recorded Angoon resident Billy Jones recounting the 1882 incident that led to the bombing of Angoon.

Jones told of an Angoon medicine man, employed by the trading company, being killed accidentally during a whaling expedition when a harpoon gun exploded. Two hundred blankets and the customary three days to mourn their leader were all that the Tlingit employees asked for as compensation.

For some unknown reason the trading company's manager, J.M. Vanderbilt, panicked at the demands and hastily boarded the company boat to race full steam ahead to call upon the United States Navy in Sitka for help.

He was familiar with the Navy through the Northwest Trading Company allowing them to charter the company boat, an 80-foot, steam-powered vessel built in 1874 called the *Favorite*, a familiar sight in the area.

Sometime during his trip, the reasonable demands of the Angoon locals turned into something far more threatening in his telling and when the *Favorite* returned it was to assist the Navy cutter *Thomas Corwin* which, without investigation, shelled and destroyed Angoon and nearby summer camps. Afterwards, a bay in the area would be victoriously named *Favorite* and retains the name to this day.

It was written up in the lurid press style of the day on the East Coast, but no compensation was made to the Tlingits until nearly a century later when in 1973 Angoon received a $90,000 settlement. It was entirely due to the Tlingits of that time that the company was somehow able to resume peaceful coexistence with them as the tribe rebuilt Angoon.

They certainly didn't seem to hold anything against us at Chatham for the destruction, although it was still within the living memory of some Angoon Elders as they and the entire village were barged to Chatham cannery.

As soon as they arrived, the cannery came to life.

Once the cannery was in operation, Linné gave the kids another tour. They were just as fascinated as the first time by the canning line where a machine turned a flat can round and then moved on to be bottomed and, after the cans were filled with fish, topped. There is something intriguing about cans racing about.

They were then sent to the "ferocious," as Dori put it, line of nine retorts that hissed like medieval dragons. Huge cartloads of canned product would be steered into the gaping mouth, then the heavy door shut and sealed like a submarine door. Inside the dark they would be cooked under immense pressure.

Rolf nets floaters out of the cooling pen.

Blaine on the *Hetta*.

**Blaine brings halibut that
he caught to the Mess Hall.**

Afterwards they were put in the large cooling pens outside, filled with running cold water. Those that floated were lifted out with a net. Blaine and Rolf would eventually be allowed to participate in this job and they loved it. (Blaine would also get to go on a buying trip on the cannery tender *Hetta* where he personally caught several halibut.)

Upstairs machines boxed the finished cans in the most efficient manner, and another glued the flaps and pressed them down. Up till WW II the canneries used wooden boxes, switching to the lighter and cheaper cardboard in the late 1940s. It made it easier for workers to handle the boxes without threat of being snagged by the wire banding and splinters. What Chatham did then, no cannery today does anymore: they labeled their own product and they put it in cases for the grocery store. Modern canneries today send the product to labeling plants.

Then the boxes were sent down to the warehouse. The kids were allowed to sit on them as a sort of fun-fare ride as they rode the conveyor belt. Linné probably shouldn't have shown them this because later they returned through the years to sneak rides on their own when nobody was looking.

One year I filmed everything—the entire operation from catching the fish to the final canned product—since the pace of the season was so much slower. You can see my photos of the entire canning operation in Appendix A.

From a friend's boat in Sitkoh Bay, I aimed my trusty movie camera at a seiner named the *Orca* as it listed toward the incoming seine net that the sunlight had turned into glittering gauze with flipping salmon embedded in it. Sea gulls fluttered about, shrieking over the grind and growl of the purse seiner's machinery.

Harry R. Beard, NEFCO's Research Director, writes that purse seiners are vessels that are "60 to 90 feet long, broad-beamed and square-sterned, and fitted with a platform aft, mounted on a pivot. Upon this turntable or 'seine-table' the seine is piled readying for a 'set' [paying out a net around a school of salmon]."

He explains:

All seines operate on the same principle. When set in the water, the seine is supported at the top by a series of large cork floats, threaded on the headline or corkline, and the bottom of the netting is kept submerged to its fullest extent by heavy lead weights attached to a rope called the leadline, which is connected to the foot of the seine. Below this line, at regular intervals, in purse seiners, a series of large brass rings is attached, through which a stout rope or steel cable is roved. The latter cable is called the "purse-line" and is for the purpose of "pursing-up" or closing the bottom of the seine when a school of fish has been surrounded.

The vessel cruises about and when a worthwhile school of fish has been located, a skiff or rowboat is launched from the stern with one end of the net attached to it. A man in it rows to hold the end of the net in position while the "seiner" with the net running over her stern moves as quickly as possible in a large circle to surround the school with netting.

As an aside, in 1958, Linné was the skiff man working for the seiner *JoAnn*. He took the job specifically to learn about seining which he felt would be an important part of his resume with his eye on managing a cannery someday. He said it was essential for a cannery superintendent to understand what a fish crew goes through to provide the cannery with product.

Beard continues:

The two ends of the net are brought aboard and the ends of the "purse-line" are taken to a power winch and hauled in. This closes the bottom of the net like the drawstrings on a purse, and prevents the fish from escaping through the bottom of the seine. Then the net is hauled slowly aboard until the fish are enclosed in a small portion of it. This latter procedure is called "fleeting in" the seine. By this time the fish are in a solid, flipping, milling mass alongside the vessel.

Then a scoop net, called a "brailer," operated by power, is dipped into the mass of fish and swung inboard to the hold or the hold of some other vessel, called a "packer," for hauling to the cannery. When all the catch has been brailed out of the seine, the seine is re-stowed on the seine-table ready for making another "set."

Beard concludes:

It must not be assumed that this operation is conducted in a leisurely fashion. Seining is a method of fishing that calls for speed, particularly in setting the net to surround the fish, and in pursing up the bottom. Very frequently the school evades the encircling maneuver and at other times will dive down through the bottom before it is entirely pursed.

As I looked through the view finder of my movie camera, I watched a man at the winch control lifting the seine over the hatch. I zoomed in, the camera rolling with the motion of the boat I was on, and focused on the glistening round white floats attached to the net as they lifted out of the water, looking like a giant's pearl necklace. Several crew members were down in the hold waiting for the brailed fish to be released.

Finally, with the net neatly wrapped and stacked on the stern it was time to offload their catch.

Happily, tenders (i.e., "packers") stood by ready to load the catch into their own holds. Refrigeration was not common at the time, though some tenders had shaved ice. It was imperative that the loads from several seiners be delivered to the cannery as quickly as possible…right away before the fish started to show their age by smelling ripe.

The *Hetta*, as mentioned before, was one of Chatham's main tenders, a barge outfitted to buy fresh salmon. My camera panned toward the cannery and there, above the open barn-like door, was my hand-painted sign stretching across the main warehouse building, easily visible to any boats entering Sitkoh Bay.

Next, I filmed unloading the *A. F. Rich*.

Fish that were on the bottom of the hold were unloaded first by sheer gravity. The gate was located on the side of the barge so fish would land on a metal scoop that narrowed into the fish elevator going up to the dock. My camera caught the tall elevator, bright orange against the epic background of sky, mountains, and water.

Men stood by to re-direct any wandering salmon and get them back on track to the elevator. Down below in the hold, members of its crew as well as at least one from Chatham Cannery nudged the salmon toward the chute. One of the young men caught my camera lens trained on him and, realizing he was a momentary film star, smiled self-consciously before returning diligently to his job.

Now, in the cannery building, human hands took over at the top of the elevators to guide each fish into a trough. I was charmed by the way the raingear clad workers would tuck a smaller fish into the belly of larger ones.

A sort of paddle in the machine swung down to press a fish in place so the "guillotine" could sever the fish heads in the right place to preserve as much of the edible meat as possible. It was, as the kids said, "fun to see the heads drop off." They were not harvested but instead sent down a grimy chute to land on the beach below where the tides and the bears dealt with them.

I focused on one woman picking out what I assumed to be uncannable waste as the fish floated in the moving trough. Her motion was quick and smooth, flowing like she was part of the machine she worked beside.

Oilskin clad slimers cleaned up fish that needed extra attention such as with the blood lines. This was a very wet process. With not a wasted motion, their gloved hands dripping with slime, the carcasses were readied for canning.

I could tell the fish they were working on were chums (dog salmon) because of the red lines on their sides and the fact that they were so big at the end of the season. Again, tucked inside each other, they were sent along from one conveyor belt to the next.

The can loft and reform line were next to be documented on movie film.

The cans arrived from the manufacturer in cardboard boxes. They were flat. The lids were in other boxes. First the cans, as noted previously, had to be made round by a machine that forced a cone shape into the flat can that forced the can to conform to its cylindrical shape. The machine was fed "flatties" by a gal who grabbed a dozen or so with a grabber and placed them in a vertical chute to be reshaped.

Open belts were everywhere, ready to snatch the clothing of anyone within reach. I always thought it was a very good thing that children were not allowed in the cannery. I was very careful of where I stood while trying to get good angles to film the reform line.

Then a lid had to be put on the bottom of the now round can. Another gal in the can loft would pick up a stack of lids with a gripper and swiftly place them in a vertical column that would send them, I think, to the rounded cans to be soldered. This area was extremely noisy. I thought it must be hard on the ears to hear that all day.

Now the cans were ready to be filled by machines called fillers. These cans would then line up and head for the Patching Table where there were "spotters' who carefully watched the scale that was weighing each can. If the weight was short, the can would be kicked out and sidelined so a "patcher" could bring it up to weight with scrap salmon. They also kept a lookout for any skin that had slipped by, or in fact, anything hanging over the side of the can.

Inadequate cans were fixed, guided and rerouted to be reweighted. I tried out several of the cannery positions just to see what it was like. I failed miserably at the Patching Table. In my zeal to catch an under-filled can I repeatedly knocked cans over, resulting in the line being shut down. I was quickly replaced.

The good thing was, I was doing the filming, so my failure was not caught on camera.

I marveled at the repetitive motion we so often hear about these days causing carpel tunnel syndrome. I wonder now what kind of medical insurance, if any, covered cannery workers then. I also wondered if Patching Table workers or others who were living attachments to the machinery dreamed all night long about the repetition they experienced day after day.

My documentarian fervor led me next to Quality Control.

NEFCO was meticulous about, and well-known for, the quality of their edible products. Back in the states their laboratory used specialized equipment such as a spectrophotometer for measuring vitamins, pH meters, a fluorophotometer, constant temperature apparatus, microscopes, low actinic glassware and many other tools used to test the quality of NEFCO canned products chosen from random lots from every one of their canneries and processing plants.

According to NEFCO's Research Director, Harry R. Beard on the subject of salmon quality:

there is just as much difference between the best canned Pink salmon and the poorest grades of Pinks, as between the finest, well-fattened young steer beef and cow or bull beef from an old animal…A housewife buys a can of Pink salmon one day. It is a good grade and she is well pleased. Later she buys several cans of "Pink Salmon" and is very disappointed because she received so-called "pale" or "river" Pinks. After one or more such experiences she eliminates salmon from her buying list.

NEFCO was determined to eliminate this outcome at all costs.

Linné was likewise vigilant toward quality and allowed no slacking off in this department. A quality control man seized random cans of salmon, dried them thoroughly, re-weighed and opened them, inspected them, took measurements of cans with a micrometer to ensure thickness of the cans themselves and wrote reports with dates and lot numbers.

Another part of the cannery was relatively dry in comparison to the sloshing about during the canning process. This is where the filled cans were racked in metal bins held up by chains.

Two men stacked one rack upon the other in readiness to push them into a yawning retort where the cans would be cooked at 240 degrees for 90 minutes. These metal retorts were lined up in a row, in various stages of cooking, belching steam from the tops.

I carried my camera back outside into the bright sunlight in time to watch the freighter *Fortuna* come into the bay riding high in the water. Ancient forklifts assembled. They were capable of lifting palettes loaded with five tiers of stacked cardboard boxes strapped together with metal bands and full of cooked salmon cans. The forklifts trundled over the warped planks of the dock headed for the freighter.

I captured children, including Blaine, riding as a passenger on one of them. What a unique experience for children to have had, an experience that would be impossible in today's safety-conscious society.

The machinery that was involved in an operation of this magnitude was staggering. When we looked around and saw the workers, though, they were all very business-like, and consistently cheerful despite the uncomfortable working conditions and long hours.

Linné was always impressed with the Native workers at Chatham cannery. The day would start at 7 a.m. with a workforce of mothers who had brought grandparents from Angoon to help with the children. They would work all day, sometimes until midnight. During the cannery-provided "Midnight Supper," they would become revitalized, regaling each other with stories.

Linné couldn't believe their spirit. "What on earth do they find to laugh about?" he would ponder. "They've worked 16 hours so far and have to go back to work after the meal."

Some of the Native workers and their children became lifelong friends to us and our kids and had a part in shaping who we became, and influenced my art.

Fishing was, unlike my first year, about normal with no unsolvable problems. Linné had a very good crew working for him. We not only pulled salmon eggs, but also milt for use in pharmaceutical research. (Milt being the reproductive gland from the male salmon.)

One thing that struck me that was different from my first year was when the entire cannery shut down for lunch or dinner. I wrote to my parents: *The sound is like a record on a turntable that is slowing down. It sort of slides down in volume, like a glissando in music. Until all of a sudden there is silence.* That was how it was when the cannery was shut down.

Every day, a couple times a day it happened. It was eerie, as if for an hour the cannery and all its workers froze in time. Same thing when the machines were turned back on. It seemed like all at once the volume and pitch of its hum would rise to its working level.

A pause in production produced a different sound, hanging there in anticipation of starting up again. The foreman, Tom Anderson, would be counting the seconds that his production was halted and how that would affect the day's production. A long shutdown was very expensive to the company. Stressful!

Speaking of Tom Anderson, the efficiency of our operating cannery largely depended on him. But toward the end of the season one year, he was forced to leave the cannery, a great loss to us. His health failed, probably from too much stress. He may have suffered a heart attack. When he left, he didn't come back. We knew at the time this was the end, so we gave him a good sendoff, full of love and hope for his recovery.

Goodbye, Tom.

I'd made a sign that he would see as he took off in the float plane. Workers lined the dock and waved as he rode by for takeoff.

Without a moment's notice, machinists led by Marvin Remlinger, would be in active mode, rushing to solve a problem that only they could do. Metal on metal sounds shrieked across the bay and lifted up to my vantage spot on the hill.

Most of the time workers kept their gloves on, but on occasion gloves would come off and everyone would have an impromptu coffee break. The machinists would have to anticipate how much time they had left in to do their repair, so they could call the workers back without losing any more time. Everything would get wet once again after workers scurried to their positions on the line.

Discussion at the coffee break would be about, "I wonder what happened?"

CHAPTER 16

Magic

An artist has to scratch an itch.

—Dot Bardarson

During one of the first days back, as I climbed the long staircase up to the house, a gruesome sight assaulted my eyes. A stream of blood cascaded down the steps in front of me. I quickened my pace, any number of horror scenes flashing through my mind.

My heart raced as I prepared to call Linné on the radio and demand a flight be sent out immediately to fly one or more of the children to the hospital.

I'd only been away a couple of minutes! What could have happened?

I found Blaine hunkered down with his pocketknife, the cause of all the blood. He was dressing out some of the fish he'd caught. He'd asked me earlier to cook them, but I'd said I wouldn't clean them, and I'd suggested that he take them to his fishing friend and get him to show him how.

Apparently, he'd decided to figure it out himself. Little did it concern him that he was covered with fish guts or that he was right on the threshold of the living room. Bless his heart, he was so engrossed in the process. We cooked the trout and scrubbed the porch. He was so happy!

By 1966 Blaine was catching more fish than we could eat. So Linné told Blaine that maybe the cannery would like to have it. Blaine and his buddy from the Village immediately brought salmon to the cannery whenever they caught one. They had great entrepreneurial visions of building quite a cash box for themselves.

One day they wrote a sort of invoice, the kind a 9 year old would write, and took it to the office to present it to the superintendent.

Linné studied it and determined that "the company can't pay for that."

He saw their faces fall and reached into his own pocket and gave them a five dollar bill.

Blaine, however, was crushed. His father giving him money out of his own pocket to "pay" for something he thought the cannery would buy. It took him a long time to forgive his dad for denying him the satisfaction of being paid for honest work. How well I sympathized!

I was happy to cook the fish Blaine brought home, but I didn't do a lot of cooking that year or any of the following years. We had new permanent cooks who, as it happened, had been right under our noses all along. Everyone's favorite from the beach gang, Smokey, and his wife Elizabeth, became the new cooks.

They were excellent—so good that for the first time in my life I put on weight, reaching 124 pounds. When I muttered about it, Linné's only suggestion was that I "lose it," providing no guidance on how I was to resist the Hansen's delicious cooking.

Smokey was a lean man with a playful, albeit dry, sense of humor who didn't seem to care a whit about status. At a time and place where professions and ethnicities self-segregated, he mingled equally with Natives, Filipinos, his fellow white laborers, the white-collar office workers, and the store owner.

Plus, he was great with kids. My three loved him. Thanks to his being the winter watchman, he was the only one onsite who had the year-around pulse of the entire cannery, so besides being the cook he also figured out maintenance issues before they became too big of a problem to handle.

Smokey and Elizabeth lived in the private quarters attached to the mess hall with their little dog Gunther. One year they received a washing machine to help with the mess hall laundry. Dori got the box it came in and she turned it into a store to sell balloons on the Fourth of July. But more on that later.

Elizabeth had to home school her children during the isolated winter months out there when they saw no other humans. Smokey's part in their education was functional with the kids following their dad around to help him shovel snow and make repairs.

Elizabeth was salt of the earth, hardworking, motherly and accepting of children. My kids were allowed to help dry the silverware by putting it in a sack and shaking it. Every day the floor was cleaned with lye and soap and the kids were not allowed in with their bare feet. Elizabeth baked Dori a memorable cake for her birthday: angel food with chocolate whipped cream for topping. Once, Dori remembers, Elizabeth was going to let them make Rice Crispy Treats, but they were out of Rice Crispys so they used corn flakes instead.

Dori says: "The mug up room was where one could go to get a snack. A favorite was cantaloupe with peanut butter. We were not really allowed in there, but we did sneak in now and then. Sometimes borrowing plates or bowls to play under the boardwalk with. We loved Smokey and Elizabeth. On occasion we would have a reel-to-reel movie for entertainment. Mom always cried [over the tearjerker movies] so Elizabeth had a special crying towel for her.

"Sometimes we kids helped by putting out the place settings. They were very good at getting help from us. Made it seem like a privilege. And fun."

Smokey and Elizabeth let the kids take turns ringing the bell at mealtimes, a privilege the kids held in high esteem. They kept careful track of whose turn it was.

I think the Hansens enjoyed my kids, as most people seemed to do.

Rolf had won everyone's heart. People said such things as, "Rolf has reestablished my desire to have children when I get married."

I wrote to my parents: *Everyone wants to adopt him. Rolf has a girlfriend, Carla, who is 3 years old, Duane and Fay's child. They are inseparable. They fight, hold hands, crayon for hours, talk, and yesterday they dug a hole on the beach and both went potty in it. This really slayed us.*

Rolf had long chats with the Filipinos, but then, so did Dori and Blaine. They went there for treats, or rather, I should say, they couldn't walk by the Filipino mess hall without someone coming out and saying, "Allou! You wait right here, now, and don't go 'way." (To me they said, "Allou, Missus.") Then they'd rush to the kitchen and come out with freshly baked doughnuts, or fresh fruit, or even barbecued beef, sliced and dipped in sesame seeds.

Last week, I wrote to my parents, *the Filipino cook "Happy" gave me an enormous kettle of sweet and sour spareribs which we ended up serving for a couple days to men who came up to the house in the evening for a drink (mostly business officials from Seattle or the states).*

Dori did all her own ironing—dresses, mostly—and loved to babysit Carla.

Seeing how well liked my kids were by Elizabeth and Smokey, I realized with a thrill that I'd have some time to paint this year. When I asked them, they willingly said they'd be glad to watch them in order for me to pursue my art. In fact, after they saw one of my paintings, they commissioned me—my very first commission!—to paint the view they had from their quarters of the main cannery building and the ways.

So, on a beautiful sunny and clear day, I finally, finally had the opportunity to paint.

And this time I wasn't going to let anything get in the way of my painting expedition. First thing after breakfast, the kids and I, like an Everest explorer with a train of miniature Sherpas, set out for the boardwalk with the first round of my gear.

Down the 79 steps, past the cannery buildings, past the office, around the wide boardwalk on pilings that turned left, then out on the main dock.

I sent the kids off to rejoice in Smokey and Elizabeth's supervision for a few hours while I painted.

As I stood there, I was glad to notice there were no freighters in, so the main dock was relatively free of motorized activity. I would have the place more or less to myself, a rare opportunity of which I was going to take full advantage.

When choosing a spot to spend the afternoon, my requirements were a place to sit where I wanted the sun to shine on the subject despite the fact that the illumination was going to change with the hours, a place where nothing was going to get in the way of visibility. Even changing my position 10 feet to the side would change the perspective that I needed in order to make the scene realistic/believable.

I glanced around for the ideal place to set up. I gazed longingly at the four-wheeled cart. It would give me a firm place to sit, a place to put all my supplies. But no, I didn't dare. There was no doubt in my mind that as soon as I used it, the beach gang would come along and need it and then I would have to move. Instead, I dragged a heavy block of wood over to a good vantage point, hoping that that wouldn't be part of today's cannery operations.

I cast my eyes about again. What could I use for a bench to lean my art board on? A-ha! I saw a lonely sawhorse separated from its herd loitering in a corner. Perfect. And a few other wooden objects that I could use to lay out my paints. Then it was time for a second trip up to the house.

It took two hands just to carry the 20" x 30" inch art board. I'd left that for last. I didn't want to turn my back on that gleaming white watercolor paper. I could only imagine how frustrated I would be if some kid came along who decided to make his own painting, or just pick it up and smear dirty, soda pop sticky hands on it.

Finally—only a little winded—I set up, brimming with exhilaration, out on the main dock with all of my gear in front of my chosen scene. It was actually happening!

When I did *plein air*, it usually drew an audience, fascinated by what I was doing. And sure enough, the first coffee break brought the workers outdoors where I was, and they gathered around until the steam whistle blew.

They were respectful, not jostling me or asking too many questions, mostly pointing at parts that had been painted. They marveled at their familiar world transforming before them into paint on paper, capturing the history they hadn't known they were living in, making them a part of history.

I was generally somewhat uncomfortable in the beginning stage of a watercolor because it often appeared that there was no hope for the piece of paper in front of me. The naked page was as vulnerable as a sleeping fairy tale princess, and I was tasked with bringing it to life with every kiss of the brush.

First, I would sometimes do a light pencil sketch, with no detail, just to position the building on the page. This time I painted with light strokes to do it. The act of moving the brush on paper jump started my muscle memory and creative imagination.

With watercolor I worked from light to dark (the opposite of opaque paints such as oils and acrylics). Once I'd covered the paper with pigment, it would be painstakingly hard to remove. The only way I could even dream of lightening an area was to saturate the area and try to lift off pigment by dabbing with a paper towel or Q-tips. Back in the day, watercolorists were instructed not to use white paint…ever…that entire technique depended on painting around negative spaces.

I used a peep hole for the design stage, and I'd found that a photo slide worked perfectly for the purpose. Held at arm's length it captured the outline of the scene and helped in figuring out my first stroke, the cornerstone that supported all that was about to be built on it. Everything rested on that first stroke, so it had to be nearly perfect.

Next, I used a ruler to discover the angle of the building receding to its vanishing point. I checked it several times before making a pencil mark. Then I looked for angles that would come to rest on the edges of the scene.

Once I had these, I was locked into the composition, and could proceed to making large areas with a loaded flat brush.

My silent observers may have wondered what form of sorcery this was, whereby the act of looking through an empty slide somehow guided my paintbrush into transferring their world onto flat, stretched paper. They whispered behind me, but it was mostly indecipherable. Perhaps, at another time, in a different place, I would have been burned as a witch.

Now is a good time to talk about the inevitable love-hate relationship in a water colorist's life: liquid masque.

Liquid masque (my peers and I called it masquoid, probably after a brand name) is a resist. That word alone, *resist*, should have warned me in the very beginning that I was entering into a toxic relationship.

The masquoid blocked a place on my watercolor that I wanted to remain the same color, maybe the white of the paper, maybe some other color. It was useful for reflections on top of water, white birds in the sky, masts of boats or flagpoles, a little white detail, or some other area that it would be hard to paint around to reveal its shape. When I swiped a brush with pigment over the area, the dry masquoid would resist the new color. After the paint dried, I could rub off the masquoid, revealing the prior color below.

At least, that was the siren song that had first pulled me into using masquoid. But, like in every imperfect relationship, things often did not go as smoothly as anticipated.

To apply, I chose a brush and made a paste with a bar of soap, then dipped the soaped brush into the masquoid and painted the area I wanted to remain the same.

It was very important to clean my brush thoroughly right away after I used masquoid. It could, as I'd discovered, spitefully gum up a brush and ruin it. I fought back with masque cleaner, then soap, reforming my brush to perfection with my lips. (This was how I reformed a brush every time I cleaned it, so that it dried the shape I wanted it.) The longer the masquoid was on the paper, the more truculent and harder to remove it became.

Masquoid had other malicious tricks. It could, and did, dry out in the jar before you were through using it. Before you realized it had dried out, you might be stuck with having to paint around something. It was very hard to reconstitute, although you could try diluting with masque cleaner. It depended upon how old it was. It was a good idea to check it before you headed out to do a *plein air*, or you might be stuck with an audience watching your struggles and eventual failure.

In my cannery days at Chatham, I always did the sky first, laying down the mood/atmosphere of the scene that would influence the entire painting and the end result. That defined the roof line. As soon as that dried (it dried fast in the sun), I would lay in large areas. With watercolor I was working all over the paper, all the time, not concentrating on a single feature.

I had to keep my wits about me. While I was painting in one area, I had to never lose sight of what was happening in another area, because as a watercolor dried, there were certain techniques I could use that had to be done at exactly the right time of drying. It was somewhat like a circus performer trying to keep all the balls in the air while simultaneously spinning plates—but doing it as creatively and artistically as possible.

It was during this stage of the process that I preferred to be alone, to manipulate the bristles quickly, and hope for an exciting drying time. If people were talking with me, I might ask them not to. I had to concentrate on what I was doing and isolate my thoughts from any intrusion.

There were other things I had to contend with while painting *en plein air* at Chatham: Weather. It changed so quickly in Southeast Alaska that more than once I had to disassemble all my supplies in a hurry to save a painting for another day. Also, shadows that I felt would be beneficial would sometimes disappear by the end of the painting. I learned to return another sunny day to see where they lay. It would be the final touch.

Today, one can take a quick photo with their phone to remember the way the sun bathes some areas and cast long shadows on others. Back then, photos took two weeks to be developed by a lab (However, one of the advantages of painting a scene over photographing it is that one doesn't feel obligated to paint exactly what is shown. One's imagination is free to add items that add to the story, like a dog, vessel, or people. Or, something that doesn't contribute to the story you're trying to tell and may distract from it can be left out, such as a parked vehicle, sign, trash can, etc.).

Bugs were another annoyance, especially at an operating cannery where fish offal stank on the beach just yards away from where I painted and lured in the swarms. I tried to always remember to bring bug dope.

The temperature could drop as winds swept through the mountains bracketing Sitkoh Bay and could completely disrupt the process. I couldn't paint when I was cold. It was also hard to paint in a coat.

Or I could have forgotten to pack something and have to figure out a way to substitute, like in cooking if you don't have all the ingredients. Or I'd dip my brush into my drinking water instead of my painting water. (It happens to every water colorist.) Also, I tended to forget to drink when I was immersed in a painting.

In fact, I'd sit in one place too long and find it hard to unwind my body. Pins and needles were normal companions to any painting expedition. And who knew what I was sitting on—certainly not a chair. It was whatever I found lying around that could serve.

Sunburn was often a danger, particularly on those deceptive Southeast Alaskan days where the clouds came and went, or the cloud cover was thin enough to let the rays through to do their mischief.

Perhaps the most frustrating obstruction was running out of time. This was really annoying. Just at the most critical and enjoyable time of finishing details, analyzing, etc., it would be time to get the kids ready for dinner, take care of a domestic issue, or chore, or act as hostess to a visiting VIP. It's not like you could capture the scene in a photograph and use that to finish it. In the 1960s it took two full weeks for a roll of film to be processed. It wouldn't be the same anyway. Somehow, being in the scene, experiencing all the senses, is part of the magic of *plein air*.

As for bears… well, although I worried about the possibility, I never encountered one when I painted. Alaskan bears, it turned out, respected art.

Once I got to the detailing stage, it didn't bother me to have visitors, though I might only respond to comments and questions absentmindedly. Sometimes (in Seattle) when I'd get back to the house, I'd find that I had phone numbers written in the margins: people who wanted me to send them the final product.

The detailing stage was my favorite part. It was when the entire image was shown, even if it was wrong. That was at about 2 hours. It was where I began to put in details that made the image come to life. It was where I tried to repair mistakes, make things stand out, or recede. I'd look back at it from almost a dozen feet and analyze it. Was there enough contrast? What else does it need? It was this stage that I enjoyed most as a painter.

Fear of failure was gone, questions by oglers were welcome. I pulled out an old cut mat just to see how the painting would look when it was matted. I loved it! Best of all the painting kept getting better and better.

Sometimes in my euphoric distraction, I accidentally drank the painting water.

As I painted, everything around and inside of me went into each brushstroke: The swirling, shrieking gulls, the constant rumble and blast of the cannery machinery, the boats coming and going, children's laughter and yells, the splash and lap of the water against the beach and pilings, the scent of tobacco as a smoker paused to look over my shoulder, the smell of the beach peas and ocean salt mixed with the stench of decaying fish, a whiff of gasoline, the red and white colors of the Native Village houses so vibrant against the spruce, cedar, and hemlock forest, and blue sky…

All of it went into the texture and colors and design of the painting so that every time I looked at it in the future, that day would come fully back in an instant.

Perhaps it was, after all, magic.

Dot's painting of Chatham Cannery Warehouse.

CHAPTER 17

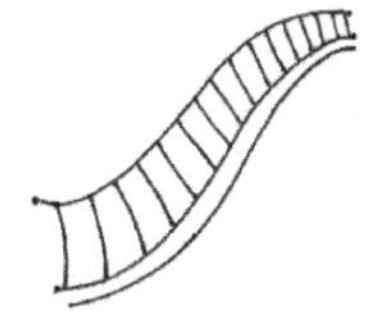

Chatham, the Musical (and Guests)

The folk revival movement included a flood of people who not only learned and passed on traditional songs, but who also wrote songs in traditional styles.

—"What was the Folk Revival?" by Paul D. Race

When the cannery's electrical plant was off in the evening, we used kerosene lamps up at the house. The warm yellow glow glinted off the panes of glass in the Mission style built-in cabinetry behind the dining room table where we'd often gather to have our sing-alongs with whomever happened to come up to the house that night.

The golden light softened our faces and glinted off polished guitars as we strummed and harmonized. The scent of cigarette smoke and coffee lingered in the air as our voices blended.

The round wood table was usually covered in Rainier beer cans, ashtrays and songbooks, including the personal books I compiled full of the songs Linné loved, including the ones we wrote ourselves.

Outside, the wilderness's great silence reigned; inside, we laughed, chatted, and shared our musical talent with deep pleasure.

I wrote to my parents:

Linne carried the ball the other night at a hilarious dinner party at the house, leading old favorites and singing new ones, including a rousing rendition of "They Built the Ship Cape Spencer." (You may remember we wrote this song after the

Cape Spencer went down in a horrendous storm. Linne had been in charge of its renovation at Maritime Shipyard.) His playing has improved so much that he confesses he is hardly aware he's playing, it comes so naturally.

For the song "They Built the Ship *Cape Spencer*" Linné stole the tune from Woody Guthrie's Titanic song and told the story of another stricken ship. It had gone down in a storm after our first year at Chatham.

The *Cape Spencer* was a 185-ton, 85-foot wooden oil screw fishing boat built in 1943 that stranded during a winter gale on the northeast coast of Akun Island on the south shore of Akun Bay in Alaska's Aleutian Islands on February 10, 1964.

I preserved the lyrics Linné wrote to commemorate it:

They Built the Ship, Cape Spencer

Oh they built the ship Cape Spencer
To sail the ocean blue
And they thought they had a ship
That the water would never leak through
But the Lord's almighty hand
Broke that cable strand by strand
It was sad when the great ship went down

CHORUS

Oh it was sad. It was sad when the great ship went down
To the bottom of the
Skipper and crew and the superintendent too
All were sad when the great ship went down

Oh they sailed from Unalaska
And were anchored close to shore
When from out of Bristol Bay
A gale began to roar
But the crew it didn't know

They were in their bunks below
It was sad when the great ship went down

CHORUS

Oh the boat was full of crab
And the sides were about to burst
When the skipper ordered Lloyd
To man the life raft first
Oh the lines were all on fire
As the skipper sent a wire
It was sad when the great ship went down

CHORUS

Oh they lowered the life raft out
O'er the deep and raging sea
As the boat was breaking up
They were nearer thy God than thee
Oh their families wept and cried
As the waves swept o'er the side
It was sad when the great ship went down

CHORUS

Four days they stoked the fire
With the wreckage of the ship
And they ate the herring bait
From that awful crabbing trip
Twas a cold and weary crew
When the Coast Guard hove in view
It was sad when the great ship went down

CHORUS

We all sang the dolorous tune with melancholy gusto, enjoying ourselves perhaps a tad too much considering the content of the song.

One of the things that made the evening so much fun was that Linné kept passing the guitar around, giving impromptu lessons to whoever needed it on which chords to strum. The people who were there that night were all married. Quite a few of the men had followed Linné's example and had their wives with them in Chatham that summer. That evening there was the store-keeper John and his wife, Berry, and Jim Nelson with his beautiful Native wife, Midge.

I was delighted and relieved that there would not be a repeat of last summer's loneliness. Not only could I paint when I wanted (and the weather allowed) but I had women my age and younger to chat with and confide in and hear their confidences. I had always loved hilarity and pulling pranks, and I fit right in with this group of merry young couples.

It was one of those parties where we laughed from beginning to end, and chuckled whenever we later reminisced about it. We served charcoal broiled steaks, salad with Marie's Bleu Cheese dressing, biscuits, baked potatoes, and hot fudge sundaes. Dori was a fabulous waitress, running in and out of the kitchen while her mother sat.

She cleared the table like a pro, asking so sweetly if she could take our plates. All the children behaved beautifully, but Dori really took the honors.

The less frenetic pace of the cannery allowed Linné to spend more time at the house with us and he liked to invite workers of every race and group up for a beer and some musical entertainment.

He wrote new words to folk songs and played guitar. I was learning to play classical guitar and accompanied him and anyone else of a musical bent joined in. When Linné and I sang together, our favorite was "Wanderin'." We harmonized with the original words, followed by "From New York City to Chatham Strait."

Music had always been important to both of us. I think our entertainment system was the first thing we bought together when we got married. Linné and my brother Dick built the sound system together. Of course, it had a record player (in those days you played one record at a time, sometimes having to change needles if they were spent).

We agreed on Scheherazade by Rimsky-Korsakov. We played it over and over. When we lived on the *Alma* at Salmon Bay Terminal, we put the two speakers in the fo'c'sle along with the turntable and a king mattress on the floor. During the winter months we would entertain friends with beer and sit around on the floor with guitars and tell stories. Sometimes people would bring their own records because nobody could afford a large library.

As for choosing which records to spend our precious cash on, we would go into a record store, select some platters, and take them into a sound booth to play to see if we wanted to buy them. It was a lot like trying on clothes. That way you were never surprised.

Our whole family liked to sing except Blaine, who sometimes held his hands over his ears. I had told my three children that they had to learn an instrument. Blaine wouldn't choose, but finally said, "Drums." At the time I didn't feel the Drums were music. His second choice was the banjo. But he never got Michael to row the boat ashore, as the old song had it.

I started with a ukulele and soon switched to guitar. Linné bought a Gretch, and just loved it. My guitar came directly from Madrid, in the luggage of Linné's cousin, Vaughn Sherman, who was returning from his stint as a CIA officer in Spain. He played guitar and so I trusted him to pick one out for me. It was a handmade classical guitar with great depth of tone.

Linné relaxing with his Gretch.

At Chatham, whenever visitors showed up with guitars, we would invite them to the house to play for each other and swap finger styles and learn new chords. During the 1960s it was the popular thing for people to do at home. Most of us were self-taught and learned from each other.

I wanted to be a better folk singer, so in the off season I found a guitar teacher in Seattle. She asked me to play something for her so she could see where I was on the learning curve. She nodded, tilted her head, and said that she could help me. "But first, you need to play the guitar."

What? I thought. *I just played for you.*

She explained, "To be a better folk singer, you need to study classical guitar."

"What is that?" I was puzzled.

"You need to learn to read notes like you do on the piano and learn hand positions that will make the guitar sing."

I sat forward. "When can we start?"

So I took off with classical guitar like a kid learning a bicycle. I practiced and practiced, wanting to impress my teacher with my enthusiasm. I fastened a small mirror to the bottom of my music stand, so I could see the position of my hands while playing the instrument. I practiced in front of the mirror so I could compare the way she looked when she played with the hand position I was using.

She was methodical with a beginner's book for me to work through. She would re-position my hand to suit her standards until I got it. She showed me how to exercise my right fingers so they would bend at the knuckles closest to the palm instead of the knuckle behind the nails. I would practice this while I was driving. Pretty soon it became second nature.

I advanced to the second book. By this time, I was playing in the second or third position well up on the neck of the guitar, challenged by the fact that you could find the same chord in different places to make different sounds, or sometimes because it was easier to shift to another position. (All beginners play in the first position.)

Through all this, Linné and I were playing together and surprising each other with new songs. He got so he could play by ear (in the first position, of course) and we both took to memorizing our songs so we could enjoy them more and perform with our family.

Linné's brother's entire family was heavy into music. I taught his twin girls chords. And Baird played a little. The most fun for me was going to "Amma's" as the children called Linné and Baird's mother, to eat dinner around her very large dining table, followed by an evening of singing with guitars.

Hootenannies were popular in the 1960s. We were not alone. Other people all over the country were gathering to exchange songs. Linné and I would work all week to learn a new song to spring on the rest of the family. Sometimes we would play and sing duets. Those were my favorites.

Two guitars.

Baird's twin teenage girls were learning guitar about as fast as anyone could and their beautiful voices blended together well. We all had yellow song books called "The New Song Fest" which included folk songs, college songs, drinking songs, old favorites, cowboy songs, rounds, and spirituals. It was put together by the Intercollegiate Outing Club Association.

The kids knew all our favorite songs, except for Blaine, who held his hands to his ears in protest. He did have a favorite song, however, called "I Wish I was Single Again" which we almost always chose because we were delighted to see him take some interest in music such as it was. It had lines in it such as "My wife she died and I laughed till I cried." Blaine would laugh uproariously, and we followed suit.

Amma would sometimes play her Irish harp and Baird, his harmonica. By this time, I was playing classical pieces too and was a member of the Seattle Classic Guitar Society. It would put together quartets to perform at various Seattle events as sort of background music. It was good practice for me to learn to play with other guitarists. I took master classes with famous guitarists who came to Seattle. But the professional musician was Baird's wife, Peggy, on the violin.

So, as I said, when we were at Chatham, we always welcomed new guitarists up at the house. We would learn so much and hope to contribute to our guest's development. One guy, in particular, played a mean guitar. He taught Linné how to sing "Rubber Tired Carriages" "Make Me a Pallette" and "The Last Leaf Clings to the Bow." He introduced a slew of new songs and strums. "Tell Ol' Bill" was Linné's first solo song and was always requested if Linné was at the guitar. Linné's personality was entertaining.

We met with Bill Carlstrom in Seattle after the fish season for a hootenanny in his living room. He gave his student cello to Linné. When Linné was 10, he had taken cello lessons. These stuck with him as something to be cherished, and he swore that he'd take up the cello again someday. (And he did, too, at the tender age of 77.)

Meanwhile, we continued to offer hospitality to a stream of diverse guests.

One of our guests was the father of the storekeeper. He came to watch his son in action. Our house was, of course, the guest house. So we escorted him to the top of the hill to take up residence.

Blaine was showing him how he could walk up the handrail of the 79 steps, and wouldn't you know, he fell off into the salmon berry bushes below, and screamed bloody murder. It turned out that our guest was a physician. He insisted on examining Blaine and came to the conclusion that Blaine had injured his kidneys, so ordered us to keep him quiet.

Was he kidding: Keep Blaine down?

Shortly, Blaine was seen escaping the house, but at least not via the handrail—at first. Soon after, though, he was observed "practicing." Even so, we remained friends with the doctor for many years.

In 1967 a Japanese woman arrived unannounced at Chatham to visit her brother. I don't think she had a clue what Chatham was or where it was, so isolated from another town.

Dori with Toshiko.

Linné called up to me on the radio: "Get a bed ready. We have another visitor. She just arrived by plane from Juneau. You will like her. She's from Japan, in no capacity here at Chatham cannery, except to visit her brother who's a technician at the Egg House."

Toshiko could speak some English. And she immediately adored Dori, who was 11. One day she dressed Dori up in a kimono, not the most ceremonial kind, yet still with two obis, and really quite elegant. We took photos of Dori on our front porch, and Linné got to see her all decked out.

Toshiko taught us a few key words in Japanese. Dori and I put our new vocabulary to use and wrote and memorized a short script which we enacted on the dock during coffee break.

Dori in Toshiko's kimono.

We were carrying an egg roe box as a prop. Our conversation with each other was about the contents of the box: "*Mushi, mushi.*" That means worm. (The technicians had found some worms in the roe that had caused consternation and much discussion about what to do about preventing them, since they had to throw out any roe that included worms.)

Basically, the script went like this: We'd bump into a group of Japanese and then apologize profusely with *Gomenasai!* (excuse me). After they realized we'd done it on purpose, they laughed so hard they almost rolled off the dock. It was after that that we began the actual skit:

Dori: *Ohayo Gozaimos* (Good morning)

Dot: *ie, Konichiwa* (No, good afternoon)

Dori: *Ikaga des ka?* (How are you?)

Dot: *Genki des, Anata wa?* (I am well, and you?)

Dori: *Daijobu des-ka?* (Are you in good health?)

Dot & Dori [bumping into each other]: *Gomenazai!* (Excuse me)

Dori: *Kozunoko* (salmon roe) *Oishii-desuka?* (Delicious, isn't it?)

Dot: *Nai* (no)

Dori: *Doushita no?* (What is the matter?)

As the big climax, we'd pull out the huge green worm that we'd made of cloth and string and say *Mushi mushi*. This got a big laugh.

We bowed to our audience.

Dot: *Ikimasho* (Let's go)

Both: *Sayonara*

Other workers who didn't understand Japanese didn't know why we were laughing so hard, but it was contagious. Pretty soon, the whole dock was rocking. Funny, how such a little thing would make the day. The harder your work and the longer the hours, the more vulnerable you were. Any break was refreshing.

The Japanese have a great sense of humor. They loved the 6-inch green worm.

Toshiko only stayed three nights, but it was good for me to have some woman talk throughout the day, and she got to see her brother. (I don't remember where she ate, with us or at the Filipino mess hall where the Japanese technicians preferred to eat due to a partiality for the type of food served there, though they were certainly welcome at the white mess hall.)

Linné's mother came to visit us in Chatham, arriving with little in the way of clothes, but with two big bags of greens from Pike Street Market and a basket of vitamins. This was her hallmark. She was always so sure we were starving at these outposts. Her lack of lung capacity kept her from negotiating the stairs very often, but we had some wonderful meals at the house with her.

Rolf Complains to Amma about his brother.

CHAPTER 18

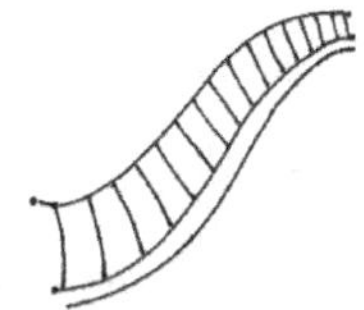

Smugglers, Contraband and Monkeyshines

There is something special about this year at Chatham. Hardly a day goes by without a practical joke or spontaneous prank.

—Letter to Dot's parents, July 1965

Naturally, incoming workers wanted to enjoy drinking. And nobody enjoyed it more than Linné. But drinking and working were an impossible combination in an industry where time was of the essence. If the fish didn't get processed within a certain time frame, it had to be discarded. Not to mention the troubles that came with alcohol…at one point we had to deal with a murder fueled by contraband booze. But more on that later.

It was Linné's job to meet every incoming plane and search the freight and luggage of every passenger for the smuggled booze. More often than not he found it and collected it, to be given back when there was a break.

Baggage inspection to sidetrack booze.

Meanwhile a mysterious Englishwoman arrived to work at the cannery doing menial work though her accent and habits suggested she was accustomed to a higher station in life. We never discovered how she found out about the cannery. Linné found a place for her in the Village, in a tiny one room house with a wood stove and hand pump for water.

She was great fun. Not adept at running machines, she was a little clumsy but a good sport and became a productive member of the team, but oh so proper. She enjoyed her tea.

Everyone liked her but no one could find out about her past.

However, *she* found out one day that the supe was serious about smuggling and he would root out the contraband booze wherever he found it, playing no favorites.

A few days after a plane came in, he knocked on Josephine's door. "I'm sorry to bother you," Linné said, "but I have to check everyone's cabin. I know you don't have any booze, but I have to be fair and check everyone."

She ushered him in, chatting merrily.

He checked all the usual places in the tiny cabin and finally came to the bed.

"Josephine, what is this box down here?" Linné asked.

She stared at him, for once at a loss for words.

"Josephine, I'm surprised at you," he said as he slid a case of beer out from under her bed.

Her jaw dropped.

The truth was, usually Linné kept all the smuggled booze he took off arriving workers in his office. (To be saved for the Filipinos so he could dole it out at appropriate times instead of dealing with hangovers "on the line.")

One day, a "shipment" had come in, but Linné didn't have time to take it up to the office, so he hid the case of beer in the first place he could find—in this instance under Jospehine's bed—until he could retrieve it later.

I'm not sure she ever fully forgave Linné for that prank although we did remain friends through the years, and she autographed several books for us that she had published. We also saw her in a one-person play during the following winter, at Pike Street Market. She was very good in it, and I've thought about her many times through the years, wondering always, what she was doing at Chatham Cannery.

One of the big wheels at the Seattle office wanted his son to be an important asset to New England Fish Co. He called Linné: "Hey, I've got my son here as a new employee. We'd like for him to experience a working cannery. Can you find him a job at Chatham?"

Linné said, "I can find him a job, but he'll have to keep it."

The young man, named Reid Rodgers, had a college degree. He arrived at Chatham in a suit, and always seemed a bit out of place. I never could figure out what he did at Chatham, but he lasted the season. Maybe Linné had him doing various jobs.

Meanwhile, to entertain the children and keep them occupied, I gave the kids scissors and my magazines to cut pictures out of them. Then I made "cameras" for the kids out of cardboard boxes. The kids went around the docks at coffee time with their fake cameras and would corner someone and ask if they could take a picture of them, just like they saw Mommy do.

They'd pretend to push a button and exclaim "Click!" and then wait a few seconds "for the photo to develop," and reach inside for an appropriate photo, i.e., a clipping from one of the magazines.

Some photos were of animals. Their favorites were monkeys in a variety of impossible poses. Everyone loved it and much hilarity ensued.

They took a photo of Reid Rodgers and pulled out a picture of the Jolly Green Giant of canned vegetable fame. He seemed perplexed, though the kids thought themselves hysterically clever. Like Reid, I could never figure out why they thought the photo appropriate, but when I looked at photos of when he was there, I noticed he'd adopted a long green army coat, and after all, he was tall. Was that it?

The Jolly Green Giant.

Movie nights were a favorite form of entertainment when a reel-to-reel projector was set up in the Mess Hall so that the crew could watch 16-mm film with sound that Linné arranged to be flown in from Juneau.

We saw the movie "Treasure Island" amidst the benches and tables of the mess hall, and the kids were mightily impressed by Long John Silver. Blaine insisted that he wanted to be a pirate. So I made a black eye patch, head scarf, and swash buckling cloth belt and long sword. He carried a flag with the skull and cross bones. Real cute, and he with no front teeth.

One day the carpenter made a bunch of stilts, and we all learned—through trial and error, many bruised posteriors and a lot of laughter—how to walk on them. Linné was the best, and definitely the tallest. But the Japanese were pros. They showed off by walking up and down stairs and over things nimbly.

Then there were water sports. Linné took the kids out in the skiff to fish and even took the time to give Dori a chance to try out water skis when she was nine. She sat on the edge of the airplane float holding onto the tow bar and the driver of the skiff took up the slack until she was pulled off.

Blaine as a pirate.

We watched in disbelief when she determinedly rose up from the water on the skis, zipping by the red buildings of the Native village, and continued way out across the bay. I was filming it with the movie camera.

She didn't fall until she almost reached the float from where she'd taken off—like a pro! We shouldn't have been surprised. Everything Dori ever tried she excelled at. And if she didn't succeed at first, she'd practice until she did.

Dori waterski's at age 9.

Dori's birthday was a continuation of the fun. For her 8th birthday we had dinner at the house at Dori's request. The Filipino mess hall supplied us with sweet and sour spareribs. Elizabeth made Dori a chocolate cake topped with candles. We charcoal broiled T-bones, had a salad, rice, and wine for everybody. Linné gave Dori a toast.

After her first series of fake spankings in the mess hall by the cooks Smokey and Elizabeth, Dori started on a treasure hunt which netted several small presents. Through clues supplied in verse at each station, she was directed to the location of various wrapped packages, including one from her grandparents in Seattle. In two places, the people involved

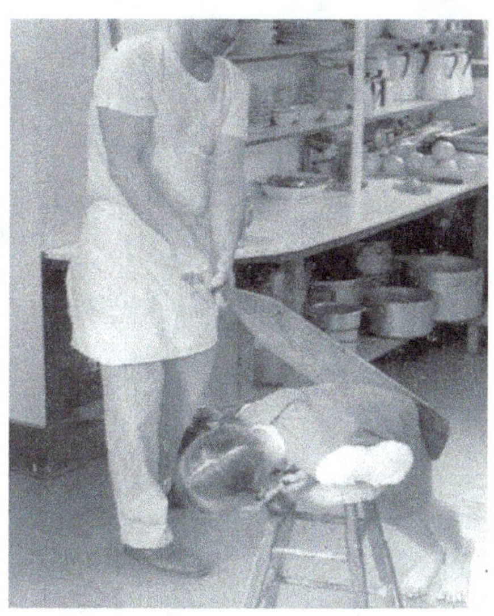

Such Trust!
A birthday spank by Smokey.

more than cooperated by hiding the prize further and teasing Dori, which made her triumph all the sweeter when she finally confounded them and discovered her presents.

The shenanigans persisted throughout the season.

Bill Anderson, an energetic young man who the kids adored, became the storekeeper in 1965. The kids were particularly impressed by the way he would climb up into a boat's rigging and do a perfect dive into the water off the highest vantage point he could reach.

One week he decided to take three days off to go out on a fish tender to see what that was like and to get away for a few days from the store.

Dori and I built Bill's effigy.

**We hung Bill in front
of the store.**

This abandonment of store duties, one and all felt, was unacceptable. While he was away, I constructed an effigy of Bill. His head was made of a mop. The handle provided a sort of support for clothes. I got someone— there were many volunteers available—to hang it over the door of the store.

We could hardly wait for Bill to return and see himself strung up. I don't know who had more fun with practical jokes, the jokers or the jokee.

When Bill came back, he wasted no time in cutting it down, opened the door, and found a long banner made of counter paper welcoming him back. He had to laugh. I got involved with tending the store while Bill was away which is why I was able to gain entrance to hang it up over the counter. I had plenty of help doing that too.

I used shelf paper to make the sign.

Then there was the head bookkeeper's wife, living in the small white house off to the right at the foot of the 79 steps, who didn't have a cannery job. However, she did have a sewing machine. When the cannery crew found out about it, they started asking her to do some mending when clothes got ripped on the job.

This, I thought, was my opportunity to indulge in another prank, deploying my unique skillset. I had the carpenter shop make me a sign board with a post to stick in the ground and I painted "The Ripper Snipper Shop" on it.

When she wasn't looking, I pounded it into the earth and then went to ground, skulking in the wings waiting for her to discover it. We had a good laugh about it. But that didn't stop her, I couldn't help noticing, from taking the sign down.

Dot the prankster:
Ripper Snipper joke player seeing reaction.

There were many other pranks, ones that I often had a hand in, too many to mention. There were plenty of ways that we entertained ourselves as well, including a forklift parade. Who knows who thought that up? Kitty Young, one of our brightest, not to mention prettiest workers, was on one of the rigs as they wound boaround the cannery buildings like a gigantic, mechanical, articulated snake.

Someone had put up a basketball hoop on the main dock for "pick-up games." There was no referee and it often turned into an absolute brawl. Linné was usually the one to break it up, and they'd resume their pick-up game. There must have been no fish on those days.

It always amazed me how children, who travelled light and stayed awhile, like at Chatham, invented their own toys and fun. Of course I'd rather forget the fun my kids had rolling tea cigarettes under the big oil tank, but I recognized creativity. Dori recently shared that they'd enjoyed endangering themselves by sneaking a climb up the vertical ladder to the top of another oil tank near the Native village in a bid to be "King of the Mountain." In fact, it is a truth universally acknowledged by all children, that a ladder wherever it is found, must be in want of a good climbing.

Chatham kids investigated every nook and cranny of the boardwalk from one end to the other. They explored buildings and played with cardboard boxes meant for canned salmon. They made up their own games. They found things to do and places to play that didn't surface in conversations with parents until years later.

The beach was their main playground and they never tired of it. A tetherball was erected and Linné tested and approved it, but the best times they had emerged from their own efforts and imagination. With collected stones lined up to make roads, and industriously dug channels

Ladders need to be climbed.

to let the water rush in for channels they could float their shell boats on, they created their own little Atlantises that were swallowed up by the tide, only to be recreated the next day. Their pockets bulged with treasured shells as they fished for anything they could find in the clear water lapping their bare feet. We called Blaine, "the great provider" for the amount of fish he caught. Fishing stayed with them their whole lives.

Old wooden boats abandoned on the beach were irresistible. The children climbed aboard and sailed away in their minds to far away places and giggled out stories of shipwreck and survival. They could stay seated in one of the old boats for hours inventing their adventures.

Kids in a boat - Dori with a gun.

Chatham float friends.

The cannery's floats were perpetually adorned with children. The fishermen were hugely entertained as the kids "helped" them tie up their boats. Their chests swelled with importance, imagining themselves crew members. The ramps, especially when they were steep at low tide, were a

challenge for the smallest in keeping up with the older children. It built Rolf's confidence as he determinedly scaled the wooden rungs behind Dori and Blaine.

Our three children coming up the ramp from the float.

When the days occasionally sweltered, the children congregated at the end of the airplane float and launched themselves into the cold salty water, sending shrieks into the tops of the evergreens, where the bald eagles looked on with brooding eyes. They paddled about, with or without lifejackets, according to their individual tastes. Adults tended to appear, taking advantage of the chance to cool off from hot cannery work under the completely legitimate pretext of supervising the children and ensuring their safety.

After all, some of them had never learned to swim. It was shallow under the floats so the kids could safely paddle and

Pushing her in off the float.

still touch down when needed, unless it was high tide. My boys, encased in their lifejackets, hung close to the float. But at least Dori had had swimming lessons in Seattle and knew how to swim.

One day hula hoops made an appearance on the oil dock. A crowd gathered as everyone demanded a chance to share their hip-swiveling talents. While there was no lack of enthusiasm, the results ranged from inept to pretty good. Then Linné stepped into a hoop. I snatched up my 8-mm camera and trained it on him, trying to hold it still against my mirth as this tall, lanky man tried to make his hips do what they just did not want to do. The entire crowd cheered and erupted in laughter to see the superintendent, who was good at everything, ruefully fail the hula challenge. Dori was happy to show her father how it was done as she rapidly improved at twirling the hoop while pop music from Bessie's radio station tinkled in the background.

One of the children's favorite people, a man named Pat Davis, had a gift with handling children. He knew how to share their delights and interests and could be counted on to tell the most engaging, spellbindging stories. The children followed him around the dock and boardwalks like he was Chatham's very own pied piper.

Pat Davis was Chatham's pied piper.

The lumber pile eventually caught the children's attention. No one else seemed to be using the 10-foot long boards, so they helped themselves. I curiously watched as the boys lined up the planks lengthwise, overlapping the one in front, one after the other, to make a continuous line of them straight down the steep hill behind the pile. Another board was impressed into service as the vehicle upon which they rode down the highway of planks. The trick was to stay aboard (literally) and not get launched into the bushes. It almost looked like an assembly line to me as the next boy on his board moved into place and shot down the hill followed by the next and the next. The organization appealed to me.

Sliding down on planks.

The carpenters refused to be left out of the fun and on a slow day at the cannery, they crafted stilts out of 2 X 2s with a sturdy wooden step for the foot. They churned out dozens of them and as soon as word got out, the boardwalk in front of the carpenter shop turned into a veritable playground for children and the Japanese technicians. Linné observed the fun from his office and in moments he was striding about, demonstrating his mastery of stilt walking. Already tall at 6 foot 6, the stilts made him a giant.

Linné demonstrating his prowess with stilts.

We all, with varying degrees of skill, learned to walk on the stilts. I, in particular, being short, loved standing tall as I pulled the pole up with each step to keep my foot connected to the stilt. Naturally we progressed to races. Children fell off left and right, laughing helplessly, but not the Japanese. They were pros, striding up and down stairs, over lumber piles, and around barriers, all the while guffawing their pleasure as we applauded in awe.

Today, I think I could still walk on stilts, for a few steps at least. It's a skill like riding a bicycle that one never forgets.

Lined up for the stilt race.

The stairs to our house were a favorite area of play. Instead of conventional slides, the children slid down the handrail, and Blaine used it as a balancing beam, eventually mastering it so that he never fell off into the bushes. Wooden sawhorses at the bottom of the stairs alongside the carpenters shop beckoned and Blaine and Dori swung their legs over them and urged them into imaginary gallops in a race toward the finish line.

Sliding down the banister.

Galloping sawhorses.

Besides all the reading we did at the house and playing in the attic, the kids got interested in the Beatles. Perhaps that was the greatest measure of the British band's fame, that they influenced children on the edge of the world in a remote, roadless Alaskan cannery. I made costumes for them with a corrugated cardboard banjo and guitar and a porcelain pot for a drum. Wigs made from mops balanced on their heads. When they heard the coffee break whistle, they paraded around the docks and "played" their groovy music for everyone who would look up from the glazed donuts. Surely the boys from Liverpool would have been proud.

The Chatham Beatles.

From somewhere Linné unearthed a bicycle and it behooved one and all to jump out of his way as he careened down the narrow boardwalks, the rubber tires jittering over the warped wooden ridges. He managed to never come to grief… and neither did the pedestrians. He even managed to ride it one-handled while holding a fishing pole. Where could he have been headed?

Everyone wanted to get in on whatever joke or prank or entertainment that was happening during every season after the first frenetic one when Linné was superintendent. It never interfered with the work, and, in fact, it probably helped it since it kept everyone in high spirits. Linné was all about high morale.

Linné rides a bicycle on the boardwalk.

CHAPTER 19

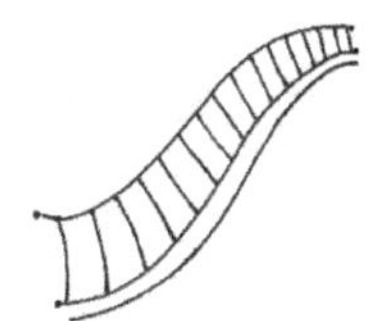

The Egg House and the Pits

*Kazunoko: Fertility. Kuzonoko, or herring [and salmon] roe,
also uses easy Japanese wordplay. "Kazu" means numbers
and "ko" means children. So, kazunoko symbolizes being
blessed with many children.*

—"Osechi Ryori: The Hidden Meanings
Behind Japanese New Year Food"
by Haruka Masumizu

During the 1960s, the fishing industry yielded to pressure from a growing Japanese market, to stop throwing away salmon roe. The pressure generated a new and lucrative industry known as *kozunoko*, a Japanese word for a New Year's roe recipe that came to be used by the cannery workers for: "salmon roe processing." Linné was eager to embrace this new option for harvesting salmon products.

The design for a roe processing building complete with refrigeration was drawn up during the winter months and was sent up to Chatham for installation in 1966.

Linné found a spot on the main dock that would accept a new building, keeping in mind that a flume would need to connect the fish house to the new egg house.

Watching its construction was great entertainment. My children took it all in, while being cautioned to "stay back." Meanwhile I, of course, had the movie camera glued to my eye as I documented everything.

The carpenter crew, aware of the dangers of working high off the dock as they often had to do, were careful to watch where they stepped and climbed. No safety devices like security straps or harnesses could be seen to prevent injury from falling. They were nimble and confident while balancing precariously on small, unsteady surfaces or while raising the trusses or roof.

Inserting the giant and heavy refrigeration units took planning ahead in order to deftly fit it in a space above while raising yet another 4-foot by 10-foot wall panel. It would take a crew of five men to raise them in place.

There were no nail guns in the 1960s… just heavy duty hammers with wooden handles and men swung them with a will, the banging echoing off the walls in a riotous cacophony.

Everything was done with manpower and forklifts that were counterbalanced by the weight of three men on the back. Everyone seemed to enjoy the challenge. And, of course, Linné was in the thick of it, driving one of the forklifts.

The roe processing building was finally built, and with more free time and older children, I was pressed into service, joining the cannery workforce in the "Egg House" (sometimes called the "roe room") as needed whenever there was a worker shortage.

But first I did the double-language signage for the Egg House. I enlisted the help from one of the Japanese technicians who had just arrived to spell out the words with Japanese characters, which I copied with my lettering brush. (This time I knew better than to expect payment from the cannery for my art, which was good since it wasn't forthcoming.)

The Egg House was a quiet place, and we were glad to get away from the noise and apparent confusion of the Fish House. The smell was salty, but fresh, the atmosphere pleasant and efficient. I rather enjoyed working there. And I did get paid for this work.

Here the young Native girls and I sorted and packed salmon eggs (roe) into wooden boxes with layers of coarse salt in between. We worked for $2.50 an hour in the roe room.

Packing roe in wooden boxes.

We readied ourselves for the job by first putting on our rain pants. Then rain jacket, then apron, then rubber gloves, and finally wristers (plastic sleeves—mainly yellow, but I saw some black ones—that went over our jacket cuffs). With this protection we were completely dry inside. If it was warm out, we might go without the jacket.

As we waited, the roe slithered down the flume from the cannery into one of the two huge circulating brine vats for washing. Then a Japanese technician turned off the vat's rotating paddles and scooped the skeins out with a blue plastic basket that acted like a large colander. Brine poured out of them as he shifted them onto a two-level table that could hold about 40 baskets.

This was typically a man's job because the wet roe was heavy. It was backbreaking work to scoop them, shake the baskets to get as much of the moisture out as possible, then turn around and slip them onto the long table for sorting.

Because I was hired to fill in when they were shorthanded, I had to know how to do both the sorting and packing. Usually a worker did one or the other. We sorted by numbers. A Number 1 was a perfect skein. A Number 2 was pretty good, a Number 3 was broken in one or two places, and a Number 4 was bits and pieces.

Linné came to film me with my movie camera and caught me sorting skeins, looking quite professional. I became so involved that I forgot, so when I glanced up and saw my own camera trained on me you can see me do a double take and smile. But I'm glad to report I did not miss a single beat sorting.

There were six Japanese technicians who came all the way from Tokyo to oversee the Egg House and were in charge of quality control. They'd bow politely and say "konichiwah" to us. (It meant "hello" in the afternoon.)

We tried with all our might not to break any skeins while we layered them like sardines in the wax paper-lined wooden boxes with Japanese writing imprinted on them. It didn't matter how carefully we did it or followed the Japanese technicians' orders—when we finished a box we would call for inspection, and they would find something not to their high standards.

We would watch intently in order to achieve perfection on the next box, but all too often we would see our efforts removed at the top by several layers and rearranged. The worst of it was we couldn't tell the difference between what we had seen them do and what we had so diligently tried to emulate. It was frustrating. It seemed like we could never measure up. We sometimes felt they meant us to come away with that impression.

Once approved, we gave the roe one final layer of coarse salt. Then we or the technicians would secure the wooden lids with nails, stamping the boxes in red ink as #1, #2, #3, or the mark of shame, #4. The date was also added.

Finished salmon roe boxes slid out from the roe room on conveyer rollers to be loaded on a forklift and taken to the warehouse waiting for a ship to come in and take them to Japan. Roe was considered a delicacy in Japan and was very expensive. About the only way I could eat it, I found, was mixed with fresh pineapple and cottage cheese, but the Japanese ate it just as we had it packed. (The roe was packed so tight it seemed to me a gelatinous mass, but each sack/skein could be carefully inched off to the dedicated eater.)

Roe boxes ready to ship.

Don Hansen, Smokey and Elizabeth's 16-year-old son, joined us in the Egg House doing general labor for one season. The following season, before he turned 17, Linné promoted him to manager of the egg operation, a position he held for two seasons. He made $2.35 an hour. (Overtime earned him another $.30 or so an hour so he worked as many hours as he could.)

Once in a while, my kids would show up to sort of "check in," but they weren't interested in hanging around while Mom worked.

I filmed everything. My camera caught the flat, raw wood boxes labeled "Salmon Roe" in English and Japanese, each of them graded. In the Egg House there were square wooden tables around which women with bandannas on their heads and clear plastic raincoats with aprons over them and knee-high black rubber boots worked, chatting and smiling.

There was a real sense of camaraderie in the Egg House that I tried to capture. One of the Native women, Kitty Young, who worked in the cannery, told me years later:

> Chatham served as a rite of passage for young people. Boys were picked to go on a seine boat. Girls began with babysitting in the village, graduating to the Egg House at 15 where there were no machines, and then to the Fish House at 18. Kids looked

forward to moving up into the adult world this way.

I learned to work as part of a team, that my position on the line was important, that if I didn't show up it would wreak havoc on its efficiency. It was like joining a club. We loved wearing our colorful bandanas and talking about how we could improve our speed or efficiency. We had responsibility. I made lifelong friends there. I learned about machinery and how important the machinists are to the operation.

It was amazing how long we discussed the importance of learning a trade, and that the cannery was a big part of our basic education. We understood how things worked in the world beyond high school.

Another photo I took captured two smiling young women carrying between them a nearly overflowing five-gallon bucket of roe from the Fish House to the Egg House.

Japanese meeting in our living room.

I even photographed the Japanese technicians gathered in my living room to discuss with Linné the way the roe operation was going. The photo revealed how at ease they felt in the superintendent's presence: one of them was seated on the wall-to-wall area rug in front of the brick fireplace complete with hearth and glass screen (with brass trim). Some were seated on our tweedy couch or a wooden stool. The basic Fifties-style coffee table was covered in beer cans, cigarettes with ash trays, and plates filled with snacks. Some of the technicians wore sneakers or sandals, most were sock footed. Some were in suits, some in polo shirts and pants. Everybody smoked.

They looked very much at home.

I kept a scrapbook of Chatham photos for all five summers we were there. One nice, sunny day, I decided that my fellow workers in the Egg House might enjoy seeing themselves and those they knew on the pages. From there it was passed around to other cannery workers.

Coffee break - looking at Dot's scrapbook.

One group spent the entire coffee break turning pages.

So I loaned the scrapbook to them to take to the Village where they didn't have to be in a rush looking at it and where more people could enjoy it. They passed it on to the Filipinos, where it was read for a couple weeks. The book suffered some from use, but that's what a book is for.

Then one day I was going though it myself and noticed something strange. Someone had taken a razor blade and slashed the photo of Linné in the office taking a radio schedule.

So, although most people liked Linné… obviously there was somebody who didn't. Perhaps it was just as well that was our last summer in Chatham.

***

Maybe it was the closer connection with the workers, being one myself, that led me to involve everyone in building a huge, community barbecue.

The first thing I did was get Linné's permission to use the fire bricks that had been stacked behind the carpenter's shop for the last 25 years.

Linné was enthusiastic. Sometimes when the cannery was short on salmon, which was more typical than our first year, there was down time. Workers with too much down time could get bored and restless, and from there fights and other trouble could break out. "What a perfect project," he said and promised full support in whatever was needed.

Shortly after this I saw some Native women coming up the boardwalk, apparently on their way to the store. They were the very ones who'd put the idea in my head when I'd overheard them tossing around the need for a community barbecue.

I was never one to let the grass grow under my feet, or let a good idea get lost in merely talk. I met them with, "Girls, we're going to build a barbecue pit and we have to get all these bricks down to the other end of the Village."

I showed them the pile and kept talking enthusiastically about the project, and at first they weren't sure if I was kidding or serious. But when I jumped into the salmon berry bushes and started hacking away at them with a piece of plywood to liberate some of the stacked bricks, they realized what was happening.

There was much kidding around (they had never seen a Mrs. Superintendent in this role) and genuine enjoyment as the women pitched in and nabbed everyone who came along including the children.

We manned a brick brigade, passing them down the line into boxes on hand trucks, which were then wheeled to the site of the construction by more "volunteers." We had a veritable parade of adult and child brick haulers headed down the boardwalk. It was amazing how quickly a lot of people can work if the enthusiasm was there.

The brick brigade.

By the time I got to "the pits" (as we called the place) with my own load of bricks, Mary Willis and Janet Jacobs were cleaning brush at the site to make room to build the barbecue. The other women plunged in, helping clear the thickly overgrown salmon berries and wild celery.

We borrowed two axes, a machete, two picks, two shovels, and a sickle and hacked away until we had a fairly level area large enough to accommodate the project. While the ladies were raking it smooth, pulling out broken glass, rusty cans and stubborn roots, I went to Gilbert, the head carpenter, for some advice. Apparently, Linné had spoken to every department head on the subject in advance, urging them to comply with our needs, and Gilbert not only gave advice on what we needed to do but cut two by sixes exactly the right length to build the forms for the concrete and some stakes to hold them.

With Blaine and Rolf "helping," I measured out where to place the forms.

Mary Willis chopping brush.

Building forms for concrete.

It was no trick at all to nail them together and level them. Linné came down that very night with several loads of pea gravel, sand, and cement.

We adults had discussed bringing the kids into it and the upshot was that we thought there'd be less vandalism if we involved every child from toddler to teen—so that's what we did. And it paid off, the kids were as proud of the end result as we were.

Linné watches Blaine mixing concrete.

So, accompanied by millions of no-see-ums and almost too much "help" from the children (Linné had them bring him only the finest gravel on the beach), he mixed it all together with water and then poured cement. He allowed the children to even help with this, and Blaine was at the forefront helping smooth it down.

We covered the cement, as it cured, with fish net to keep little fingers out of it. The soft expanse was just so tempting to write one's name in it.

Pouring concrete into the forms. Dori wants to help.

There was a chap on one of the boats who had worked with brick, so we planned to con him into "helping us" by laying the bricks himself. We didn't have to do much conning, as it turned out. He was enthusiastic about the idea. Everyone was.

The beach gang helped on making the steps up to and down the other side to facilitate cooking and serving and even added the tables.

Tom lays the bricks for the barbecue.

For the grill, Linné gave us some old can coolers from the cannery which he cut down with a torch. We even got help from two machinists who cut strips of sturdy metal for us to support the arches of the fireplace.

I wrote happily to my parents, *We now have a firepit, the location of our forthcoming 4th of July celebration. That is when we will christen it. Salmon barbecue…Ummmmm!*

The finishing touch was added when three Native women took their outboard skiff across the bay to gather wildflowers—maidenhair ferns, columbine, wild iris—with which they decorated the barbecue. *The result is almost too beautiful to describe,* I wrote in the letter to my parents.

But I was content that they'd get the full effect when they watched our Chatham home movies once we returned to Seattle, for I had, of course, captured the entire construction project on film.

CHAPTER 20

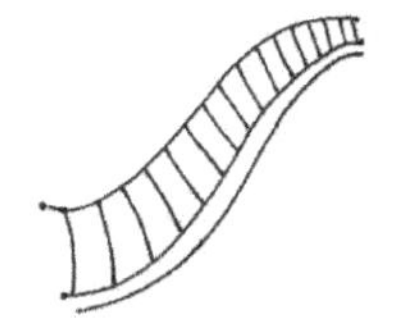

The Fourth of July

At Chatham we didn't ask Dad for anything. But what I wanted more than anything was a ride in that boat. So, the rest of the summer I bailed out the boat every day hoping that Dad would notice, and offer to take me out in it.

—Blaine Bardarson

The cannery laborers worked hard, and they played even harder, especially when it came to the Fourth of July. I, of course, filmed and photographed everything, except when I was a participant in the hijinks. Then I'd hand my 8-mm movie camera over to someone I trusted.

We did some prep work ahead of time. For instance, someone went around and collected coins to use for game prizes, and I put up posters all over the cannery ahead of the great day advertising a five-lap speedboat race at 1:30 on the Fourth designed to draw a crowd. There were three boats participating: a powerful craft with a small cabin, a 40-hp tiller-handle vessel, and Linné in a boat he'd bought for $100 that had blown up and burned.

The fire pretty much gutted the boat, even burning out the ribs, and there wasn't much left of it. It had even melted the hoses. It did still have an outdrive on it though and Linné got it running again. But there was no way to steer it.

So Linné rigged a system whereby the boat was steered by someone pulling on two ropes while facing aft as the port engineer handled the throttle.

Linné and his team practiced for days. Linné sat in the bow and verbally steered the boat. He was captain but with no controls. The guy who actually steered the boat faced aft, pulling on the ropes. He couldn't see what was going on. Linné shouted orders to him over the sound of the engine as the boat careened across the bay, carving the water aside when they practiced turns around a buoy. When Linné yelled "Go to the right" the man operating the ropes had to steer left. Linné also directed the throttle man controlling the speed of the boat.

Finally, the 4th of July arrived and the much anticipated race was announced. Boots and shoes and bare feet hurried across the weather-warped boards of the dock as people of all ages and sizes lined the bull rail where they had an unobscured view of the entire bay. They were dressed in rolled up jeans and flannel shirts over white Tees, the men wearing halibut hats and the ladies with bandanas over their big curlers, and the occasional fashionable young woman adorned with a beehive hairdo. A warm breeze under scudding clouds carried the scent of motor oil, fish, seaweed and sun-heated clover and beach grass.

One and all knew that this would be a spectacle the likes of which they'd never seen. Of the three craft, bets leaned toward the red and white boat that was fully endowed with not only a cabin but an actual functioning steering wheel.

However, Linné's boat was much faster than the other boats. They whipped around the first three orange buoys, and then again during the second lap. Linné was in his element—in his twenties he'd liked to imagine himself as a race-car driver. On the third lap they hit a wave that threw everyone to the bottom of the boat and by the time they got back to their places, the other boats had caught up and passed them.

With just two buoys to go, now it was a race! When Linné came around the final corner, there was only about 20 feet between the racing boats and the dock lined with cheering spectators.

Captain Linné shouted: "Full throttle," and called out orders to the ropesman, taking the inside route between the final marker and the competition at their side, barely slipping by the last buoy, and hardly avoiding a catastrophic collision which would surely have sent both boats to the bottom of Sitkoh Bay.

Linné won by a nose.

**Boat race on Fourth of July.
Linné won by a nose.**

The astonished audience couldn't believe what they had just seen, and they yelled and laughed and cheered. And promptly exchanged dollar bills from the bets they'd made.

Blaine was perhaps the most excited person in the crowd. For the rest of that summer the one thing he wanted more than anything else was a ride in that winning boat. So every day, of his own initiative, he bailed out the speedboat (as it would otherwise have sunk from its burn wounds) hoping his father would notice and offer to take him out in it.

Unfortunately, Linné never did and sold the boat for a hundred dollars.

Meanwhile, up on the dock post-race, we had things organized for various contests and we started with the little children, alternating with adults. The weather vacillated between brilliant sunshine and dark squalls. Winners in each race won blue ribbons (made of stick-um sail cloth) and a dollar. A red ribbon and 75 cents was awarded for second place, and a green ribbon and 50 cents for third.

Before the Fourth of July, I'd assigned Bill Anderson the job of making the shaving cream roulette game, a task which he attacked with glee. He attached 5 cans (one empty, four full) to a wheel to be spun.

The night before the 4th, I heard a commotion on the boardwalk just below our house. A group of men (including the office crew) got into a shaving cream fight, a spinoff of the testing process. Evidence of shaving cream extended from the office to the Filipino house.

The shaving cream roulette was reserved for the children. "Step up, step right up," Bill urged them on the day. "Put your face right up here next to the nozzle. Take a chance! One can is empty, four are filled."

Watchers leaned in close to see who got whip creamed next.

The kids lined up to stand bravely in front of the wheel and put their little faces close, bracing themselves as Bill spun the cans and hit the discharge. It was a risk they wanted to take.

Out flew a blob of cream onto their noses and they squealed in delight.

Most, including Dori who I captured on film getting her nose dabbed, accepted what came forth, almost always the shaving cream. But one little Native seven-year-old girl took her squirtings and threw them back at Bill, which unleashed a free-for-all.

For the adults we had a nail-driving contest that involved a huge fir timber with 16-penny nails, practically impossible to drive into the hard wood without bending.

Driving 16 penny nails is hard.

The women were first. Only two succeeded in sinking their nails. The men had such a good time that we ran the contest twice, the second time with galvanized nails which would bend more easily. (The galvanizing process that comprised dipping nails in boiling zinc—to prevent rust—took some of the temper out of the nails, which had the side effect of making them less hard.)

The boat race wasn't the only race that day.

There was the gunny sack race, suitcase race, three-legged race (that Linné and I practiced well in advance—the photo of us practicing is almost comical due to the difference in our heights), egg-in-spoon race, potato-on-the-head race, and more.

Dot and Linné practice for the 3-Legged race.

Perhaps the one that caused the most merriment in the onlookers was the suitcase race—especially the one between Linné and Mary Willis (another time it was Martha Kitka, the canning forelady, against the head bookkeeper). Each one had to run with the suitcase to a chalk mark on the dock which was lined with spectators to watch them open their suitcases.

Linné's suitcase had women's clothes. Mary's had men's clothes. Men, in particular, had the hardest time figuring out what the clothes were and how to put them on (One year I brought in my suitcase a corset that I'd picked up at the Goodwill in Seattle. It had garters hanging down. It had hooks and eyes to secure it, once wrapped around the waist. A man-befuddling garment if ever there was one.).

The clock was ticking.

Each had to run with his or her suitcase and put on all the clothes in it and return, take them off, and finish by closing the case. That first Fourth of July, Mary's suitcase had a pair of men's trousers and a white terrycloth bathrobe. Linné's contained a ruffled, very feminine nightgown, a necklace, and a bonnet for putting over curlers, but he thought, using his famous "reason and deduct" skills, was a pair of underpants and he couldn't find the holes. There was much shouted hilarious advice and helpless laughter.

In a future race, it was ridiculous to see a man in the Goodwill corset running with garters swinging to and fro as he raced back to the starting line to remove everything and put it all back in the suitcase. Each year I'd think of some new diabolical thing to add to befuddle the men.

The men's and women's footrace around the cannery was about a quarter mile long, with obstacles. I entered the women's race and was gaining on the two leaders who were running out of steam. Success seemed achievable to me, but they spread their arms out to keep me from passing on the last leg in a narrow corridor.

So I came in third, I reported to my parents. As I told them, I learned from the 4th of July that friendly cheating was not only expected at a community shindig but a big part of the fun.

For example, the relay race balancing the potato on our heads turned out to be a straight-up cheating match! The men just couldn't keep it from falling off, so Paul Kowalski broke his spud in half and ran his leg of the race with the flat parts on his head. While he was returning, Mary Willis bit a hole in the bottom of hers so it would stay on better, so Paul deliberately jostled her, but in so doing both lost their potatoes and had to start over.

It was claimed that I was the biggest cheater in this race simply because my thick, curly hair provided a perfect nest for the potato, and it remained in place to the end.

The pie-eating contest used pies donated by Elizabeth and was as much fun for the participants as the onlookers. But I think the "Pass the orange under the chin" took the honors. There were men's and women's teams. Each was given an orange which had to be passed without the use of hands. You can't imagine the positions people got into as the orange slipped down the chest, even to the knees, while the next person in line tried to grab it under his chin. Most of our office crew were in on this including the storekeeper Bill Anderson and Paul Kowalski.

Several of the men were growing beards which complicated the maneuver.

There was an egg-in-the-spoon race in which eggs went splattering to the dock en route to the finish, the three-legged race, and a potato sack race where the men literally threw themselves across the finish line in an effort to be first.

Potato on
the Head race.

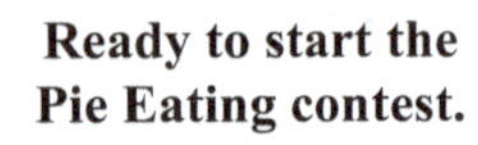

Ready to start the
Pie Eating contest.

Pass the
Orange Under
the Chin race.

The Egg in Spoon race.

Best of all was the tug of war, one of the last games played. One man handled the fire hose, dousing the centerline of the hefty hawser, marked by a red scarf. It was the men against the women, which hardly seemed like a fair fight. I was captain of the team. It was nip and tuck at first, and then it looked like a losing battle as I began to be pulled toward the gush of water. But just within two inches of being drenched, I felt strength on our side and slowly the men began to lose ground, and I would take up the slack forcing the men through the stream.

Tug of War in the warehouse.

About 12 men got drenched before they realized that the women were walloping the men repeatedly. This was mighty suspicious until it was revealed that Mary Willis was tying our side of the rope off to a dock bollard every time we got some slack, making it impossible for the men to regain any lost ground.

Who said cheaters never prosper? They obviously never attended the 4th of July at a remote Alaskan cannery!

Then there was the volleyball game in front of the Filipino House. (I had asked the Filipinos to rig up a net made out of fish net.) Everyone was invited to watch. I don't know how it got started, but two fire hoses were spraying on the boardwalk in a retaliatory splash down between the men and women. Whoever escaped in the tug of war was soon caught in the water fight including the poor volleyball players.

Dori selling balloons on 4th of July.

Meanwhile, Dori sold balloons from a booth we had made from an enormous and sturdy washing machine box which she decorated with signs and balloons. She took in $6.50 and was allowed to keep a quarter. I had asked Mike Standard to have Dean Goodwin fly out some balloons. "Oh, about 500 penny ones would be fine," I'd said casually. The order was misinterpreted as so often happens when ordering remotely. When the balloons arrived, there were seven gross with an accompanying bill for $47.50. They were beautiful balloons with monsters on them, but you can imagine our horror. We were able to send five gross back.

Perhaps the highlight of the day was the 4th of July Parade. Folks dressed as local Chatham characters and took up their positions. The children loved it and fully participated. Blaine went as the storekeeper Bill Anderson complete with beard and a handcart for hauling merchandise.

Start of the 4th of July Parade.

Dori and Rolf teamed up to be "the Chatham Bear." I'd helped them create the costume using burlap bags for their legs, a large, brown-painted box for the body and a mask made of brown paper. Rolf was in the front and could see, though his vision was hampered by the mask. Dori was inside the box bent over and could not see at all, so had to depend on Rolf as to where they went. All went well until Blaine got impatient with the slow moving Chatham Bear and cut in front. Over the bear went, legs flailing in the air.

Much to my pride, however, they managed to right the ship—or bear—and finished the parade in style, which earned them the grand prize of five dollars. (Which, according to Dori, they redeemed at the store for candy, something I was not aware of at the time.)

The Chatham Bear in the parade.

While we much preferred, of course, the sunny days when we could have all of our fun and games outside, and work the barbecue and eat a la fresco, we sometimes had to have our fun indoors on rain-misty days thanks to Southeast Alaska's damp climate.

Imagine our dismay when one year on the 4th of July we woke up to rain—not just drizzle, but rain big enough to raise welts on unprotected skin. We didn't cancel. We could never have done that. Instead, we moved into the warehouse where our laughter and competitive voices rang out in the spacious room and reverberated against the wooden walls, ceiling, and floors.

Girl's race in the warehouse.

Boy's race in the warehouse.

My flash didn't work well inside, so I didn't take many photos, but I was able to grab a few action shots of the fun, though they weren't the best and had a red tinge. Back then we had to buy flash bulbs, insert one for each photo into a sort of rounded shield attached to the camera. It was unwieldy to say the least, and it took extra time for each photo to make the adjustments for focus and exposure. The photographer had to be quick to catch an action shot, and there was nothing quick about handling flash bulbs...and they cost money on top of film and developing. That's why there were so few indoor photos.

That first year that we had the barbecue, though, we had glorious weather and we gathered around it promptly at five. We asked everyone in the village to contribute something from a food list. Elizabeth had made a macaroni salad and all kinds of goodies. I had put together a huge potato salad, enough to feed a hundred. Roberta made cakes. The Filipino contingent was in charge of cooking the salmon that Linné contributed from the cannery and added Chop Suey and roast pork. Mrs. Jack (a Native elder) contributed three cases of soda pop and a halibut in celebration of the 40-day party for her nephew. (A party given 40 days after the death of an important person.)

The barbecue worked fine except for the can-cooler grill which didn't work at all. We had to make a mad dash to the mess hall to borrow its oven racks to make a quick substitution.

People were shaking their heads over their dinners in amazement. They'd never imagined they would ever see a barbecue picnic at Chatham.

The barbeque.

Dishing up.

Barbecue picnic
table.

Barbecue picnic
- find a seat.

Following the barbecue, which everyone agreed was a smashing success, was a movie in the white mess, and later on, a Filipino dance. The dance itself seemed pretty dull in comparison to others I'd attended, but our usual invitation into the galley for a "nip" was hilarious. Mary Willis was there confessing all her methods for "winning" and we just had the best time recounting the day's festivities.

The 4th of July celebration every year, whether it was inside or out, was everything we hoped for and more. I have never laughed so hard over such a long period of time as we did on the dock during the races.

CHAPTER 21

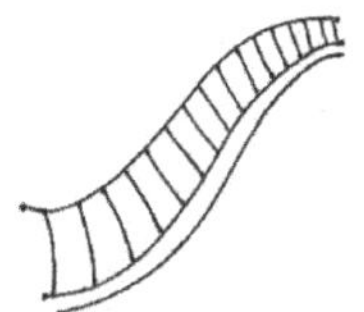

Emergencies: From Birth to Murder

No way!

—Pilot who was called in to Chatham
to fly out a pregnant woman
who was about to give birth.

Letter to my parents
July 19, 1965

Probably my most memorable letter to my parents was written during my fourth year at the cannery. Here it is in full:

> This morning I reached the pinnacle in Chatham adventures when I was asked to escort a woman in labor to Juneau via a Cessna 180 "in case she needed help." I wanted to go to Juneau anyway to look over photos the Air Service [or, rather, pilot Dean Goodwin] that was commissioning Christmas cards from me.
>
> Her contractions were at 3 minute intervals.
>
> So I grabbed a few items in a flight bag—a couple of pieces of string, a clean bath towel, a pair of scissors, and of course, my camera. The children were involved in Bible class provided by the floating mission for most of the day, so I singled out each child and told them Dori was in charge and they were to stay around the office between classes to be near Daddy while Mommy was away.

Impatiently I waited at the airplane float. But women kept coming to the float to give me a progress report. It appeared that the contractions were now 30 seconds apart and there was doubt that Genevieve would be making the trip. The women were excited, clucking like chickens and running back and forth. So naturally I had to investigate the situation.

From the busy little shack, I could hear the plane landing. A blanket had been strung across the tiny bedroom to act as a divider between the activity and the mother's 3 very small children who were sitting on a metal double bunk. A porcelain dish pan of gently boiling water was on the coal stove, sterilizing a pair of scissors. One gal seemed to be in charge, a nurse, someone said. She turned to send somebody for some string so I fished around in my flight bag and pulled out the 2 carefully prepared pieces of twine which we dropped into the boiling water.

Just about then, pilot (Dean Goodwin) was coming up the boardwalk wanting some answers. Was she coming and if so, let's go. No, he wouldn't wait around for her to have her baby and then take her to Juneau—she probably wasn't going to have the baby for 3 days anyway…Stand-by charge is $45 an hour, etc., etc.

By this time Linne had come on the scene and was wringing his hands and pacing the boardwalk, chatting nervously with Dean and moaning, "Oh my God, I can't stand it." I ran back to the little dry shack just in time to see the little baby boy emerge.

Everything really seemed quite simple. The baby simply arrived, quietly…too quietly I thought, and worried while this blue thing just lay there doing nothing. Amy Walker picked him up by his feet in the classic manner and rapped him gently on the bopo and it seemed like a long time before his ribs began to move. But they did, and sure enough he began to cry. They tied the string about 2 inches from the baby's belly and then again about a foot from that, then, Snip! went the scissors between the two knots.

I produced a fluffy white towel from my trusty satchel, wrapped him in it and gave him to his mother, clucking like all the rest. The only sounds in that tiny room were the ooohs and ahhhs of admiring Native mothers and my sniffing the tears back.

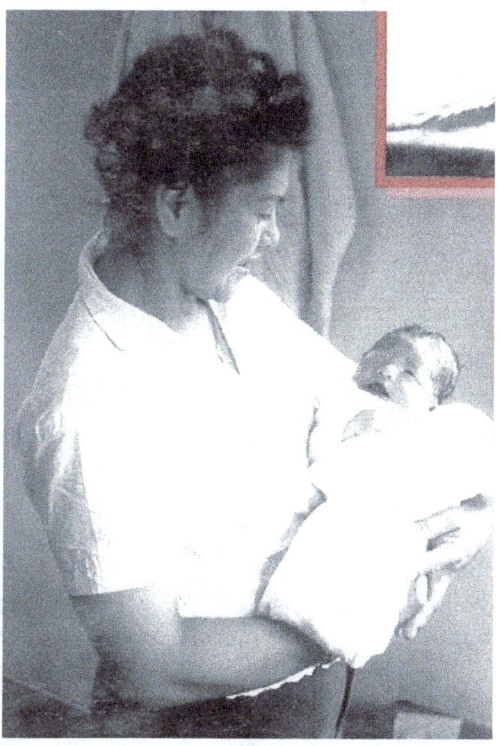

**Bessie holds Ricardo Linné
while the mother rests.**

The mother was tired so only held her baby briefly, then handed him back to me. I stepped on a bathroom scale which had been located for the occasion, and figured the baby weighed 7 pounds and I had gained 3. Already his coloring was changing to a lovely pink. He was perfect in every respect. The mother responded to massaging and the afterbirth followed normally.

During all the excitement Linne asked me if I still wanted to go to Juneau. "Of course not," was my answer as we continued to cluck away.

Someone ran to the store to buy a box of cotton balls. Another ran to her house to pick up some Wesson Oil (Chatham style baby oil). I was appalled at the skimpy stack of thin, old dish towels that had been gathered to receive the baby and the dirty mattress cover on the mother's bed. There was just a dab of water on the stove now. Everyone washed with cold water. After struggling with the cotton balls which just slid around on the baby's skin and accomplished little, I sent 2 girls to my house to bring back 3 freshly laundered, fluffy bath towels. These worked slick. In no time the vernex was scrubbed off. The baby was clean.

Discussion followed as to what WE should name the baby (It never occurred to anyone apparently that the baby's mother might have an opinion.). I took several pictures of the baby. Then Dori arrived from Bible school. Imagine her thrill at seeing this brand-new baby, by this time, clean and adorable.

The natives decided the mother and baby were fine despite a small tear in the peritoneum, and that they would not go to Juneau after all. The other children were hustled off to other quarters.

Dori Meets Ricardo Linné Willis.

After lunch I prepared a casserole dish for the family, the cook made an angel food cake, and the carpenter made a cradle from an empty nail keg. I have just finished making a mattress and coverlet from our scrubbed dining room drapes (very fancy). Of course now the dining room doesn't have drapes, but then, if Scarlett O'Hara could do it, so can I.

And so another normal day at Chatham draws to a close, and another page in the annals of Chatham lore.

Love,

Florence Nightingale

P.S. *The mother named her baby Ricardo Linne* [complete with the accent, which my typewriter still continued to balk at] *Willis*.

***

There were other emergencies over the years at Chatham. Including bear-related ones. Like the time I heard a sound on the back porch, a place I seldom went. It was where I kept the garbage. Our first days back a bear had gotten in it, so I'd kept the garbage inside for half the season until the bear gave up… I thought.

When I heard the noise on the back porch, I suspected the bear had come back. I went into cat burglar mode, approaching the back door all bent over so the bear (if it was a bear) wouldn't see me through the window in the door.

I slowly raised my head to peer out, hoping to catch a glimpse of the intruder.

My eyes met the eyes of a grizzly approximately six inches from my face. If the window hadn't been there, we would have exchanged breaths. His ears were *huge*.

Cardiac arrest felt imminent.

The door with the window in it was suddenly incredibly flimsy as it stood between my body and the massive predator on the other side of it. If he just bumped it with his head he would be inside, in my lap.

As my eyes held the bear's my thoughts raced.

Where were the kids? I knew they were playing outside. Were they near the back porch? If they weren't, what if the bear moved around to where they were? Should I get them inside first, or get to the radio and get someone with a gun on their way up here? Even if I got the kids inside, the bear could break in and I had no way of stopping it.

One thing I knew beyond question: I wanted Linné present, preferably with a gun, *right now*!

I ducked down like an infantry man in a trench and headed as quietly as I could to the living room to call Linné on the radio. My ears tingled, listening for the bear's actions on the porch.

I keyed the mic, speaking as quietly but insistently as possible. "Are you there, Linné? It's Dot."

What if he wasn't in the office?

He came back, his tone preoccupied, "I'm really swamped down here, can we talk later?"

"No!" I whisper-shouted. "There's a b-b-b-bear!"

"Where?" Linné demanded, immediately on alert.

"On the back porch. And the kids are outside playing."

"I'll be right up."

He probably flew up those 79 steps taking two or three at a time with his long legs after grabbing the cannery rifle, but it felt like a year to me.

I had to wonder if I went to the front door and called the kids, if the bear would hear and come around. If I did nothing maybe the bear would stay where it was. Or would he break in? Should I go outside and take the kids down the steps? I had too many choices and none of them felt good.

Fortunately, Linné got there quickly, out of breath and ushering the kids inside under armed escort. I pointed to the kitchen. "Back door."

Linné gingerly let himself out onto the now empty back porch. He could see the silhouette of Mr. Bear between some spruce trees, standing, ears forward, as if aware of the human predator behind him.

The kids and I watched wide-eyed as Linné flung the rifle up to his shoulder and pulled the trigger. The shot deafened us.

"Did you get him Daddy; did you get him?" the kids shrieked.

Linné muttered something that didn't sound particularly victorious.

The bear had shifted his weight just as Linné's rifle shattered the peaceful afternoon quiet of the forest.

An expletive burst out of Linné. "I missed." He'd always been proud of his marksmanship, and now he knew the story would make its way into the mess hall and all over the cannery. He swore aloud.

The big brownie disappeared into the woods. It didn't make me—or the kids—feel safe to know he was still out there.

Linné may not have shot his bear, but somebody else shot one. So I had to get the children out of bed to go see it. By the time we got there, it was 9 p.m., and its nose had already been cut off, and a man was admiring its teeth in its hands. Ugh! The kids loved it.

Fortunately, the bear I'd met never returned to our back porch—maybe he'd been as scared as I was. The entire time I was at Chatham, I never lost my fear of bears.

***

Blaine tells of the time a department head (chief machinist) didn't show up for lunch. Linné said, "Hey, Blaine, are you through eating? How about going to get Marvin? I think he's in the plant, working on the Pelton wheel belt. We had a problem with it this morning. He must be trying to finish up before lunch."

Marvin Remlinger was extremely dedicated to his job of fixing things. I had photographed him multiple times as he worked over machines and consulted with Linné about cannery equipment.

Blaine ran out of the mess hall, down the boardwalk, and into the cannery up to the can loft where Linné had said Marvin would be switching a belt to diesel power.

The belts were hung together with staples. One of the staples had grabbed him, and there was Marvin with his severed arm in his lap.

Blaine's face lost all color, and he ran back to the mess hall, shouting, "Marvin lost his arm." The cook house completely emptied out.

Another time Linné had to remove a halibut hook from a man's thigh. At the time, a Native hand-carved halibut hook was 5 ½ x 11 inches with a 2 ½ inch bone barb. Imagine trying to dig a nearly foot long hook out of someone's leg! Linné poured bourbon into the patient and then poured some on the wound. It took three men to hold the patient down during the operation. Linné used wire cutters to cut off the barb and forced the shaft out with brute force. I cringed as I wrote to my parents about it, envisioning the man's pain.

Removing halibut hooks from men was not part of Linné's job description, but he took it in his stride as he did all things. He seemed, unlike me, to actually enjoy a crisis and be at his best during one.

I wrote to my parents about another emergency: *Last week the bakery oven in the mess hall exploded as Elizabeth lit it (gas). She was not burned deeply except on her wrist, but burns covered a large area, her arms and face, and singed her hair. She was flown to the hospital, but returned that same night and has been working ever since. About 5 of us got the evening meal served that night.*

***

And then there was the murder.

We were entertaining Jay Gage (General superintendent of New

England Fish Co.) in the mess hall sitting around chatting over coffee after dinner. Chatham, for whatever reason—perhaps because of how isolated it was—had never been Jay's favorite NEFCO property to visit. Linné, aware of this, always wanted everything to go as smoothly as possible while the VIP was there.

"Everything is going well," Linné had just reassured Jay.

Along came, Buddy Elession the Filipino head honcho.

The Filipinos never came to the white mess hall, so immediately Linné knew something was up and his stomach sank.

"Mr. Bardarson, you'd better come."

Linné shot an apologetic glance at Jay and quickly left with the anxious worker.

As Maxine Fred, one of the young Native workers at Chatham, would later tell me, from what she saw at the cannery, the Filipino workers simply didn't seem to care about dying. They were always fighting and showed no fear of death, especially the older men. (To be fair, there were a lot of rumors about the Filipino contingent. One of her girlfriends had a Filipino boyfriend and the word on the boardwalk was, according to Maxine, that he could be preparing to sell her. Which never happened, but it seemed possible at the time to her friends and relatives.)

Linné would have known of their penchant for fighting, so it must have been at the forefront of his mind as he followed the agitated worker down the boardwalk.

They reached the Filipino mess hall. Linné stepped into the galley and saw workers with scrub brushes and mops and a bucket full of pale red water. They were

Happy - A Filipino cook.

scrubbing blood off the floor.

"Who got hurt?" Linné looked around at the men in front of him.

There was a jumble of replies all at once, but Linné managed to get the truth out of them. It was the cook's blood on the floor, but he wasn't "hurt."

He was dead.

With a bullet hole in him.

Not Happy! Linné thought. Happy was one of the Filipino cooks and he radiated kindness itself. He loved children and was always smiling or breaking up a fight. He was one of two cooks who brought glazed doughnuts to the cannery for break time. The cannery would be a worse place without his bright presence. (Maxine said she and her friends grew up with Happy and he seemed to be from a different world with how "happy" he always was. "He was always glad to share something from the kitchen," she remembered.)

They'd already moved the body, which Linné asked to see.

It was indeed the cook, but it wasn't Happy. It was the head cook and he had been fatally shot. It didn't take much sleuthing on Linné's part to figure out what had happened.

Although he had confiscated as much of the alcohol being smuggled in as possible, some of it slipped through. Both the cook and a worker had indulged heavily. The worker decided he was going wash his hands in the galley sink, something the cook never allowed (understandably, I thought— he didn't want his galley, where he prepared food, being contaminated by people coming in to wash their dirty hands).

According to Maxine Fred: "The Filipinos were very clean people, but they didn't have hot water in their bunk house. The only hot water was in the kitchen, but the cook wouldn't let anyone wash their hands there." It was an ongoing bone of contention between the workers and the cook.

The altercation rapidly escalated until the worker stormed off.

He returned minutes later with a gun and shot the cook dead.

Linné confiscated the weapon and locked the perpetrator in a room.

Mathew Fred and some of his buddies searched every room and took away all the weapons in the entire bunk house. Mathew was the best person to take charge of this delicate job because of the Filipinos' high regard for him—they called him "brother-in-law." (He was the one who helped them coordinate their all-important dances in the mess hall. In addition, Mathew was highly respected as a musician, playing any number of instruments.)

Linné called the nearest sheriff who arrived via floatplane in a couple of hours with a body bag. All of this, of course, happened during Jay Gage's visit to find out how well Linné was handling the cannery.

What could Linné say? To be fair, it was the only time during his tenure that anyone left Chatham escorted by a law officer in or out of a body bag.

That cut no ice with the General Superintendent of NEFCO.

"Going well," muttered Jay, shaking his head. "I'm out of here."

CHAPTER 22

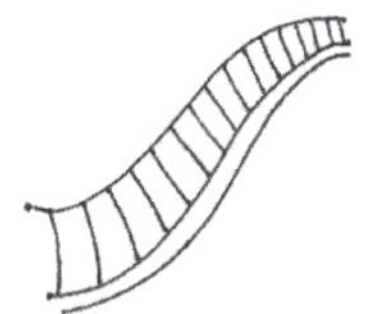

My Two Loves (Family and Painting)

My two great loves have
always been family and art.

—Dot

Smokey and Elizabeth came and watched a bit while I painted my first Chatham painting, which was the one of the big warehouses on the main dock. After they saw how it turned out, they wanted a watercolor for themselves.

My vantage point had all the right requirements.

The view they wanted me to capture was of the scene they saw from the Mess Hall deck when they took a break from cooking. They had a couple of chairs out there for themselves.

283

The scene was of the "ways" where the boats could haul out for repair to their bottoms. Behind the ways was the part of the cannery that was reserved for storage. I don't remember any machinery in that part of the building. So that building was in the background of the painting. The carpenter shop was on the left and there was a little white generator building at the back.

I was beyond thrilled to have an actual commission. It was validating as an artist to know that someone valued my painting enough to spend their hard earned money on it.

To get the correct vantage of the commissioned painting, I sat on the little deck just outside the mess hall's galley. The deck wasn't very wide, just wide enough for me to fit in a chair and lean my plywood against the railing. Behind me, as part of the galley, were boxes of goods, tubs, etc. with the beautiful wood and glass door and windows behind them.

"Chatham Ways" - Commissioned by Smokie Hansen.

Smokey and Elizabeth brought me anything else I needed, like paper towels or water, a snack (if I even remembered to eat it) and showed up occasionally to watch the progress. They were so excited.

My art prospered in Chatham and that first commission gave me a tremendous amount of confidence.

***

My family life began less auspiciously than my art life. When I first married Linné, I didn't realize just how relentless the fish industry was. I almost didn't get my husband-to-be from its grasp in time for the wedding (a story for another time), and afterwards I was drawn into the industry myself. Little did I know then how many times it would pull him away from me, and how my little family and I would always follow.

Here are excerpts from some of the letters he wrote to me while he was on his own at Chatham in the years before we joined him. (The letters, in full, can be found at the end of the book.) Linné had been promoted to assistant superintendent by this time:

June 21, 1960

Dear Dot,

What a true bastard I really am. I have a horrible guilt complex. You are undoubtedly the most understanding wife in the world, and the sexiest and the most loveable. How is that for throwing in the hat.

The weather has been absolutely miserable. I have not seen the sun since I left Seattle. The first thing I saw was the Annette Island Airport at 1,000 ft. Thank God these planes have radar.

What have I been doing? You name it, I'm doing it. Everything from writing letters to fishermen to building brailers for the tenders. Most of my time goes into taking care of the fishermen and learning the operation methods of this cannery…The Bering got here last night and as I went into the stateroom to pick up my stuff I thought to myself, "By Golly, I hope Dot didn't forget the candy!" You see what you have done to me. A bloody addict…I have gained 24 pounds. I now weigh 204 pounds of throbbing muscle. What do you think of that? You had better watch out when I get back…

I have a radio schedule now at 6:00 P.M. so that's it. I miss you very much sweetheart. Send me some pictures if you have any.

***

July 9, 1961

My darling wife,

Busy, busy, busy. The season is exactly opposite from that of last year. Fish all over in our area. Last week we got just about all the fish we could handle. We canned fish until 1:00 a.m. every night. This week every seine boat in Southeast Alaska will be in our area. I'm worried, the Neptune was four hours out of Chatham tonight and Ketchikan called her back. She was going to pick me up at 2:00 a.m. this morning and help us out in this area. I don't know why they called her back but I'm so mad I can't see straight. It seems that I've been going constantly since I arrived. Tomorrow morning early I will start out early in my instrument of torture (17' Glasspar with 80 hp Mercury) for the fishing grounds 90 miles distant. The other night while charging through a black raining night at 2:30 a.m. soaking wet, spray flying all over the place, I thought to myself what the hell am I doing here? The finest family in the world on the San Juan Islands and here I am. What a business.

Today we have a five year old girl. How I wish I could be there to celebrate with you all. Good times, happy times, times to remember. How lucky I am to have someone like you at the controls while I'm gone. I'm in love with my wife. She is the finest thing I have ever known.

I'm having some moccasins made for Dori. It will take a little while. I hope she doesn't think her daddy has forgotten her. I enjoy the pictures you send in your letters, that one of Rolf asleep by the phone is excellent.

The watchman is about ready to turn out the lights so its goodnight sweetheart, I wish it were with you.

All my love,

Linne

Besides Linné's mentioning of the usual family concerns and his homesickness for us, he always kept me fully involved in the business that fed us and did not talk down or soft peddle anything. It had always been his way from the start, and I appreciated that.

It allowed me, after my first lonely season at Chatham, to fully immerse myself in and embrace the challenge of the fish-oriented world of the cannery. I felt empowered to plunge in wherever I saw a need, whether it was at the store, the Egg House, helping build a community barbecue, taking a leading part in arranging the 4th of July games, and even pranks that helped build our sense of camaraderie.

Keeping an eye on my children, however, was an altogether different challenge at Chatham as they got older and expanded their investigative territories and tested their independence.

Dori running away from home.

Once, Dori decided that she'd had enough of my parenting and was going to set out on her own. She packed her suitcase, clapped a straw hat on her head, tucked her doll under her arm, and headed for the boardwalk — barefoot. Blaine (likewise unshod), intrigued by this rebellion, packed a gunny sack with odds and ends and accompanied her all the way to the airplane float.

Finding nothing that could transport her to a new, independent life, she, with Blaine still in attendance, retraced her footsteps and decided home wasn't such a bad place after all.

Another time, I misplaced my youngest child.

As soon as a boat tied up, all the kids would clamber aboard to "help" One time Rolf got left aboard when a landing craft backed away from the beach.

When the crew found him, they turned him over to the captain who radioed the Chatham office that they had the superintendent's kid, and would somebody motor out to take him back to the cannery? So Linné jumped into the skiff, fired up the outboard, and ran out only to find Rolf happily eating breakfast aboard the scow and in no hurry to depart.

The kids missed not eating family style so enjoyed the experience of a home cooked meal at the house from time to time. Dori was always a willing helper. (Rolf would "generously" offer to wash the dishes at 8:30 pm…right at bedtime. Pretty clever, I thought.) After dinner, we'd play one of Dori's birthday gifts: Bingo. It helped Blaine learn his numbers better.

Rolf wanted to play on the beach since there were no dead fish like our first year. I didn't like the looks of the beach, so I set out with some boxes to pick up glass and trash. My three kids were enthusiastic and did their best to do more than their share of filling the boxes and in no time there were about ten Native children help-ing. Pretty soon word got around and Berry,

Rolf hauls trash with a hand truck.

John and Fay pitched in. With their help the beach started to improve rapidly, and we enjoyed a huge bonfire.

***

Linné took advantage of his free time to spend time with his family, taking us on annual expeditions to inspect the dam.

The dam at Chatham had been created upstream on the river so water could back up behind the dam to create a reservoir. The meandering hike paralleled the river until we reached a bunch of big, felled logs that had been strategically wedged between its banks. It certainly wasn't very sophisticated but did the job.

Hiking to the dam.

After a particularly rainy summer, it was even more imperative to inspect it and make any repairs. It would be devastating to have the dam give way under the enormous pressure from the lake since the cannery's entire operation was dependent upon this water supply.

On the other hand, a rainy season, besides helping the fish up the stream to spawn for future generations of canning stock, gave us good flow through the penstocks (10-inch wooden pipe wrapped with wire) which also had to be monitored.

Resting at the penstock.

A spillway at the dam was built to accommodate a surplus of water, helping to regulate how much we were getting at the Pelton wheel which created electricity for the plant.

Linné carried a rifle in case we ran into an aggressive bear. The cannery boardwalk branched off on a tangent up to the dam. It was quite steep in parts to navigate the elevation needed for the penstock conduit carrying the water.

Eventually, we arrived at the dam built of sturdy logs. "I'm going to go on up to check the lake," Linné said over the sound of the water. "Anyone want to come with me?"

Blaine immediately scrambled up to stand with his dad, but Dori and I hung back, and I kept a grip on Rolf when he tried to follow. The route up to the lake did not have the benefit of a walkway and was far too precarious and slippery for him.

So while Linné and Blaine checked out the lake, checking its water level and making sure beavers hadn't clogged up any important arteries or diverted water from the reservoir with their

Examining the reservoir.

own beaver dams, Dori, Rolf, and I rolled up our pant legs and dipped our toes into the cold water below the dam and cooled off from the hike.

I hoped no bear showed up in Linné's absence, since he had taken the gun with him, of course. Fortunately, we never did bump into one at the dam.

Amma made it all the way up to the dam.

When Linné's mother came to visit, Linné talked her into making the trek up to the dam. I wondered how she would navigate the uneven path when she had so much difficulty climbing the stairs. But Gertrude was always a mystery to me. Her "Viking son," as she called Linné, could talk her into anything and she never wanted to be left behind.

Wading in the cold water at the dam.

Hiking up to the dam in Chatham was much less of an arduous affair than some of the adventures he'd plunged her into. In fact, trekking to the dam was always a great adventure for our entire family, one we always looked forward to every year.

But we weren't the only ones who enjoyed the dam. Kitty Young, one of our best young workers who carried off with panache a fashionable beehive with her flannel shirt and rolled up jeans, remembers that one of the things she and her fellow young women workers thought fun to do was to hike up to the reservoir.

"A bunch of us gals, when we had a break, walked upstream on a trail to the dam that was fed by a man-made lake. It was a treat to jump in for a swim. Some guys thought we were skinny dipping, so they sneaked up on us to take a look. They were disappointed. We were wearing bathing suits."

When Linné got wind of it he took them aside and told them that they couldn't do that anymore.

"Why not?" Kitty asked.

"Because," he explained, "you're swimming in the cannery drinking water."

Don Hansen, the son of cooks Smokey and Elizabeth Hansen, who care-took the cannery in the winter, remembers that his parents had the work of "shoveling the walkway to the dam after a heavy snowfall. If you recall," he later told me: "the walkway was sturdy but not built to hold six feet of wet snow. So, usually every winter, Mom and Dad would start at the end of the Village and shovel their way to the dam. I know things always look bigger when you're small, but I walked that as an adult and that was a lot of territory to shovel. No power tools at the cannery."

Somehow the dam lasted all the years the cannery was in operation.

***

Another episode that sticks out in my mind was when Linné had an hour to spare and he gathered us up for a boat ride to the other side of the bay where a Chinese worker from the earliest times of the cannery's presence was buried, and where there was a real sand beach (rare in Southeast Alaska).

It was just four of us, Linné, me, Dori and Blaine. Rolf couldn't go. He'd been caught putting a broom handle in the compressor at the mess hall to enjoy the irresistible rat-a-tat sound that the fan made when interrupted by the stick. Elizabeth said she'd take care of him. He had a wonderful time being the center of her attention.

Meanwhile, the shoreline we landed on was festooned with large, bleached logs that were stacked like dinosaur bones under the skirts of the forest where beach grass, beach peas, and clover divided the dead trees from the living ones.

A jaunt with Dad.

At the beach we waded out into the cold water but didn't go swimming.

We gathered driftwood and rocks to take back to make candle holders and other art forms. No matter where we went to live, I would gather found objects to decorate our home. We also made our own candles by melting old ones. I had bought wicks in anticipation of this activity.

Sometimes the found art forms were enough without candles. They could be add-ons to native flower arrangements or arranged as a centerpiece at the dining table (where we seldom dined). I had a compulsion to improve the interiors with what I could find, wherever we were. After all, we arrived with just suitcases. We had to make do with things we found once we got there. It was the artist in me.

I discovered, though, at Chatham that I was not the only one foraging for "parts." Harvey Jacobs (11 or 12 years old) was one of the talented Natives in the village with a right brain. His art form was making boats out of seine floats which he carved to create model seine boats. He then rigged the tiny boats with masts and string rigging. They were accurate to detail and floated nicely as he pulled them along in the water with a pole and fishing line. I bought one from him to take to Seattle.

Blaine fishes while Rolf watches Harvey tow his little seiner.

* * *

It was a gorgeous day, the water like glass, bees droning through the tall beach grass, with the golden sinking sun burnishing the forest and gilt-edging the moment forever. Across from us the red buildings of the cannery stood out from the evergreens climbing the hills behind them and reflected in the water.

Although we didn't know it, we were living a part of Alaskan history that would soon be gone forever.

We were writing the final chapters of a long, productive tenure of remote expensive-to-run canneries in Alaska that were about to shut down and cease operations in the coming decades. They were soon to be replaced by large, modern industrial canneries located strategically on the road system along with big floating processors.

Its time had come. We had been a memorable part of a large network of salmon canneries scattered throughout Southeast Alaska, now part of Alaska history.

How could we know that those buildings adorned with my large sign emblazoned with the words *NEW ENGLAND FISH COMPANY, CHATHAM ALASKA*—an invitation to fishermen, tenders, freighters and a variety of official visiting fishing industry insiders—would soon be consumed by fire?

We were thankful later when someone retrieved from the scorched wreckage the steam whistle that called the workers to their stations. Linné was thrilled to receive it and put it back in use at a later cannery where he was manager. But more on that in the next book.

Chatham's steam whistle installed at Seward Fisheries in 1994.

Chatham taught me so much. How my husband earned our living, how to be a cog in the wheel, how to run a business, how to be a manager, how to do without when there were no stores, how to mix with other cultures. It taught me more about children than I'd ever known: their self-reliance, their adaptability, the ease with which they adjusted to a new environment. They learned how their father made a living and how they would too someday.

All of us would look back on our time at the cannery as some of the best times of our lives. Chatham was a milestone for us. We often would refer to an event as "before Chatham" or "after Chatham." Linné referred to Chatham as his "Camelot." Our children speak of it as if it was a magical place. My memory of it has been stimulated by writing this book, and like with people who have died, it tends to get sunnier and sunnier with time.

Now, I release my part in a dying breed to readers out there who relish the personal touch of a serious business. Fish! I never thought I'd write about it. But I did with all the enthusiasm of a beginning fisherman.

It was a wonderful family outing that day, the kind that is always remembered fondly. Playfully, Linné demonstrated his manly strength by hoisting both children up at once, one on each arm. Although Linné, the love of my life and stalwart companion in adventure for 60 years, is gone now, I will always see him like that: tall and broad shouldered with a Viking smile of triumph.

And of course, I got a great photo.

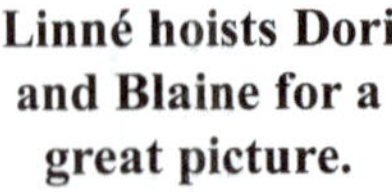

Linné hoists Dori and Blaine for a great picture.

Epilogue

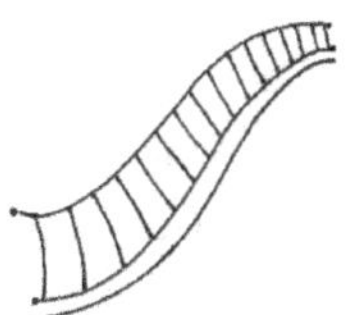

Return to Chatham: 1998

Many [remote] canneries have succumbed to fire, coastal erosion and piecemeal disassembly for prized lumber [and other hard to get materials], salvaged by locals. These relics stand as poor testaments to the vibrant people who once lived and worked in them.

—The Canneries, Cabins and Caches of Bristol Bay, Alaska, by John B. Branson

On our second return to Chatham, we moored the *Bardy* on the remaining dock, an island in itself, now detached from where the cannery used to be. We took the Zodiac to a float, so we could get out and explore the ruins.

The *Bardy* tied up to the old cannery dock.

Rie Munoz made a couple of trips with us on the *Bardy* when we were exploring Southeast Alaska in the late 1990s and was with us when we returned to Chatham the second time.

Rie was about 10 years older than me, a famous Alaskan artist who took every opportunity to explore Alaska, spending much of her time in the Arctic with Eskimos. A lot of her art was about their lives.

She was loved wherever she went. People knew her. Children would run up to her and throw their arms around her. She was constantly sketching in a 5" x 7" journal and used her sketches for future paintings. She was very good at capturing gestures but paid no attention to faces. She had decided early in her career, that if she got roped into portraits of people, she would have to give up spontaneity. She could do a sketch in 30 seconds that captured work, emotion, and movement…really quite amazing.

Rie commented to me that my ink drawings in my 8 x 10 journals were complete in themselves, filling whole pages, capturing an entire scene with colored pencils. They took one to three hours to complete. She used her quick sketches of people in creating a fictitious scene of family or work, mostly Eskimo.

We were a mutual admiration society with different approaches to art. She did not carry her watercolor paints with her. Neither did I. Soft colored pencils were easier to pack. But I didn't discover them until the 1980s, so I didn't use them at Chatham.

Linné and I weren't the first Bardarsons to return to Chatham. When Blaine was visiting his in-laws in Juneau he made a side trip. He chartered a plane to Chatham Cannery to see what was left of it. He took his little girl, Breanna, with him. She was four and a half, a year older than Rolf was on our first summer there.

What struck him the most was how small the usable area was. As a child running up and down the boardwalks, it had seemed like a long way from the white bunk house to the last house in the Native Village. As an adult he figured the distance to be possibly a quarter of a mile.

The big tank that we'd watched the beach gang replace, using ancient Egyptian methods, or so it had seemed to us, was still there when Blaine visited. As a young boy he'd watched the procedure thinking there was no way a big tank like that could be man-handled into position.

Later when describing his visit, he said that he believed he learned so much during those summers at Chatham, so much that it became the basis for what he does today, building warehouses, trucking fish, converting containers for housing at the local cannery in Seward and shipping them all over Alaska.

The big difference in today's world is that he owns his own heavy equipment and builds warehouses. Rolf owns a tool rental business where he rents big machines. Both men got their foundation for businesses at Chatham despite their young age at the time. It all sank in. Both are land barons in Seward with over-the-top projects, and they love their work.

All three of our children say they learned lifelong lessons at Chatham. When they were hanging around the cannery, they sort of grew up in the business, seeing how their father made a living, picking up on the synergy of an operation in motion, how if someone dropped out he'd need to be replaced immediately, or the entire line would shut down until they could figure out how to do without someone. They experienced the camaraderie and saw how workers who came didn't want to leave. They came back year after year.

Dori, my sidekick, wanted to do art like me (I taught her silk screening when she was ten). She wound up making quilts and did some leather tooling, and she sews. She made a really good watercolor when she was 12 when she painted on location with me one day on San Juan Island but didn't pursue it. She sure could have. Instead, she made a name for herself as a world champion dog musher and now a dog trainer along with her husband Daryl Hollingsworth.

Chatham was still in pretty good shape in 1987 when Blaine wandered the boardwalk, except for the disappearance of the cannery buildings from the fire. Nature hadn't yet rotted the underpinnings of the other key structures.

The same could not be said of the cannery during our first trip back in 1996 (the Filipino mess hall we'd explored collapsed in the bay six weeks after our visit, probably during a storm) and definitely not in the summer of 1998 during our second visit.

The steps up to the house were more rotted than ever, and Rie and I had to be extra careful, warning each other of any missing steps or soft spots in what had looked like solid wood. They were covered in moss and decaying leaves from top to bottom, the railing spongy with rot.

Front steps of our house.

Up at the house we found more decay. What a mess the place was. I never could understand why, when we explored old, abandoned structures, the places were always a mess. I would've thought the last surviving person would sort of clean it up as he left.

The rest of the house wasn't much better. It was funny; I had the urge to do some housekeeping but resisted it. It almost seemed to me that it was sacred ground, that I shouldn't "take" anything, or for that fact, even move anything, like I wanted to honor its existence. Why did I hesitate? Was it a shrine? I think, if we hadn't had company with us, I would have taken something or straightened things up. I'll regret pulling back from that for the rest of my life.

The basic furniture in the living room was the same. Only gone were the fireplace that I had so lovingly lit whenever I realized Linné was coming up, and the sink in the master bedroom that I absolutely loved and used. The bathroom no longer sported the old-fashioned tub with feet where the children had taken their bubble baths before going to the mess hall for dinner. The bathroom had been modernized and was now totally lacking the old-fashioned charm we had so loved.

The dining room looking into the living room.

Looking into the living room.

Dot surveys the dining room and remembers.

The children's dorm/play area upstairs had been completely remodeled and was now cordoned off into several rooms. That was a big disappointment to me. That was where I had hoped to find things we'd left behind in 1967, so sure we'd be back in 1968. I couldn't identify anything of our children's.

"This must have been a great place to grow up," Rie said as I described how I'd originally arranged the upstairs. "Not just here, the whole cannery."

"Our kids thank us for letting them grow up here all the time. It's probably just as well I didn't know everything they got up to at the time, though."

"Like?"

"Like one of their favorite games being something called 'Stretch,' when they'd stretch themselves between two barges. Rolf's legs weren't as long as the others and it didn't take much barge movement to find the limit of his 'stretch' so he fell into the water. Dori fished him out."

"Kids." Rie shook her head, smiling.

"They also confess to throwing rocks on the conveyor belt to see which ones would ride all the way into the cannery. Oh, and apparently Blaine and his friends found .22 shells and used pliers to pry open the bullets and spill out the powder. They'd somehow re-stock it, put the bullets through a knothole, and when a Filipino worker walked by, they'd ignite it which would sort of shoot the shell out."

"The little devils."

"Thankfully no one was hurt."

We carefully joined Linné down on the main boardwalk.

Looking up at the superintendent's house with its birds-eye view of the entire area and the workers bustling below, I thought about how everything at the cannery had operated on a sort of "soft segregation" basis.

It struck me how I'd never noticed that privilege at the time either. In fact, to be honest about it, Linné and I had been OK with the arrangement, except that I had felt New England Fish Co. should have fed the Natives since they fed all their other workers. That didn't seem right to me.

Linné explains as he walks past the carpenter shop.

We'd accepted the hierarchies as the way canneries were run back in the 60s, probably because as long as there was an unprejudiced, empathetic person at the helm, it worked. Linné was that person.

Dori has mentioned how as an adult she looked back and realized the unrecognized privilege she and her brothers had as white children of the superintendent. But she's also noted that the hierarchy and class system in the cannery was only able to work as well as it did, during her father's tenure, when respect was shown to all walks of life. As Dori wrote to me after reading this manuscript:

> The slimer respected the fisherman who brought their fish. The patcher admired the slimers for tirelessly and quickly preparing the fish, the retort man esteemed the patcher for not missing a single can. And the superintendent respected all those working for him. From the cook preparing nutritious meals once Marla was gone, down to the family living in the very last cabin of the Native Village. The Japanese were respected for their egg knowledge and the machinist for keeping the cannery running. Never did I feel as though I was better than the Native kids that lived in the village. We respected the kids and tried to emulate them in such things as carving cork boats. But no one could carve a boat like Harvey Jacobs. His boats were masterpieces. Hard work and a good sense of humor were valued above where we were born or what nationality we might fall under. So although we had our different housing designations, we all worked together corporately in our cannery kingdom.

On that second return visit to Chatham, as we went from one decrepit building to the next, I thought about the people who had lived here, who I'd known, and where they'd ended up—at least the ones I knew about. Including the baby whose birth I was present at.

In 1978 I was the featured resident artist at Sitka Fine Arts Camp where selected Alaskan students from all over the state had the opportunity to spend a couple weeks in the summer learning to develop a variety of artistic skills. In my class I met, and sketched, a talented 13-year-old young man named Ricardo Willis.

Sketch of Ricardo Linné Willis.

I asked him, "Would your middle name happen to be Linné?"

He looked at me wide-eyed. How could a stranger possibly know his unusual middle name, and even pronounce it correctly?

"I was there when you were born," I said, and told him the story of his birth in a cabin at Chatham Cannery. I had even done a *plein air* painting of this row of red houses.

Painting of three village cabins.

I think he was embarrassed at that age by the story of his birth, but later, when he was an adult, Linné and I met him again when we stopped in Angoon that year in 2001 when we revisited Chatham. There he was at the top of the boat ramp. Someone pointed him out to us. He had grown into the story of his birth and didn't hesitate to share a hug with his namesake. I, of course, got their photo.

Ricardo Linné Willis meets his namesake.

During that side trip to Angoon, we met many of the people we'd gotten to know and care about in the 60s. As it turned out, many Angoon residents who'd worked at Chatham and lived in the Native village moved on to run their own businesses, join the legislature in Juneau, and one became the Mayor of Angoon.

Mathew and Bessie Fred were cultural leaders amongst the Tlingits both at Chatham and afterwards when they returned to Angoon. At Chatham, Mathew was what Linné had called an "all around guy," valuable at a multitude of jobs. Bessie worked on the can line and operated a local radio station from her village house at Chatham. Mathew was clan leader of the Deisheetaan (Raven) Moiety. Later on he was also the vice president of the Angoon Community Association and sat on the board of Alaska Legal Services. In his seventies he led a delegation to Washington, DC to try to convince the U.S. Navy to apologize for bombing Angoon in 1882. This proved to be successful on October 26, 2024 when Admiral Mark Sucato officially apologized on behalf of the U.S. Navy to hundreds of Lingits gathered for the event in the Angoon gym.

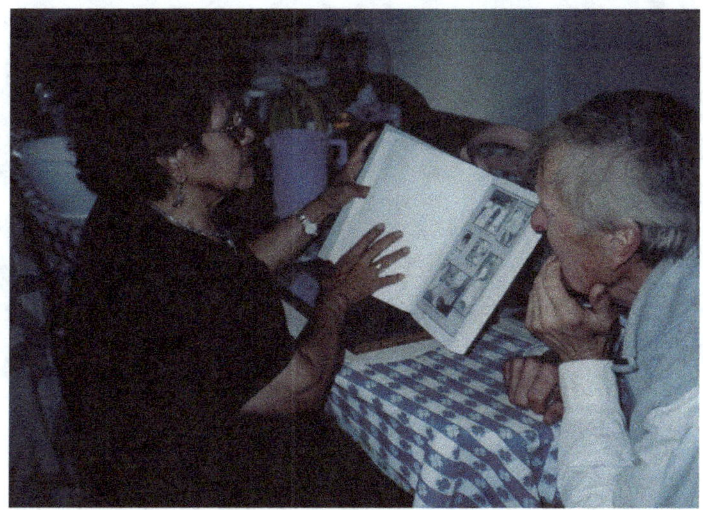

Bessie and Linné look at my first Chatham book.

During our 2001 visit, we were delighted to see their children all grown up. Their son Eddie was an accomplished poet, who had just won a prestigious award and their daughter Maxine (who pulled eggs with me at Chatham when she was 18), earned degrees in Office Management, sociology and psychology. She was an accomplished businesswoman who later was voted in as Mayor of Angoon.

Maxine shared her thoughts about Chatham with me for this book, and some have been included in the text. One of the things she talked about was the autonomy of Natives in Alaska. She spoke a little about the churches coming in to educate them because they thought they were "stupid." The churches didn't acknowledge that Natives had their own sovereignty based on survival. Native languages were lost due to the paternal interference of the new, White, owners of Alaska. This was an incalculably great loss, and later generations blamed their parents for not keeping the language alive. Despite this, even to this day the Native Elders have tremendous sway on Native communities.

Maxine Thompson shares her Chatham stories.

"How is it," she asked during our phone interview for this book, "that in the Native community Elders are revered and in the White community old people retire and are no longer sought out for advice? It is the young people who are revered. Or so it seems."

I didn't have an answer for her.

Here is what she said about Chatham, particularly when Linné was superintendent:

It was kind of like a vacation. It was a place where a community atmosphere could be allowed to be fostered. At Angoon [where we lived in the off-season] there were no bathrooms with hot running water, no all night lights.

Life was easy at the cannery. Teenagers could babysit and earn money. We couldn't wait to be old enough to work at the cannery where we'd start at age 15 by pulling skeins of eggs. Young Natives wanted to move up the social ladder of progress. Chatham was the perfect place to do that. A girl could start at 15 in the Egg House, from working up to packing roe in boxes, to sliming, to working on the line with machinery. As they advanced they would move up the pay scale.

Slimers liked to challenge each other. Competition on the line was strong to see who could out-perform the other line. There were two 1 pound Talls and the one and a half pound line. We'd call over, "How come you guys are going so slow? We're going to be here all night."

Fishing was highly competitive. If you were top dog for the opening, you "Flew the broom" letting everyone anchored around you know who you were. Natives came to that naturally from many years of settling fights with war canoes.

For those of us from Angoon, Chatham was a vacation despite the hard work and long hours. It was at Chatham that we had hot running water in the village and lights on the boardwalk. In Angoon there were none of these amenities.

The Village had impromptu dances in an empty house. Workers would come home so tired at the end of the day, and just want to go to bed, but they'd hear the music and know that something was happening and they'd get a second wind. They just had to get up the energy to investigate. It might just be Mom [Bessie Fred] firing up the radio and taking requests for music [for the small radio station she ran out of her house].

Or Dad [Mathew Fred], jamming with his band, or even an unannounced dance in an empty house for which they had to get approval from the "supe." They always had energy for a party.

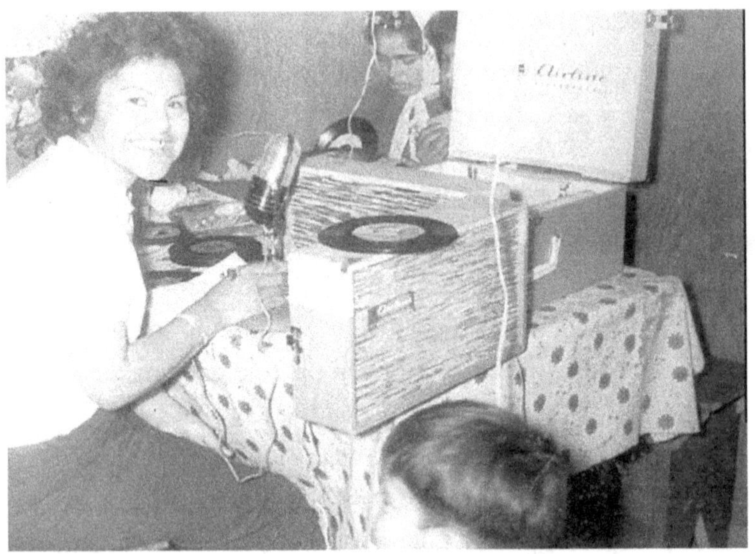

Bessie Fred's radio station in the Native village.

I was happy to learn of this from Maxine Fred. As a White woman, up on the hill with three children and being the supe's wife, I was not aware of the fun they were having in the Village after work. Looking back, I wonder how they found the time or the energy after a busy, work-filled day.

I asked Maxine to share her favorite memory of Chatham. Here was her response:

Favorite memory of Chatham? Chatham provided for us a piece of the puzzle that made us who we are. Music was very important. We were surrounded by it every day. Dad played a lot of instruments and was a driving force for entertainment and helped the Filipinos organize a dance. Mom, as I mentioned, had the little radio station that she would crank up after work. Her transmitting station had a short battery life.

When Mom was in Juneau shopping with us girls, we

talked her into buying more current music than she was playing over the waves in the Village. We told her it was Old Fashioned.

Mom didn't have to cook. That was the job of the other members of the family who didn't work in the cannery. Each person was responsible for a portion of the work. In laundry, even that was divided into parts—washing, hanging on the line, folding, etc. so members worked together for a common cause.

The grandmothers would pick berries and hang salmon. After they put the jam up in jars preparing for Winter, they'd take them down to the guys at the retorts to get cooked in the tail end, after all the canned salmon was done that had been processed that day. They called them "ties to your clan."

Mathew and Bessie Fred's younger daughters Margaret and Lillian came to visit us at our home in Seward. Recently Dori told me that Lillian, with whom she'd maintained her childhood friendship, had been going through some hard times and called her to talk about it. Dori suggested that what might help was to think about something special, "Some place where you were especially happy." And Lillian immediately said: "The Native Village at Chatham."

Maxine told me that the families from Angoon so looked forward to returning to Chatham every summer. It was their chance to leave the usual worries and anxieties of everyday life behind and be a part of the camaraderie and energy present at the cannery. That was especially true, they told us during our Angoon visit, when Linné was superintendent.

They never forgot the aura of fun and efficiency that had accompanied his management of the cannery. We were gratified to realize that they had truly loved him. From what they said, none of the following "supes" had encouraged the community camaraderie that had marked Linné's tenure.

Other Chatham alumni included Herman and Martha Kitka who had been a force at Chatham, and they had a lasting impact on their community. Herman was a cannery fisherman, owner of the *Martha K*, and Martha had been the canning forelady. She was almost regal in the way she led our workers, and she expected high standards. Later Herman became the clan leader of the Sitka Kaagwaantaan (Wolf) Moiety as a respected Tlingit Elder. He was active in developing the Alaska Native Claims Settlement Act in 1971 and became the first president of the Shee Atiká Corporation board of directors. Herman was invited to lecture at the University of Alaska-Southeast to anthropology students on the subject of Traditional Ecological Knowledge (TEK). He received an honorary doctorate degree in 2009, shortly before his death at the age of 95. In 1998, during a stop in Sitka, we hoped to give Herman a personal copy of the Chatham photos and letters that I'd compiled into a hardbound book, but he wasn't home.

Chatham Cannery's forelady, Martha Kitka.

Ichie Sawa was another "all around worker" who could do anything he put his hand to. We kept in contact with him, and he has visited us in Seward. He was also there when we visited Smokey and Elizabeth Hansen in their Sequim, WA home just a few weeks before Elizabeth died. He had come to Chatham as a Japanese exchange student and now lives in Juneau.

Smokey and Elizabeth were very special people in our lives. Smokey ended up following us all over Alaska. He was at Unalaska when Linné ran a crab plant and then in Seward as well. He used to tell people, total strangers, that Dori was his wife and they just got married. "We got some strange looks because of the age difference," Dori recalls with a smile, "But it was rather fun to shock folks. Especially since we knew we would never see them again."

**Smokie (Harold) Hansen
at Seward Fisheries, 1971.**

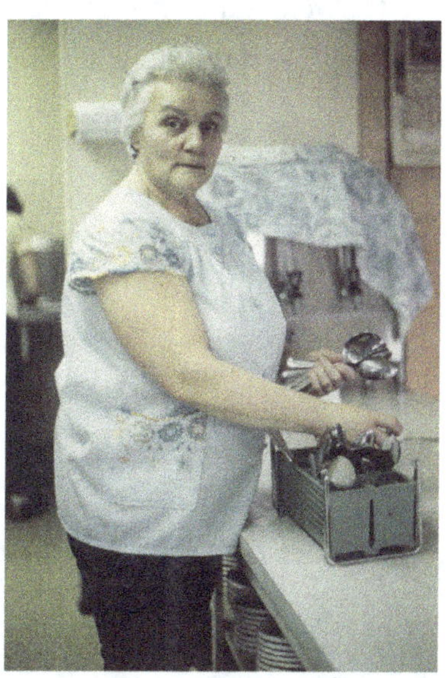

**Elizabeth Hansen
at Seward Fisheries, 1971.**

What became of the bull cook, Martin Ebona who had the terrible accident with the fish ladder? According to his grandson Brian Ebona, Martin worked at Chatham into the 1970s until it burned and then moved to Juneau where he worked in the gold/coal mine. "I remember that because his hardhat had a light affixed to it. Later he was given a breathing apparatus that sat next to his recliner, very small with a clear tube and mask that hummed like a V8 diesel. This was needed in part because of the dust from the mine. Dr. Rude occasionally dropped in with his large worn leather bag that could fix anything and despite his name was very kind."

**Martin Ebona
at Chatham.**

Ten years after his accident, to the month, Martin Ebona died at the age of 75. "He never touched alcohol or smoked." His wife, born in 1900 died in 1991.

There was also Kitty Young, pretty and fashionable regardless of the job she held at the cannery, her hair up in a beehive and all the young men crowded around her during coffee breaks and at the 4th of July barbecues. When Linné became the manager of Seward Fisheries in 1970, Kitty was one of the Chatham workers he called. She flew up to work on the line in 1970 and 1971. She lived with us in our rental house in Seward.

Kitty Young and friends at Chatham barbeque.

Kitty eventually moved to Petersburg, Alaska, where she lives now and is recognized as an accomplished Haida basket weaver. Her woven cedar hats and baskets are displayed in the Clausen Museum in Petersburg. She talked to me about her memories of Chatham for this book:

The Village houses had running water and toilets. But with most houses one had to go to the Laundry Room to take showers. I lived a few doors down from Martha Kitka and I shared a house with two other women who were Tlingit. I was the only Haida in camp. At first there was a little tension, but as we got to know each other it was fine. I did have trouble with the way they would look away from the person they were talking with. I finally told them, "You have to look at me when you talk."

I wasn't aware of any problems with the hierarchy of the cannery or how the housing was set up at Chatham. We by nature, didn't cross social barriers of racism. It was just sort of understood, but not an issue. But, when we walked up the boardwalk to the cannery we would have to go right past the Filipino house where the men usually sat on a bench outside, just a few feet on either side of the boardwalk.

It didn't seem right to me that we wouldn't acknowledge them with a greeting, so one day, I deliberately went up to them and said, 'Hi, I'm Kitty.'" After that we got nice waves and sometimes some rice.

They were the ones who brought the donuts and coffee for our 15 minute breaks in the cannery. We appreciated them. I also ventured to the white mess hall area upon occasion and was friendly with everyone.

Don Hansen, the son of Smokie and Elizabeth Hansen who were the winter caretakers of Chatham and eventually the permanent cooks (and my 16-year-old boss in the Egg House), had the most unique experience of Chatham since his family members were the only ones who lived there year-around.

Don Hansen, 2024.

He shared his memories too:

The Chatham experience had a profound impact on my upbringing, and probably my adult life. It was so simple. [In the winter] we had school work to do, so we did it. For me, school was in the morning hours. I worked as hard as I could so I would have the entire afternoon for trapping, hunting and exploring. And school was seven days a week unless the weather was good enough to get the mail plane in. I think the mail came on Mondays, weather permitting, and mail day was a holiday. It is amazing what you can accomplish when not distracted by meaningless chatter and fluff in the curriculum. I even studied Latin in the eighth grade, something I would bet is not offered in any public school [today].

The winter watchman's job was pretty basic. The only real "work" I remember was painting the interiors of the mess hall and bunkhouse. Mom and Dad would paint and Ron and I would play. It was during the mess hall painting that I fell into the bay from the walkway along the mess hall during high tide. Good thing it was high tide. If not, I would not be here today [due to the height of the drop from the mess hall walkway to the beach below].

The way Mom told it, Ron came into the building without me and she asked "Where is Donnie?" Ron's reply was "He's looking at fish." Well, Dad didn't swim so he went out on the ways to climb down the timber bracing to get to me and Mom just went over the railing and into the water.

Mom said I was floating face down when she first saw me and I don't remember anything about it until I was up on the boardwalk shivering. I think that was when I was in first grade because that was the last winter we spent there until we children were much older. I think it scared the heck out of them. In my version of the story I always say that Ron pushed me in. He didn't, but it made for a better story.

I think Dad did walk the whole camp every day, but I

guess it never occurred to me it was a job. The reason I knew he did that is because he would always discover the mischief we got into and the mess we would leave behind.

Evenings were always family time. We played lots of games and read lots of books. In eighth grade I taught myself how to do taxidermy and so the house was always filled with stuffed birds. We didn't have need for a lot of clothing so I set up my taxidermy shop in the closet off the bedroom. Everything went well until I dragged a crow into that little space. What a godawful smell!

Ron and I also collected stamps and pasted them into a stamp book. We would clip out coupons for mail order stamps that would come in envelopes through the mail and then we would try to find the appropriate place for the rare one that had not already made it into the book. I still have the stamp books and stamps and occasionally get them out to browse through. I have some Adolph Hitler stamps from WWII Germany and those are quite the conversation pieces. It wasn't long after the war ended that we began the stamp collecting.

Evenings were also a time for music or stories over the radio. No television, just radio. We also had a weekly schedule with a ham operator in Juneau to check for messages about family, or to send our own message out if there was something of importance. Otherwise messages went by mail, weekly or whenever the plane could fly. I do recall Mom ordering new shoes for us via the mail from a shoe store in Aberdeen. Ron and I would stand on a piece of paper so she could trace feet and send that to the store to be measured and the order filled. No one cared about style or color, they were just new.

Mom was a genius when it came to entertaining us. One of her favorites was to give us each a tablet and pencil and sit us down in front of the anemometer gauge in the house. Our task was to carefully observe the gauge and write down our observations. There was no way to prove anything however, so it always resulted in an argument amongst us as to who really saw the highest gust of the day. Her other trick was to bundle us up and put us out on the walkway that went around the store so we could see the corner of the dock that stuck out into the bay. This was important so we could have a good view of the waves and mentally record the highest wave strike on the piling. The tide was predicted from the tide table. We just sat there and watched until it was obvious the big one had already passed.

**Hansen kids ready with snowballs,
revolting against Cod Liver oil, 1956.**

I do remember there was a murder at the Filipino bunkhouse but I don't remember any of the details. Did you know there was a burial site across the bay where one of the Chinese laborers had been buried many years before our time? Dad took me by it a couple times when we were running the trap line or hunting. I know it was not well marked and there was only one grave.

My first job was washing dishes, peeling potatoes and carrots, and otherwise helping around the mess hall. I did that when I was 14 and 15 I believe because you had to be 16 to work in the cannery. I recall asking Dad if he had heard about a wonderful invention called instant potatoes because the work was tedious. He wouldn't have it though. It all had to be fresh. I worked each meal and when Mom and Dad were down for their afternoon break, I would grab my fishing rod and head up to the second creek to fish. I did that pretty much every day when the weather was good and the tides were right. At high tide the beach was not passable so the tide had to be down somewhat in order for that to work.

Once Don turned 16, like so many of the Native teenagers, he went to work in the Egg House. (He says that after his first season in the Egg House he took all the money he earned and paid for a private pilot course. "That was my dream and ultimately led to the phone call [in 1970] from Linné inviting me to come to Seward and fly for Seward Fisheries.")

He adds:

I particularly enjoyed the company of the younger Japanese technicians [in the Egg House] and one, Hiro (Hiroyuki), became a friend I stayed in touch with up until my time at Seward. I would take them [the technicians] to the head of the bay at Chatham for sport fishing and for Dungeness crab. They, in turn, introduced me to sake and raw fish. The sake was ok but I swear that the first chunk of raw flounder was stuck in my throat for a week. I don't think Linné ever knew, or if he did know he didn't say anything, But Ichie [Sawa] and I used to borrow a skiff and make the occasional run to Angoon to buy liquor and bring it back. I guess I got into the liquor business at a very early age.

I think Dad had a number of jobs over the years. He talked about working on the fish traps, being a cook on the tenders, working the oil dock, the store, the beach gang and the mess hall. I don't recall him ever talking about working inside the cannery. I think he probably made a higher wage on the beach gang but the mess hall offered more overall because Dad and Mom got to work together.

Remember, he was a bit older than most other workers with children our age. He was in his late forties, early fifties when he was on the beach gang, and that was hard work. The mess hall was hard too, with very long hours, but it seemed to fit them both quite well. I have no idea what his hourly wage was but I do recall before he passed, he told me he had never in his life made more than $10 per hour (as a straight time wage obviously). They lived quite comfortably though and we never lacked for the necessities.

He only finished the eighth grade before dropping out of school. He was a very bright guy but he had that speech impediment that plagued him until his later years. He said he dropped out to help earn money to support the family, and while there may be some truth to that, I believe the peer pressure and lack of resources in the school probably made it untenable for him. I think many thought people with a stutter just weren't very bright, but I can tell you with 100 percent certainty that is not true. He was a kind, compassionate and gentle soul, and read and wrote amazingly well for someone with an 8th grade education. I have tried to model my life after him in many respects. I do get wound up on occasion but I guess people don't see it. I overheard my daughter Kim tell one of her friends recently that "I have never seen that man (me) lash out in anger or be disrespectful to anyone." It caught me by surprise, but after thinking about it, I decided it was a very good thing for her to feel. Kind of humbling.

Mom, on the other hand, was the one with the temper and the opinion, and she was not shy about expressing her opinions. Many inebriated individuals got a good talking to when they got out of line.

There were so many, many people—so many that if I was write to about all of them, I'd have to write another book on the subject.

It wasn't just people, either. When we reached the part of the boardwalk, during our visit in 1998, that used to lead out to the cannery wharf before the heart of the cannery had burned, I thought about the boats that had visited Chatham while we were there and had had such an impact on us. One of my many paintings at Chatham was of a freighter tied up to the dock.

My painting of a freighter at Chatham.

The *Southport* was sold in 1964, the year after we'd enjoyed our formal dinner aboard at the captain's table, to Bildberg Rothchild Co. Inc. Its name was changed to the SS *Oduna*. On November 26, 1965 she ran aground at Cape Pankof, on Unimak Island, Alaska and became a total loss.

According to reports: "The vessel stranded in heavy seas on the east side of Unimak Island. The radar aboard the *Oduna* was inoperative and strong currents dragged her onto the rocks. The Chief Mate was at the helm when the disaster occurred and was blamed for the stranding. The crew was removed by breeches buoy and helicopter to the [Coast Guard] Cutter *Storis* and a tug, but several men organized a salvage effort and were able to save much of what was onboard, including 200,000 pounds of frozen crab in refrigerated container vans."

**The *Oduna*, the former *Southport*,
aground on Unimak Island, 2022.**

Then there was the missionary boat, the *Anna Jackman*. In the early 1970s it was bought by the State of Alaska and the *Anna Jackman* became a floating library. The Alaska State Library used it to deliver library books to the roughly 8,000 people living in Southeastern Alaska's remote coves and bays. It carried about 400 books, along with some cassettes and battery-operated tape-players for the sake of those without reliable electricity. The floating library primarily visited isolated logging and fishing towns, including Hanus Bay, Five Finger Lighthouse, and Meyers Chuck.

Chatham Cannery, commissioned by Bob Thorstenson.

And what about our magnificent cannery barbecue that everyone, from the youngest child to oldest Native elder had participated in building? What had happened to it? We couldn't find it during either of our visits. We were told, when we stopped in Angoon, that when Al O'Leary took over as superintendent at Chatham in 1969, he had the barbecue destroyed. We wondered why, but there seemed to be no answer.

We had left Chatham in 1967 but not before I had painted one last scene of the cannery, a scene commissioned by Bob Thorstenson. We fully expected to return in 1968 but that never came about.

Linné, Dot and children say goodbye in 1967, expecting to return in 1968.

Before leaving Chatham after our final visit in 1998, Linné and I stood there hugging each other and gazed at the gaping hole where the cannery buildings used to be. It left an ache in us that it didn't seem possible to assuage.

But then I thought, one day I'll write a memoir and bring Chatham back to life. The people who lived, laughed and loved here will walk the boardwalk again, eat at the mess hall, stand in the slime line—boats will arrive and offload their catch as masses of sea gulls cry overhead.

And one more time, Linné, the children, and I will climb the 79 steps to go home.

Dot and Linné say their final goodbyes, 1998.

Appendix A
The Canning Process in Pictures

Linné directs a delivery of fresh salmon to the cannery.

Someone had to make sure that the boat tied up to safely line up with the fish elevator.

A cash buyer delivering at the dock.

The *A.F. Rich* was one of our biggest tenders.

Unloading salmon from a tender.

Crew members guide salmon into the fish elevator to prevent a jam.

The Fish Elevator.

Unloading fish at the dock. Someone was watching from every vantage.

The revolving elevator would have to be stopped immediately should a problem occur. Burt Wold was there to stop the fish elevator and clear out the problem salmon in case of a jam.

Burt Wold worked for the cannery.

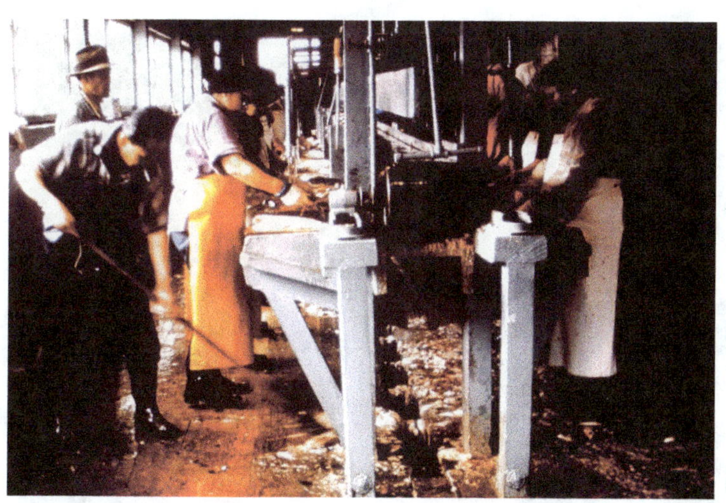

Slimers on the Slime Line.

Once the salmon reached the cannery itself, they entered the Iron Chink which cut off heads and fins. The slime line cleaned out the belly and sent the fish to be canned.

We had two lines for 1-pound talls. We added a half-pound line. Here Kitty Young is at the controls.

Cans are filled.

The Patching Table.

Machinist, Marvin Remlinger, watches the gals on the patching table where they bring shorted cans up to the perfect weight.

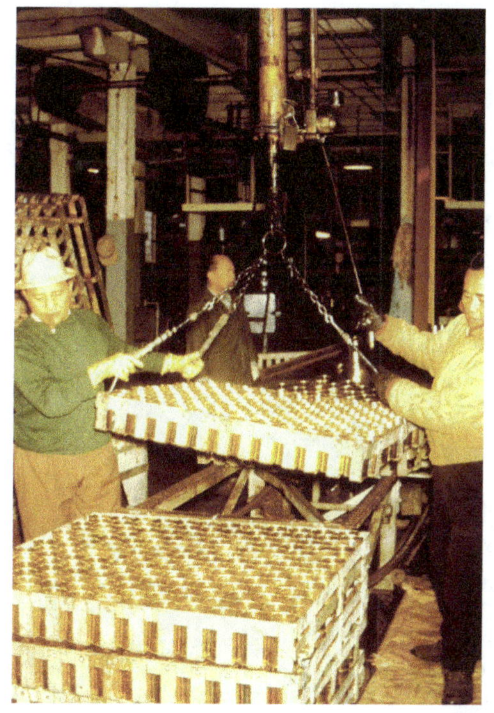

The filled cans were placed in racks that would fit into the retorts.

Racking the cans ready for the retorts.

Filled cans loaded into the retorts.

Cans were cooked in the retorts for 90 minutes at 240 degrees.

Appendix B

Linné's Chatham Correspondence, 1960-1965
(Dot, Mother, Kids Too)

June 21, 1960

Dear Dot,

What a true bastard I really am. I have a horrible guilt complex. You are undoubtedly the most understanding wife in the world, and the sexiest and the most loveable. How is that for throwing in the hat.

The weather has been absolutely miserable. I have not seen the sun since I left Seattle. The first thing I saw was the Annette Island Airport at 1,000 ft. Thank God these planes have radar.

What have I been doing? You name it, I'm doing it. Everything from writing letter to fishermen to building brailers for the tenders. Most of my time goes into taking care of the fishermen and learning the operation methods of this cannery.

The Bering got here last night and as I went into the stateroom to pick up my stuff I thought to myself, "By Golly, I hope Dot didn't forget the candy!" You see what you have done to me. A bloody addict.

When I first read your letters about the merging lane, I just about had a stroke. It would be better to burn the house down. If they just didn't have to take the trees down. Hang signs on all the trees saying "Woodman, spare that tree." As far as the fence goes, unless they tell you specifically to take it down, why just leave it up. If they knock it down we'll sue the bastards. From my observations the cars come up new Westminster in groups. The reason or this is the light at 155th and Aurora. It would be impossible to get into these groups riding on the back of a Bumble Bee let alone a car. You have to wait until one of these groups passes by and then go. Consequently, I don't see any great improvement by the construction of a merging lane. The end result as I see it is the devaluation of the Slatters and our property and the same traffic situation. Another result is that it will now be impossible for any car on 149th to get onto New Westminster in the morning because there will be a solid line of cars blocking 149th waiting to get onto N.W. I don't know how to advice except to stand by your guns, whatever that is. It's hard to talk with someone (like Ashley) on a subject which one person doesn't give a dam about and it means so much to the other person. God, I hope they don't chop those trees down.

I'm sorry to hear about the house rental problem. I was hoping that you and the children would be enjoying yourselves at "Bardvista" by now.

I miss you all very much. What a wonderful family I have been blessed with.

All my love sweetheart,

Linné

~

June 21, 1960

Dear Blaine,

I am working way up in Alaska. I hope that some day you can come up with me and work also. I miss you very much Blaine and wish we could play together again at "Bardvista." We could chase the rabbits and have a good time. I will be home in about three months and then we will be together again.

I love you very much,

<u>Your Daddy</u>

~

June 21, 1960

Dear Dori,

Here I am, way up in Alaska. I thought that you and Blaine and Rolf and Mommy would be up at Bardvista by this time but I guess you are still in Seattle. Maybe when you do go up to "Bardvista" you and Blaine can sleep upstairs in the room that I built for you. I wish I could be there too so I could play with you. But I have to stay up in Alaska a little longer to work. I will come back again soon so that we will all be together again.

I Love You Very Much,

Your Daddy

~

July 20, 1960

Dearest Dot,

I am enjoying my work more and more. When I first came up I didn't know exactly what the story was going to be. However, the things that I have wanted to do and the ideas that I have had have all been accepted by John. I don't know what he thinks, he just says, "That's fine, Linné, that's O.K. with me, you do what you want." And that's the way it's been. I chartered an inboard speedboat from a fellow and have been using it constantly since the beginning of the season. John and I work together in dispatching the tenders, he from the cannery and I from the grounds. I have worked with John in negotiating with the Alaska Fisherman's Union. On two occasions I feel that I clarified certain points in the contract and in correspondence pertaining to the contract that saved this company quite a few dollars in overtime. It was nothing really big and the company will never know about it because I clarified it for John, but it made me feel good anyway.

Two weeks ago I was in Juneau and last week I was in Petersburg. It was good to see Bob again. I had meals with him several times at the PHE cannery and Monday night John Lions who is San Rubenstein's personal representative, Roland Able outside man for Naket [sic] Packing Corp., Bob and myself went to dinner at the "Beach Comber," which is kind of a night club out at Scow Bay. Went to the "Ellis" with Clara and George and spent most of the evening table hopping. Saw Ray and Arline Ottness, Tom Rustad. Neil and Jan and most of the people we know in Petersburg.

The way things are shaping up the NEFCO cannery at Chatham is going to sustain a terrific loss financially. I have never seen or heard of a season that's as bad as this one is so far. To date we have canned 8,000 cases and it doesn't look as if we were going to get too much more. It really looks black. Fortunately, NEFCO is knocking them stiff in Bristol Bay. That's the fishing industry!

Today is the third day I've seen the sun since I've been up here. It's enough to drive a guy crazy. I haven't been back to the cannery in over two weeks so I don't know what is going on at "Bardvista." I do know this though, I have the best family in the world and know I miss them. I find myself thinking about getting back to Seattle much more than I have in the past. If there were more fish it would be better.

I suppose mother is back from Eugene by now. Have you had much company at Bardvista? How are the kids, etc., etc.?

I don't have the foggiest idea when I will get back home. J. was saying something about going to Ketchikan after Chatham closed sometime in the latter part of August.

I wonder if those bastards have built that merging lane yet? Did they cut the trees down??

I have a radio schedule now at 6:00 P.M. so that's it. I miss you very much sweetheart. Send me some pictures if you have any.

All my love,

Linné

~

July 20, 1960

Dear Dori,

I am still up in Alaska on a boat but I wish that I was at Bardvista with you and Mommy and Blaine and Rolf and Emma. I'll bet you have a good time with Blaine down at the beach playing in the sand. Are there still a lot of rabbits at "Bardvista"?

I am working very hard up here in Alaska, but one of these days I will be at Bardvista and then we can all play together. I miss you very much Dori and I love you very much too. Say hello to Emma for me. Goodbye for now.

All my love,

Daddy [sketch of the tender *Beryl-E*]

~

8/10/60

Dear Dot,

Just a note before the mail plane comes, things are so damn slow around here I can't stand it. Within the next two weeks the plant will probably close. What I will do then I can't say for certain.

I had a long talk with J. Gage when he was here about what I was going to do this winter. It was a very interesting talk, but I still don't know anything. I think he thinks I have a few brains. Really snowed him, eh??

The company is discontinuing the Houghton Operation which I think is a good deal. All the Bents will now be tied up in Ballard.

I understand the weather in Seattle has been blazing hot. I keep thinking about our well at Bardvista. Is it dry yet??? Your art lessons sound very interesting. I'll bet you are enjoying them.

I'm looking forward to spending a few days at Bardvista before move to Seattle so don't be in a hurry to leave same.

I suppose the kids are brown as berries by now. It sounds as though you have been doing a lot of work around the house and property. I'm really looking forward to being there. I hope it won't be long now until I can take you to bed and ________

All my love,

Linné

~

August 14, 1960

Dearest Dot,

My God! Time is dragging. This is the first time in Alaska that this has been so. In the last 21 days we have had only 5 ½ days fishing due to closures. As far as I can see, Southeastern Alaska has been a complete failure. Our total pack to date is 13,300 cases as compared to last years 64,000 cases. The break even point is 45,000 cases, so you can see where we stand profit wise. We are now waiting out a 7 day closure before we can start fishing again.

S   H   I   T

I need more letters, shorter, but more often. We have a mail plane in 3 days a week. I keep wondering about that ding-dong well of ours, is it dry yet? Could you give me a comparison of the water level in the two wells? I just can't imagine Rolf with a mouth full of teeth when I get back. I'm going to notice a big change in him I'm sure. When I read your letters, they bring me almost to Bardvista. What a wonderful home, away from home, that must be. Everyone sounds healthy, happy, and well-adjusted. We should really count our blessings.

I've gained about 8 pounds this year. Not much, although I eat quite a bit. I miss you very much sweetheart, and long for the <u>day.</u>

All my love,

Linné

~

August 15, 1960

Dear Mother,

Surprised? I can't remember the last time I wrote to you. Years I guess. You have been so good about writing me and I appreciate it. It sounds as though you are all getting along splendidly. Life at Bardvista seems to produce health and happiness. You can imagine how I am looking forward to spending at least a little time there before summer ends.

I think that I will be coming to Seattle when Chatham closes. However, it is not definite. The last few days I have been working on a little project of mine which is obtaining and compiling specification and description material on all our floating equipment. (Tenders, seine boats, skiffs, etc. etc.) The purpose of this is for quick reference and to eliminate purchasing errors. I will be glad when they close this place and I can go somewhere and sink my teeth into something. When there are no fish it is hard to see where one is productive.

Roger's promotion sounds great. I'm waiting for more details on the event. It appears that he has done quite well and I am very happy for both of them. Say hello to Linnea and all.

Love,

Linné

P.S. To Dot, You can do as you wish with regard to your planned trip, sweetheart. However, I don't seem to be able to generate much enthusiasm over it. Reasons furnished upon request. Love to all, Linné

~

August 22, 1960

Dear Dot,

The plane will be in here in a few minutes, I'll try to get this off. The cannery is closed, the *Beryle-E* went to Sitka, and the *A.F. Rich* went to Juneau with all the Native cannery workers. Tomorrow, the Filipinos fly out, and on the 26th the machinists fly out—leaving only 9 of us. The fishing season will remain open so we are staying. My God, it's really going to be quiet around here.

Tomorrow I will be out of my twenties—LIFE IS OVER. Cheer me up sweetheart. I need your support in my hour of trial. Will you still love me? Do I still have sex appeal?? Do you still want to go to bed with me even though I'm old and haggard? Stand by your old man, will you?

I saw Roni Price yesterday. He said you had dinner over at Patty's. I suppose that is when you saw the renters off. What have they done with the merging lane?? Trees? Property?

I love you sweetheart, I love my family, I'm a very loving fellow.

All my love,

Linné

~

July 9, 1961

My Dear Dori,

Today you are five years old. My, my how big you must be getting. I'll bet you have a real nice suntan also. I hope you don't think that I forgot your birthday. I am having one of the Alaska Indians make you a very nice pair of moccasins for your feet. However when the Indians make them it takes longer than if I bought them in a store. That is why you won't get them until after your birthday. I miss you very much, Dori, I'm sorry that I have to go away each summer. Take good care of Mommy.

All my love, Daddy

P.S. I haven't had a cigarette in over a month.

~

July 9, 1961

My Dear Blaine

Gee! How I wish I were at Bardvilla so that we could all play together. Wouldn't it be fun if you and I could go for a ride on our raft in False Bay? I'll bet when I get home you will be a great big boy.

We sure are getting a lot of fish up here this year. Some day you can come up and help Daddy can all these fish. This fall when I get home I'm going to take a vacation. Then you and I can play together every day.

All my Love,

Daddy,

P.S. I don't smoke any more.

~

July 9, 1961

My darling wife,

Busy, busy, busy. The season is exactly opposite from that of last year. Fish all over in our area. Last week we got just about all the fish we could handle. We canned fish until 1:00 a.m. every night. This week every seine boat in Southeast Alaska will be in our area. I'm worried, the Neptune was four hours out of Chatham tonight and Ketchikan called her back. She was going to pick me up at 2:00 a.m. this morning and help us out in this area. I don't know why they called her back but I'm so mad I can't see straight. It seems that I've been going constantly since I arrived. Tomorrow morning early I will start out early in my instrument of torture (17' Glasspar with 80 hp Mercury) for the fishing grounds 90 miles distant. The other night while charging through black raining night at 2:30 a.m. soaking wet, spray flying all over the place, I thought to myself what the hell am I doing here? The finest family in the world on the San Juan Islands and here I am. What a business.

Today we have a five year old girl. How I wish I could be there to celebrate with you all. Good times, happy times, times to remember. How lucky I am to have someone like you at the controls while I'm gone. I'm in love with my wife. She is the finest thing I have ever known.

I'm having some moccasins made for Dori. It will take a little while. I hope she doesn't think her daddy has forgotten her. I enjoy the pictures you send in your letters, that one of Rolf asleep by the phone is excellent.

The watchman is about ready to turn out the lights so it's goodnight sweetheart, I wish it were with you.

All my love,

Linné

~

August 7, 1961

At the end of last week we canned a total of 114,000 cases. That's 4,000 cases more than has ever been packed in the 61 year history of this cannery. The fish are still pouring in and there is no end in sight. I bet one of the fellows here that we would still be canning in Sept.

I read your letters with great pleasure. How I wish I could be there to share your lives. Somehow I can't believe that Dori can do the Hula-Hoop. Impossible!!! I don't know when this Native gal can make Dori's moccasins. I might have to buy them in Juneau when I get there.

I was glad to hear that you and Rosalie had such a good time together. For some reason I like her although I have never met her. What are her plans?? I hope by this time you have the water problem straightened out. With all their people it must have been a mess. Is Rolf beginning to talk yet or is he going to be like me? I couldn't talk till I was 3. It sounds as if the patio were finished. If you could send me some more pictures I would appreciate it.

I have gained 24 pounds. I now weigh 204 pounds of throbbing muscle.

What do you think of that? You had better watch out when I get back.

All my love,

Linné

~

August 18, 1961

It was wonderful to talk to you last night. You voice came in as clear as a bell. I just talked to Jay and now I'm not sure when I will be coming home. Possibly this month. He wants me down there when the first tenders from westward arrive in Seattle. I suppose it's ok to rent Bardvilla for the month of Sept. if it's for people who are <u>vacationing</u> I don't think $150.00 would be out of line. Use your own judgment sweetheart. I am enclosing two newsy letters, one from Baird and one from Peg. It sounds as if they are having a wonderful time.

Every day I remind myself how fortunate I am to have such an outstanding wife and children. I am forever grateful.

All my love,

Linné

~

August 20, 1961

Dear Linné,

A busy week has just transpired.

I'm about expired.

Bobbie Bremner with Davin and Eric, and Marty Duggan with Robbie (age 5) spent three and half days here. It rained for two days, so you can imagine the confusion in the house. We had a lovely time and talked a blue streak. Bobbie is getting along well with her hand. Finds diapering difficult because her thumb hasn't healed completely yet. A bone was removed and fancy stitching done. The nail is black and blue and about to come off and her thumb is in general sensitive. Her attitude is typically Bobbie, and she won't let you do anything for her.

Marty's main concern now is that with the Berlin crisis Bob might be called to active service. Some squadrons have been already. His could be next. She stopped working in July and is five months pregnant.

Those poor gals missed the early ferry from Anacortes by about ten minutes. They saw it leave the dock. They had to then cool their heels in the rain in Anacortes from 9 until 2 pm. When they left here, they missed the 11 am ferry (our clocks and watches were wrong and we didn't even know it. I had set our clock by Bobbie's watch which is haywire) They then had to wait until 5pm. Dick and Ruth arrived on the 9:15 ferry (which didn't dock until 10.00 pm). They came on foot carrying the car bed and pushing Gregory in the stroller. I of course had to meet them. With the extra wait and all the kids were pretty restless and tired by the time we got home.

I can't get over how clear the phone call was from you the other night. That was certainly enjoyable.

Mom and Dad called last week to say hello. Nothing of particular interest was mentioned.

Dick repaired the well pump and switched us over to our own water. Then he built a box to enclose the valves next to the house. Then he fixed the spring pump so it works at the flick of a finger. Then he tried to patch the roof with new shingles but found that every time he would kneel down on the old roof, shingles would disintegrate. He announced Linné is right, the old shingles will have to come off when you re-roof. He is willing to come up some time in the Fall and help you roof the house. Then he built an extra step at the top of the stairs to facilitate that last big step into the Grabite hole. He sprayed our thistles again. He installed a swing for the children. Ruth helped me paint the house. It looks like a patchwork quilt. We can't reach the high spots. The front of the barn is done except for the top boards.

Love, Dot

~

8/22/61

Sweetheart,

Tomorrow I'm 31. How ghastly! Will you still love me when I am old and gray? Everyone at the cannery has Going Home Fever. However there still seems to be lots of fish around. For today's canning we had 25,000 fish for 2,000 cases which is very good for this time of year. Before the season is over we will have over 150,000 cases canned at this cannery plus another 30,000 canned at other canneries for our account. This is somewhat phenomenal. But at last I think I can see the end of the road for this season.

It sounds as though Baird and Peg are having a marvelous time on their trip. I think it's nice that they have good friends their own age over there. Mother and Mrs. Johnson I'm sure are living it up in the big house. I wonder who has their kids?

I love to hear what extent our children talk. I'm sure I am going to be surprised when I see them. I keep wondering if Rolf can say anything. I certainly do miss my wonderful family.

NEXT DAY

The mail plane is due in about 10 minutes. It won't be long now sweetheart. Give a kiss and a hug to my children. All my Love, Linné

~

DOT – August 21, 1961

Dear Linné,

The children have spent the afternoon making these birthday cards for you. We are planning to have a cake when you come home. The children wanted one this week but I convinced them that you should be invited to your own birthday party.

I am simply delighted that Jay wants you in Seattle so soon. The prospect of going home was definitely not full of anticipation as in other years. I have a birthday present for you which I shall save for your return since it is on the large side and rather awkward to mail.

I am frantically doing signs for Madd, hoping to allay any obligations I may have toward the Baves for use of their water. If this was a commercial job I'd be making plenty.

Better stop now and get dinner. I don't suppose anyone there has fixed you a cake. We are all thinking of you honey. I always remember with pleasure the spontaneous parties we had on the boats on August 23 when whoever was around got in on the celebration. (Remember the time when we had the baby aboard and all those seiners sleeping in the galley, rough seas, etc. Chocolate cake as I recall.)

All my love sweetheart. The kids are climbing all over me, jamming fingers in the typewriter, etc. It'll have to be supper now.

Love, Dot

[Handwritten P.S. "Brenda and Roger and Kerry are coming tomorrow for 3 days in case you wonder why there are never any pictures of Blaine, it is because when he sees the camera he acts up, won't let me near him.]

~

June 16, 1962

Dearest Dot,

Mail day again. I have enjoyed your letters immensely. I was especially pleased by Dori's report card. It sounds as if by the end of the summer Dori and Blaine will be able to swim. That would really be something.

The *A.F. Rich* arrived last night from Seattle loaded with odds and ends for the cannery. They had an uneventful and non-stop trip which is usually the case with the skipper, Pat Davis. He will be 71 in July.

The way things are shaping up we will have over 100 seine boats operating out of Chatham at the start of the season. With any fish at all, we should be able to put up a decent pack.

Leo Larson, who used to be on the *Hetta*, and who went deck-handing on the "Sand Point" this year, died last week in Bristol Bay.

All my love,

Linné

~

July 2, 1962

Dearest Dot,

Enclosed you will find the results of the company's profit-sharing plan. We have been a part of this plan for one year and one month. I am very pleased and somewhat surprised at the amount. Be sure and put this in a safe place.

At the end of the first week of fishing we had canned (7,400 cases: We have had as many as 92 deliveries in a single day. If any fish show up we could have a good pack.)

I had planned to leave for Bristol Bay today, however, Tom, the cannery foreman, went to the hospital yesterday with bleeding ulcers. We shall hear tonight whether he will return. I don't know when I shall leave now.

I was very pleased to hear how well the kids did with their swimming lessons. Have they started again at the Island? I think with some concerted effort this summer they could master it.

How lovely it must be at Bardvilla in the summer. It seems a lifetime since I have been able to wear just a pair of pants with a shirt. I don't think of summer weather often but it is somewhat depressing at times. It has rained here almost every day since my arrival.

One thought however, keeps recurring in my memory. It is that of two young, beautiful naked bodies making love by the mirror in our bedroom. You are indeed a woman through and through. Sexually, and in all ways, you are as appealing and necessary to me today as you were eight years ago—lasting qualities.

All my love,

Linné

~

July 10, 1962

Dearest Dot,

As usual the mail plane is about to arrive. I have just returned from a grand tour of Western Alaska and the famous Bristol Bay area. It was one of the most interesting trips of my life. I will write you in detail soon.

Our little girl is now 6 years old, Dot! In 8 more years she will be going out with boys. What do you think of that? Give her a big hug and kiss from her daddy.

Those pictures of Blaine are beginning to look like mine at that age. You haven't said anything about mother. Is she at the island or where? How many guests have you had, etc. etc.

I miss my family very much and hope they miss me also.

All my love,

Linné

~

May 25, 1963

Dear Dad,

I took a skating test and passed. I got one (I) in swimming lesson. Roger got a heater put in his pool. We are going to swim in Roger's pool tomorrow if it's a nice day. We've had lovely weather.

Thurs. May 26 was the Girl Scouts Award. I got nine badges. I got the sign of the arrow. And I got the one year pin. At school I sung in the spring program with the fifth and sixth grade. I only have to play one piece and there is one more [?]

Last night we had Molly for dinner and charcoal broiled steaks that was good. Jennifer is learning to walk in her walker.

I miss you very much.

With love,

Dori   xxxxxxxxxxxxxxxxxxxxxxxxxxx

        xxxxxxxxxxxxxxxxxxxxxxxxx

~

May 21, 1965

Dearest Dot,

I was going to wire you the day we arrived but our radio transmitter is inoperative on the ACS frequency. I saw you and the children faithfully waiting by the window at the airport until we took off. We arrived at the cannery at 12:30. Fine trip.

We have had outstanding weather since our arrival. Absolutely clear skies every day. We have removed the old diesel generator set and put the new one in its place. The freezing units will be installed today. Cannery work is coming along very well.

I have spent the last 2 days in Sitka talking with our fishermen and getting them squared away for the coming season. Going over the cannery workers list with Martha Kitka was an experience. We hire one cannery worker and we get 10 humans beings that we are supposed to house along with the one worker—children, babies, old people, friends, etc. Gad! Some of the workers have worked at Chatham since the 1920's.

I left Sitka yesterday afternoon and the pilot let me off on the beach in front of the Angoon village. There I was greeted by about 20 children. From the beach I walked up to the one and only main street. As I walked up the street it seemed like the total populace of Angoon was standing outside their houses to see the new superintendent of Chatham. It was a one man parade.

We all sat around and smoked the peace pipe, discussed Indian tradition, and who would be working at Chatham. After that the great white father disappeared into the sky on a great a (sic) thunderous eagle. For some reason my course in personnel management did not cover that situation.

All my love to you and the children.

Linné

~

Appendix C

Dot's Christmas Cards and
Christmas Verses from Chatham, 1963-1966

1963 - Christmas Card from Chatham

Christmas time in Chatham
Is a time for taking stock
Of brailling pinks and iron chinks
And working 'round the clock

Last summer was an active year
The plant was swamped with salmon
Of fishing in Alaska
It's either feast or famine

But now it is December
We take time out to extend
Best wishes for the Holiday
To every NEFCO friend

1963 - Christmas Verse from Chatham

1964 - Christmas Card from Chatham

For an off-season year '64 produced well
   It just goes to show what you cannot foretell
This card shows our cookers belching forth steam
   Completing the work of our fishing team
We send greetings from Chatham on Christmas Day
   To our Nefco friends from Sitkoh Bay

Merry Christmas!

NEW ENGLAND FISH COMPANY
Chatham, Alaska

1964 - Christmas Verse from Chatham

1965 - Christmas Card from Chatham

New fish house, chinks, more working space
Our girls continue to keep pace
No matter how we modernize
No fish escape their watchful eyes
This card depicts our skillful crew
At work that no machine can do

Greetings from Chatham on
Christmas Day
To our Nefco friends from
Sitkoh Bay.

Merry Christmas!
New England Fish Company
Chatham, Alaska

1965 - Christmas Verse from Chatham

1966 - Christmas Card from Chatham

Early this summer the fishing was slim,
Our weekends were long and our pack guess was grim.

Amazed by mid-summer by what we had packed
We realized at last it was sleep that we lacked.

The item this year our card would enshrine
Is this tireless filler for our new half pound line.

We send greetings from Chatham this Christmas Day
To our NEFCO friends of Sitkoh Bay

Merry Christmas!

Chatham Cannery
New England Fish Company

1966 - Christmas Verse from Chatham

Acknowledgments

I would like to thank and give credit to the following people for their help in making this book possible:

Linné Bardarson: He and I often reminisced about Chatham. He called it his Camelot. He helped me, over the years, to remember the names of his repeat workers and gave me added insight about the cannery's process— many things I would have never known if we hadn't talked about them. I also kept my ears open when'd talk about Chatham with our friends. How he would love this book now, were he still here. He left me with his guardian angel in 2014 after 60 wonderful years.

Blanche "Dolly" Day: My mother had been a stenographer who could type fast, and since there were no copy machines available to us in the 1960s, she retyped my Chatham letters to be able to send carbon copies to friends. Thanks to her, the letters that form the backbone of this book were preserved.

Loranne Bardarson: A granddaughter who read a few chapters at the beginning of my project and made some helpful suggestions.

Dori Hollingsworth, Blaine and Rolf Bardarson: These are my children who recently gathered around my computer to watch the home movies I had made at Chatham Cannery. They were so animated and involved: telling stories I had never heard before and sharing observations from a child's point of view. They added so much to the experience I was trying to write.

Dori gets special credit for reading the unfinished manuscript from cover to cover. She made some wonderful and usable suggestions that enhanced the telling of the story.

Maxine Fred Thompson: Our long phone conversation unearthed feelings and attitudes of her family and friends from Angoon, Alaska and gave me insight into the unbridled enthusiasm they had for their hard work at Chatham. She also helped me understand some Native spirituality and some of the problems that have been solved after the appearance of the White man.

Kitty Young: She gave me a better understanding of what went on socially in the Native Village and in the Filipino house.

Ichi Sawa: He came to Chatham as a working exchange student from Japan. Many years after Chatham, he visited me in Seward, Alaska. And of course we reminisced.

Brian Ebona: He conversed directly with Tara, my ghostwriter, about life at Chatham from his viewpoint as a child and shared what happened to his grandfather Martin Ebona, one of the cannery's bull cooks after he left Chatham.

Don Hansen: He grew up at Chatham and was home schooled there, and worked there from the time when he was 14 peeling potatoes in the mess hall galley. He had stories of his own to share. He knew everybody and every inch of the cannery.

Brad Warren's book *The Rise of Icicle Seafoods—from the Roots of Alaska Statehood* and NEFCO's book *From Sea to World Markets: The Story of New England Fish Co.* by **Harry R. Beard** were the sources of some technical information.

And the ghostwriter of *Boardwalk Footsteps,* **Tara Neilson**. We bonded with each other right from the start, being immersed in the book in ways that were personal as well as informational. Almost every day there was an email from Tara wanting me to clarify something or answer a specific question. I loved the way she managed to sound like me in the writing. Sometimes when reading the script, I wasn't sure who had written what. She could take my paragraphs, reword them, or enlarge them in ways I hadn't thought about. Sometimes she used my words exactly, when appropriate. She and I were never offended by criticism, and we certainly had opinions. I love that woman.

Aerial view of Chatham remains,
***Alaska Southeaster*, March 2000.**

About the Author

Straight out of college, Dot Bardarson found herself aboard a fish tender in Alaska as a bride, dramatically changing the scope of her abilities. Her early years of marriage demanded her full attention as a cannery superintendent's wife and Mom of 3 children, but underlying was her creative brain wanting to get art down on paper.

This finally became possible when her family moved to Seward, Alaska and she won her first Best of Show with a watercolor she had painted at Chatham Cannery.

This launched her career, from one show after another and in galleries throughout Alaska. Her involvement in the arts continued, not only as an artist but as a leader in arts organizations.

She served 6 years on the Alaska State Council on the Arts, transformed her painting style several times, immersed herself in print making and finally published 58 limited edition watercolor prints to satisfy a developing market. She was commissioned by the State of Alaska for 17 public art pieces.

She owned and ran the art gallery, Bardarson Studio, at the Seward harbor for 20 years representing herself and 35 Alaskan artists. She is well known in Alaska, not only for her award-winning watercolors, but also as an art juror, an artist in residence, a muralist, and a set designer for amateur theater.

During the last 20 years she has been master artist for 4 murals, was named Queen of Arts by the Seward Arts Council, a favorite American artist by TOSCA, and chosen for the Alaska Governor's for the Arts award, "Alaska Lifetime Achievement in the Arts."

Her current main focus is on her large family and writing.

~

Contact Dot — email her at: dotbardarson@gmail.com; phone: 907-224-3131

About Cirque Press

Cirque Press grew out of *Cirque*, a literary journal that publishes the works of writers and artists from the North Pacific Rim, a region that reaches north from Oregon to the Yukon Territory, south through Alaska to Hawaii, and west to the Russian Far East.

Cirque Press is a partnership of Sandra Kleven, publisher, and Michael Burwell, editor. Ten years ago, we recognized that works of talented writers in the region were going unpublished, and the Press was launched to bring those works to fruition. We publish fiction, nonfiction, and poetry, and we seek to produce art that provides a deeper understanding about the region and its cultures. The writing of our authors is significant, personal, and strong.

Sandra Kleven – Michael Burwell, publishers and editors

www.cirquejournal.com

Books From Cirque Press

Apportioning the Light by Karen Tschannen (2018)

The Lure of Impermanence by Carey Taylor (2018)

Echolocation by Kristin Berger (2018)

Like Painted Kites & Collected Works by Clifton Bates (2019)

Athabaskan Fractal: Poems of the Far North by Karla Linn Merrifield (2019)

Holy Ghost Town by Tim Sherry (2019)

Drunk on Love: Twelve Stories to Savor Responsibly by Kerry Dean Feldman (2019)

Wide Open Eyes: Surfacing from Vietnam by Paul Kirk Haeder (2020)

Silty Water People by Vivian Faith Prescott (2020)

Life Revised by Leah Stenson (2020)

Oasis Earth: Planet in Peril by Rick Steiner (2020)

The Way to Gaamaak Cove by Doug Pope (2020)

Loggers Don't Make Love by Dave Rowan (2020)

The Dream That Is Childhood by Sandra Wassilie (2020)

Seward Soundboard by Sean Ulman (2020)

The Fox Boy by Gretchen Brinck (2021)

Lily Is Leaving: Poems by Leslie Ann Fried (2021)

One Headlight by Matt Caprioli (2021)

November Reconsidered by Marc Janssen (2021)

Callie Comes of Age by Dale Champlin (2021)

Someday I'll Miss This Place Too by Dan Branch (2021)

Out There In The Out There by Jerry McDonnell (2021)

Fish the Dead Water Hard by Eric Heyne (2021)

Salt & Roses by Buffy McKay (2022)

Growing Older In This Place: A Life in Alaska's Rainforest
by Margo Wasserman Waring (2022)

Kettle Dance: A Big Sky Murder by Kerry Dean Feldman (2022)

Nothing Got Broke by Larry F. Slonaker (2022)

On the Beach: Poems 2016-2021 by Alan Weltzien (2022)

Sky Changes on the Kuskokwim by Clifton Bates (2022)

Transplanted by Birgit Lennertz Sarrimanolis (2022)

Between Promise and Sadness by Joanne Townsend (2022)

Yosemite Dawning by Shauna Potocky (2022)

The Woman Within by Tami Phelps and Kerry Dean Feldman (2023)

In the Winter of the Orange Snow by Diane S. Carpenter (2023)

Mail Order Nurse by Sue Lium (2023)

All in Due Time by Kate Troll (2023)

Infinite Meditations For Inspiration and Daily Practice by Scott Hanson (2023)

Getting Home from Here by Anne Ward-Masterson (2023)

Crossing the Burnside Bridge & Other Poems by Janice D. Rubin (2023)

A Variable Sense of Things by Ron McFarland (2023)

Tiny's Stories: An Athabascan Family on the Yukon River by Theresa "Tiny" Demientieff Devlin with Sam Demientieff (2024)

If Singing Went On by Gerald Cable (2024)

May the Owl Call Again: A Return to Poet John Meade Haines, 1924-2011 by Rachel Epstein (2024)

Out of the Dark: A Memoir by Marian Elliott (2024)

Kissing Kevin: An American Nurse in the Vietnam War by Sara Berg (2024)

Boardwalk Footsteps: Memoir of an Artist at a Remote Alaskan Cannery by Dot Bardarson (2024)

Bury Me in Cherry Blossoms by Eric Braman (2024)

A Wonderful-Terrible God by Judith Lethin (2024)

Last Call of the Dark by Mary Eliza Crane (2024)

Dancing Away by Robert M. Fagen (2024)

Taking Time: Sailing Away with My Family in Southeast Alaska by Larri Irene Spengler (2024)

Lost Last Poems by Shannon Gramse (2024)

Seasmoke, Spindrift and Other Spells by Shauna Potocky (2024)

The North Face of Summer Russell Tabbert (2024)

CIRCLES

Illustrated books from Cirque Press

Baby Abe: A Lullaby for Lincoln by Ann Chandonnet (2021)

Miss Tami, Is Today Tomorrow? by Tami Phelps (2021)

Miss Bebe Goes to America by Lynda Humphrey (2022)

AK192B